Cognitive Technologies

T0189671

For further volumes:
http://www.springer.com/series/5216

Cognitive Technologies

Managing Editors: D. M. Gabbay J. Siekmann

Editorial Board: A. Bundy J. G. Carbonell
M. Pinkal H. Uszkoreit M. Veloso W. Wahlster
M. J. Wooldridge

Janos J. Sarbo · Jozsef I. Farkas
Auke J.J. van Breemen

Knowledge in Formation

A Computational Theory of Interpretation

Janos J. Sarbo
Jozsef I. Farkas
Auke J.J. van Breemen
Radboud University
Faculty of Science
Institute for Computing and Information
Heijendaalseweg 135
6525AJ Nijmegen
Netherlands
janos@cs.ru.nl
fjozsef99@yahoo.com
a.vanbreemen@science.ru.nl

Managing Editors
Prof. Dov M. Gabbay
Augustus De Morgan Professor of Logic
Department of Computer Science
King's College London
Strand, London WC2R 2LS, UK

Prof. Dr. Jörg Siekmann
Forschungsbereich Deduktions- und
Multiagentensysteme, DFKI
Stuhlsatzenweg 3, Geb. 43
66123 Saarbrücken, Germany

Cognitive Technologies ISSN 1611-2482
ISBN 978-3-642-26869-4   ISBN 978-3-642-17089-8 (eBook)
DOI 10.1007/978-3-642-17089-8
Springer Heidelberg Dordrecht London New York

ACM Computing Classification: I.2

Cover design: KünkelLopka GmbH, Heidelberg

Printed on acid-free paper

Springer is part of Springer Science+Business Media (www.springer.com)

Preface

With knowledge representation we face more or less the same problem as Augustine (354–430) when thinking about time: if nobody asks what it is, it seems clear enough, but being asked it proves to be very difficult to provide an answer.

At the beginning of our research we thought that a solution for the problem of knowledge representation depends on a solution for the problem of natural language processing. But this was wrongly taken. Our experience with practical applications of grammars developed by linguists has shown that formal grammars, at least those we had access to, cannot capture the full complexity of language. As a consequence of an analysis of our 'results' we drew the conclusion that a reason for the fiasco we experienced must reside in the formal, i.e., *static, detached* character of our approach. Natural language and human communication in general are basically dynamic processes. We surmised that the sources for the dynamics of language can be found in two fields: in human information processing and in human communication. We also realized that any modeling of the first requires a theory of cognitive activity, and any understanding of the second needs a theory of signs. As the two fields are torn asunder, in the beginning it was not clear whether it is possible to establish a link between them. It was clear, however, that if we could find a solution for the problem of language interpretation, we would be able to find an answer for the problem of human knowledge representation as well.

This was the situation when we started our research in order to develop a model of knowledge representation that respects the properties of human information processing as well as the properties of signs. Soon we found out that a proper understanding of the relation between the theory of signs and the cognitive model of knowledge representation taken is harder than expected. Similar to experiences with problem solving in other fields, for instance, chemistry, which requires some understanding of the properties of chemical elements, we found that the definition of a model of knowledge representation asks for some understanding of the rules pertaining to the propagation of signs. We had to realize that signs are not some special kind of 'things', but consist in complex systems of dependencies.

A promising result of our research is the development of a theory that, in our view, provides an answer to our original problem. Results of various tests and experiments of our theory show that the approach taken could be correct.

About the book

This book consists of three parts. The focus of the first part is on the properties of signs and sign interpretation. This is followed by the second part, in which we introduce a model that complies with the conditions for sign processing set by the first part. In the final, third part we delve into various applications of our model. We concentrate on the presentation of a theory of knowledge representation and illustrate this theory with a number of examples. In order to assess the practical value of our theory, in past research we conducted a couple of experiments in the field of geometrical problem solving (by individuals) and problem elicitation (by a team of participants). Preliminary results of these experiments provide some evidence for a naturalistic interpretation of our model (Draskovic, Couwenberg, & Sarbo, 2010). Earlier presentations of the theory of this book can be found in (Farkas, 2008) and (van Breemen & Sarbo, 2009).[1]

About the reader

As for the reader, we assume that (s)he has some interest in human information processing and knowledge modeling in different domains such as natural language, logic, mathematics and reasoning. Natural language is considered in the obvious sense, familiarity with linguistic theories is not required. Sign theoretical concepts are restricted to a manageable subset, which is introduced gently. Some familiarity with basic concepts of propositional and syllogistic logic may be useful.

Readers who would like to make acquaintance with the central ideas only may wish to read the chapters: Introduction, Signs and sign interpretation (Chapter 1), From signs to interpretant (Chapter 2), A world of signs (Chapter 4) and Reflexive Analysis (Chapter 10).

Acknowledgments

This book could not have been written without the help and support of many persons. The authors wish to specially thank Rein Cozijn, for his encouragement and for proof reading the manuscript; Guy Debrock, for the initiation he provided in the work of C.S. Peirce; Vera Kamphuis, for her guidance in the field of language parsing. We thankfully acknowledge inspiration and help from our colleagues (in alphabetical order): Peter-Arno Coppen, Irena Draskovic, Wim van de Grind, Claudio Guerri, Stijn Hoppenbrouwers, Dick van Leijenhorst, Bernard Morand and Joost Wegman. A special word of thanks goes to Kecheng Liu and his group at University of Reading (UK), and to Meurig Beynon and Steve Russ at University of Warwick (UK), for their inspiration, help and hospitality on different occasions. For their criticism and remarks on an earlier version of the manuscript we thank: Lou Boves and John Sowa. With pleasure we thank our students Maikel Couwenberg and Eddy Klomp for their efforts in experimentally testing our theory.

---

[1] See also www.cs.ru.nl/kif.

Finally we feel indebted to a number of colleagues for their encouragement and friendly support (in alphabetical order): Henk Barendregt, Jean-Louis Bouquard, Herman Geuvers, Arjen Hommersom, Tom Heskes, Mary Keeler, Emiel Krahmer, András Lörincz, Peter Lucas, Csaba Pléh, Gary Richmond, Pieter de Vries Robbé, Toine Tax and Theo van der Weide. The authors would also like to thank the editor at Springer, Ronan Nugent, for his contribution during all phases of this book project.

Last but not least we would like to thank our families for their patience, support and love.

Nijmegen, November 2010

Auke van Breemen
József Farkas
Janos Sarbo

Contents

Introduction

In 1671, in a letter to the Royal Society for the Improvement of Knowledge, Newton gave a first account of his theory of colors based on the prism experiments he started in 1665. Notably, it was not the colors that drew Newton's special attention. The refractory potential of glass prisms was commonly known at that time. He was struck by the oblong form and the specific order of colors in the spectrum (Sabra, 1981). In his 'experimentum crucis', Newton showed that those light rays are primary in a twofold way. First, by merging them in a single bundle, white light arises again, and second, leading the separate color rays through a second prism does not lead to further refraction. Newton writes (Newton, 1959/1671): "Light it self is a Heterogeneous mixture of refrangible Rays". Elsewhere he writes: "[Colors are] original and connate properties of the rays just as their respective degrees of refrangibility were".

What, might the reader want to ask, does this talk about light and color have to do with information and information processing? Looking at Newton's experiment through the glasses of information science, one can observe similarities between a prism that reveals the spectral colors involved in the white light and an interpreting system that processes information.

One of the similarities is nicely captured by the term involvement. As it is possible to refract light into ultimate constituents, characterized by frequency, and merge them again into white light, so it is possible to analyze input for information processing into ultimate perspectives and merge them again into an informative response. A clear description of these perspectives and their processing is the main goal of this book.

Another similarity has been aptly indicated elsewhere (Stamper, 2009) with the term *actualism*. It is only when there is an *interaction* between a white light ray and a prism that the spectral rays can be sorted out (by the prism) and revealed as colors and refractory properties. Just so, it is only when an information agent 'refracts' the input that the constituent parts can reveal themselves and show their properties.

A last similarity we want to mention here concerns the emergence of ambiguous terminology. As *light* may mean the already existent white light and its involved, but to be refracted, colored light, information may mean the input that offers itself for interpretation, but also the involved, hence to be discerned, constituent perspectives on the input.

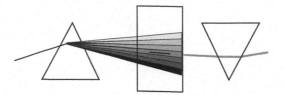

Figure 1: White light analyzed by glass prisms

The mind's eye

The idea that signs can be sorted into nine sign aspects that are involved, is due to the American mathematician-philosopher, C.S. Peirce (1839-1914). In his view, sign aspects represent perspectives of interpretation. Sign aspects can be ordered in a dependency structure on the basis of their dependency and subservience relations. By virtue of the completeness of the collection of nine sign aspects (perspectives), the interpretation of the dependency structure as a system of relations amounts to a process aiming at consistency as its goal.

In order to reach its goal the process of interpretation must take the input as a sign, 'refract' the involved sign aspects –take the aspects as signs themselves– and combine them into a new, responsive and, on account of that, informative sign. In order to realize its goal the process must consist of an interaction sequence between an input signal, appearing as an *effect*, and an observer, that is affected while being in some specific *state*. Although an analysis of the interaction established by the observer (interpreting system) represents the observer's view, the resulting relations are at least partly determined by the input signal.

In this book we will suggest that human information processing can be modeled as a sign interpretation process. Information conveyed by external stimuli (input) is analyzed into sign aspects on the basis of internal knowledge already acquired by the mind (interpreting system). Metaphorically speaking the mind fulfills the role of the prism. The main difference consists in the former's flexibility to develop new habits in comparison to the prism. Habits arise through learning. We recognize that learning is orthogonal to habitual input processing and frankly admit that in our book we restrict our focus to the procedural aspects of habitual interpretation. In particular, we will show that information conveyed by the input can be sorted into types of relation and arranged in a structure that is isomorphic to the Peircean dependency of sign aspects.

Interaction and knowledge

Through interactions we experience, via learning we know reality. Although knowledge representation is basically concerned with the latter, any authentic theory of knowledge representation must respect some of the properties of the first. As any experience presupposes the possibility to sense qualities that in principle are independent from us, we conclude that knowledge must arise from interactions forced upon us.

All interactions involve an action between two or more entities. By considering one of those entities to be 'the observer' and the collection of all other entities to be 'the observed', the interpretation generated by the observer can be called the observer's reaction. Following this line of thinking, below we will suggest that a model of interpretation can be derived by making use of Newton's fundamental law of action–reaction. In this section we introduce the blueprints of such a derivation, a more detailed account will be given later in this book.

Action–reaction phenomena

A theory of forces can be found in Newton's work (Newton, 1999/1687). In his 3rd law of motion he postulates: "For every action there is an equal and opposite reaction". An illustrative example of a nail, hit by a hammer is depicted in Fig. 2. Following Newton's 2nd law ($F=m*a$), the applied force (F) accelerates (a) the nail much harder, by virtue of its smaller mass (m), than the reaction force ($-F$) accelerates the hammer. In the end, the nail may get deeply driven into the underlying piece of timber, while the hammer only gets slightly bounced back in the opposite direction.

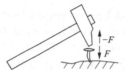

Figure 2: A sample action–reaction phenomenon

Monadic view

Newton's 3nd law, in combination with the 2nd law, not only predicts the reaction force, but, in specific cases, also the possible consequences of the action, such as the driving of the nail. Remarkably, in Newton's world, there are only action–reaction phenomena. This may explain why in everyday life the term reaction ambiguously denotes a force as well as the effects triggered by that force.

From the point of view of information processing, Newton's model of action–reaction phenomena may be conceived as too narrow: by knowing F and m, everything else can be computed. Being neutral to the direction of time, this monadic model lacks the notion of a development, for instance, from action to reaction (see Fig. 3).

Dyadic view

If we are interested in the way in which reactions arise from actions, we may introduce the hypothesis that, in everyday phenomena, action and reaction are

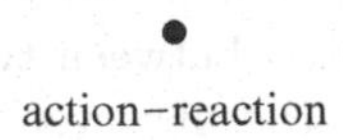

action–reaction

Figure 3: A monadic concept of action–reaction phenomena

related to each other according to a relation of dependency. Assuming, for the moment, causal dependency, the result is a dyadic concept of action–reaction phenomena (see Fig. 4).

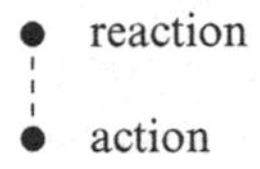

● reaction

● action

Figure 4: A dyadic concept of action–reaction phenomena. A dotted line is used to express a dependency between events

Triadic view

We may further refine our model by assuming that reactions arise from actions through an act of interpretation. Indeed, even at the physical level, the ability of objects to show different reactions to different actions may be seen as their potential for *interpreting* actions by '(re)cognizing' them and 'generating' a reaction. Just as, in principle, physical objects involved in action–reaction phenomena must be independent (otherwise their co-occurrence cannot appear as a phenomenon), interpretation assumes the existence of knowledge about those objects and the possible consequence of their co-occurrence. For example, in Fig. 2, the nail may be said to interpret the appearing force, by '(re)cognizing' its measure and 'generating' a counter force, as well as a diametral piercing movement. In sum, through the introduction of the concept of interpretation, the relation between action and reaction can be split into two relations: one between action and corresponding knowledge (recognition) and another, between that knowledge and a corresponding reaction (generation). See Fig. 5. With the assumption of an involved dependency between action and reaction the concept of development comes into sight.

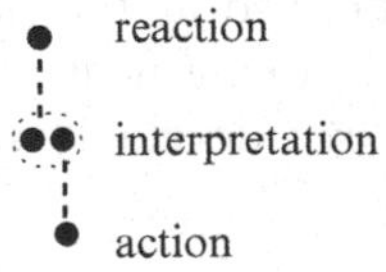

reaction

interpretation

action

Figure 5: A triadic concept of action–reaction phenomena. A pair of nodes that can be merged in a single node is indicated by a dashed circle

Knowledge through internal processing

In Newton's world, action and reaction are unambiguously related to each other. Objects occurring in the Newtonian world simply do not have the potential of changing their 'reaction strategy'. The 'knowledge' in the node 'interpretation' in Fig. 5 remains the same. What happens if we extend our focus and include in our model objects that do have the potential to acquire knowledge?

Obviously, Newton's 3rd law holds for such entities as well. However, the potential to generate more complex reactions enables the introduction of more refined models of action–reaction phenomena. Through memorization, the interpreting system obtains information about occurring action–reaction events that may prove useful in later interactions. If the interpreting system has the potential to observe itself and to memorize its observations,[2] it will be able to distinguish information about external actions from the possible consequences those actions can bring about to the interpreting system. The latter kind of information may be called the system's knowledge about itself. Through abstraction and generalization the interpreting system may introduce concepts that can favorably be used to predict the consequences that emerging external qualities may have. This potential of the interpreting system to predict future events assumes an ability to cope with modalities other than the mechanical one such as wave-type qualities, for instance, the observation of light rays in visual action–reaction phenomena: if we see the qualities of a hammer moving in our direction, we may step away or shout in order to prevent certain unfortunate effects.

Matching mode operation

Arguably, Newton's theory considers action–reaction phenomena from the point of view of an external observer. If we are interested in the question of how interpretation may capitalize on memorized information for the generation of reactions, we must switch perspective and analyze action–reaction phenomena from the stance of the interpreting system itself. Following this view we suggest that the interpreting system occurring in some *state* is in interaction with the external force (quality). This external force appears as an *effect* in the interpreting system. The qualities of this state and effect will be called the input state and effect qualities or, briefly, input qualities. The relation between *this* state and effect is the ground for the reaction generated by the observer.

The aforementioned interaction is stored by the interpreting system in a collection of (unanalyzed) 'input', 'state', 'effect' and (interrelated) 'state–effect' qualities. See Fig. 6. These 'storing events', which come down to establishing relations, are all triggered by the external force ('action'). Interpretation can be successful only if these events consistently *match* memorized information. This informational relation underlying the generation of reactions is depicted in

---

[2]An *observation* is defined as an event interpretation of an interaction, for instance, by a perceptual judgment.

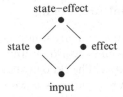

Figure 6: Informational relation underlying interpretation. A continuous line is used to represent a flow of emerging information, not just a dependency

Fig. 6. A schematic model of the corresponding 'matching' mode operation of information processing is depicted in Fig. 7.

Note that all 'storing events' included in Fig. 7 are internal. They are related to the occurring action and reaction, which are external. The latter relations are expressed by means of dashed lines, connecting the nodes 'action' and 'reaction' via the nodes 'input', 'state', 'effect' and 'state-effect' relation, refining our model in the node 'interpretation' (see Fig. 5).

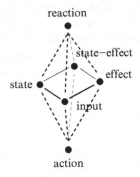

Figure 7: Matching mode operation

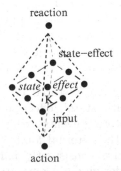

Figure 8: Analysis mode operation

Analysis mode operation

Through abstraction and generalization, perceived data obtained in past experiences may be transformed into knowledge. In the case of indeterminate input qualities the generation of a state–effect relation may require an *analysis* of (all) possible matches as well as the selection of a solution, on the basis of some strategy. As part of this analysis, different interpretations of the input state (cf. 'state') and effect (cf. 'effect') as well as their relation (cf. 'state-effect') can be generated internally by means of the system's knowledge about corresponding state and effect qualities.

Following the above considerations, a model of action–reaction phenomena can be derived as follows. By considering the input state and effect qualities to be external (cf. effect), in relation to the system's knowledge which is internal (cf. state), the interaction between the state and effect qualities on the one hand, and the system's knowledge on the other can be modeled by two instances of a 'matching' mode process. As the observer's knowledge is shared by those process instances, it can be represented by a single node ('K'). In Fig. 8, the two sub-processes are marked by the labels *state* and *effect*. Note that the above 'internal' refinement of our model (in the nodes 'state' and 'effect', in Fig. 7) does not affect the dependency between 'action' and 'reaction' (cf. dashed lines).[3] In Fig. 8, the nodes between 'action' and 'reaction' represent the nine types of relation as well as the nine sign aspects mentioned earlier.

By the introduction of analysis and selection in the interpretation process, the possibility of anticipatory responses and habit formation are added to the mechanistic Newtonian model.

An overview of the model

In sum, complex information processes, such as the human, can be characterized as follows. External triggers (actions) appearing as data ('input') are analyzed in state and effect qualities by making use of memory knowledge ('K'), and merged into a relation ('state-effect'). This relation, which is the interpreting system's response to the question: 'Why is this effect occurring to this state?', may form the basis for the 'generation' of a reaction. If, according to the system's knowledge, the input qualities can be merged into a relation in many different ways, the generated reaction as well as the underlying state–effect relation will be recognized as hypothetical.

An overview of the above derivation of our last model can be found in Fig. 9. Note that on each level (except level (1)) a representation of the model is defined, by means of a combination of two instances of the representation introduced on the immediately preceding level.

---

[3] In Fig. 8, dashed lines connect the nodes 'action' and 'reaction' with the nodes 'state' and 'effect' comprised by the two sub-processes, respectively. The labels of the latter two nodes are omitted in the diagram.

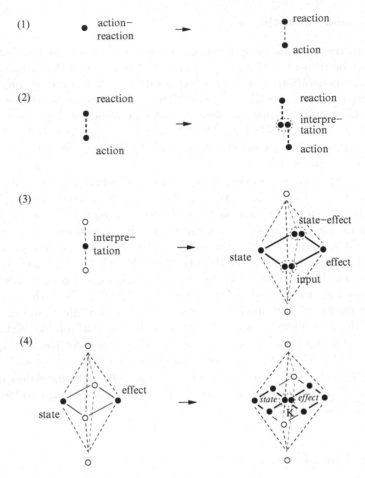

Figure 9: An overview of the transformational derivation of the model introduced. Nodes and edges involved in a transformation are emphasized by means of thick lines and black bullets. On each level, (1)-(3), the output of the transformation is used as the input on the next level

Summary and related research

The focus of this book is restricted to the properties of 'analysis' mode information processes. In the context of this program we will consider the potential of our theory for uniform knowledge modeling in different domains. To this end, we will offer a logical analysis of our model, which is necessary for a computational realization of our theory. As a side effect of this analysis we will suggest that our model of information processes can be used as a theory of our innate logic or the 'logica utens'.

Differences with traditional views

An important difference with traditional views on information processing or knowledge representation lies in our conception of data, knowledge and information. In contradistinction to more traditional views we do not regard data or knowledge as monolithic kinds of entity, but as relational entities that comprise a multitude of involved perspectives of which in each interpretation process one surfaces. Which one will surface in any given case depends on the state of the interpreting system and on the goals that are operative during the process of interpretation.

The assumption that knowledge arises from the observation of interactions is not without consequences. As interactions are dynamic, their representation, including a model of cognitive activity, must respect this dynamic character. According to the received view of cognitive theory (Solso, 1988) however, the brain processes stimuli in samples, which are static snapshots. Is it possible to bridge the gap between the static input and its dynamic interpretation?

In this book we will maintain that dynamic representation may arise through a process of interpretation of static snapshots. According to this view, interpretation moments in input processing contribute to representations that are in the process of becoming a sign. Such representations are the intermediate nodes lying between 'action' and 'reaction', in the models of Fig. 9. The intermediate interactions only have existence from an analytical perspective.

That the brain is capable of interpreting static information dynamically, can be illustrated by the phenomenon of apparent motion perception. In this phenomenon, a series of steady pictures (cf. 'action') are presented. Although each picture can be meaningful in itself, combined they can be interpreted as parameters in the experience of the entire series of pictures as motion (cf. 'reaction'). It is a conjecture of this book that an analogous relation may exist between the individual interpretation moments of cognitive processing on the one hand, and the experience of the entire process as meaningful on the other.

Limitations of the proposed approach

In order to construct a naturalistic model of knowledge representation we need to be able to cope with external qualities. A theory of mapping external qualities to internal representations or qualia, on the basis of physical properties, is suggested by Gärdenfors (2004), and Pribram (1971) and Prueitt (1995) (research by the last two is related to the fundamental work by Gibson (1997)). An axiomatic characterization of the conditions for a representation of qualities (cf. stimuli) by means of qualia is due to Ramachandran and Hirstein (1997).

The definition of a mapping from qualities to qualia however is beyond our scope. In this work we restrict ourselves to the introduction of a set of *conditions* that such mappings have to satisfy. By focussing on conditions on qualia, not the qualia themselves, we circumvent, but certainly do not solve, the problem of symbol grounding (Harnad, 1990).

An introduction of conditions on the properties of qualia will be part of the definition of models of information processing in a number of knowledge domains. Roughly, a *knowledge domain* will be considered to be a 'closed' collection[4] of signs representing a certain perspective of interpretation, such as syntactic, logical, mathematical (Mackay, 1987).

Knowledge domains that we will deal with are natural language, 'naive' logic, mathematics and syllogistic reasoning. Those qualia conditions being abstract, a representation of qualia that suits a computational implementation will not be provided. Achieving that level of concreteness, in some knowledge domains at least, is a primary goal of our current research.

The various strategies of interpretation –top down, bottom up, anticipatory, etc.– are beyond our horizon. Since our main interest is in the procedural aspects of information processing, basically our focus is on bottom up processing.

Related research

An overview of some of the goals of traditional KR research can be found in (Davis, Shrobe, & Szolovits, 2009), as well as in (AITopics, 2009). The approach presented in this book differs from those mentioned in these studies, by virtue of its semiotic orientedness and cognitive foundation. The theory of this book is also related to Intelligence Augmentation (IA). The main goal of IA is to develop tools and methods to support and possibly improve the effectiveness of human intelligence in solving complex problems (Engelbart, 1962). To achieve better efficiency and effectiveness of computer systems for knowledge representation, a human-compatible formal model of knowledge representation is needed, linking IA with the model presented in this book. The nature of qualia has been extensively studied in philosophy as well, for instance, by (Harnad, 1987), (Churchland, 1997), (Fodor, 1998), (Pylyshyn, 1987), and (Dennett, 1991), but the list is far from complete.

---

[4]Webster gives for 'collection': a group of objects [. . .] accumulated [. . .] for some purpose or as a result of some process.

Part I

Signs and interpretative processes

Chapter 1

Signs and sign interpretation

Let's try to answer the question: What is involved in any interpretative process whatever? Our basic assumption will be that there must be something capable of being interpreted in order to make an interpretative process possible. We will call that something a sign. Since on this assumption interpretation without signs is not deemed possible our first task will be to specify what we understand signs to be. The example sign we will work with is the following message, written down on a note by the model maker in an information system building project and passed down to the head of the IT department.

From: Bernard
To: Peter

Dear Peter,

   Do we have to evaluate the model of the personnel administration with all
   the members of the personnel department before we decide to realize it in
   its current form or can we work with representatives of that department
   in order to validate the model?

Best,
Bernard

The standpoint we depart from is that of the head of the IT department at the moment he takes up the note and is turning his eyes towards the surface of the paper on which the sign is written. It is important to note that at this point the head of IT presumably has already done some sign interpretation since he singled out the note in his field of vision as a sign that somebody wants to communicate something to him, and he also must have decided that it is worth his while to find out what it is. This comes down to saying that the note, itself conceived as a sign, already did its intended job at the moment the head took up the paper in order to read it.

For a first understanding of what is involved in sign interpretation it is good to dwell a little upon the case of the note conveying that there is some message. A question that might be asked is: Where do we draw the border of the process that we designate with the words 'sign interpretation' in this case? Is it when the head recognizes that there is a note? Is it when he recognizes that the note is stating its demand to be picked up? Is it when he makes the resolution to actually pick up the note? Or is it when he actually picks it up with the aim of reading it or deliberately does not at that moment for some reason? Wherever we draw the border, it will be clear that, in general, the interpretive possibilities a sign offers will depend on characteristics of the sign. In the next section we will investigate the properties of signs as an introduction to the study of interpretive processes.

1.1 The basic terminology of Peircean semiotics

Before we start analyzing the message, we need some basic distinctions in order to guide the tour. On the note we have a sentence that is communicating something to somebody or –abstracted from the receiving actor– we have a sentence (sign) that expresses something about something else (its object) and that has to have an effect (an interpretant) in order to realize its function as a sign. At this point it might be tempting to settle for the thought that thus our sole business will be with the sentence apart from its relations to the object and interpretant. But then we study the sentence as an object and not as a sign, which is not what we are after. That is the reason why Peirce defined a sign as something relational:

> A *Sign*, or *Representamen*, is a First which stands in such a genuine triadic relation to a Second, called its *Object*, as to be capable of determining a Third, called its *Interpretant*, to assume the same triadic relation to its Object in which it stands itself to the same Object [...] (CP 2.274)[1]

For instance, in our example sentence above, the written message (representamen) stands for the decision to be made (object), triggering a course of action (interpretant). But there are many more possibilities, as we will show below.

---

[1]A reference to the Collected Papers of Peirce (Peirce, C.S, 1931-58) is given by CP, followed by volume and paragraph.

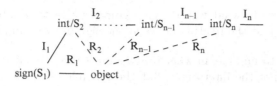

Figure 1.1: Diagram of the 1903 definition of a sign

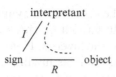

Figure 1.2: Partial diagram of the 1903 sign definition (R: relation to object, I: relation to interpretant)

A diagram of the above definition is provided in Fig. 1.1 for several instances of a sign that realizes its possibility to determine an interpretant. Each instance of int/S_i ($1 \leq i \leq n$) represents a sign as an interpretant-that-becomes-a-sign by actualizing its relational capability I_i; and that, as a consequence, stands in a relation R_i ($1 \leq i \leq n$), to its object.[2] That relation to the object is 'the same'. So, R_1, R_2, ..., R_n are the same, in short R, and I_1, I_2, ..., I_n are the same, in short I.

Note that the R_i, I_i themselves are signs, not just binary relations. For instance, the object of R_1 is the relation between S_1 and its object; the interpretant of R_1 is an expression of the nature of that relation.

Later, when we shift our attention from signs to processes of interpretation, we will refine this definition in order to cover cases in which the interpretant sign is qualitatively more informed than one of its preceding signs. For the moment it is sufficient to take only one moment out of the sequence (see Fig. 1.2). Notice that we drew a curved, dashed line between interpretant and object in order to underscore that the sign always mediates the relation between an interpretant and its object.

Since it is not sufficient solely to investigate the sign vehicle, we will also have to pay attention to the ways in which the sign is related to its object and its interpretant.[3] These relations give rise to the threefold distinction that structures this exposition:

1. If we analyze the note, the sentence written or whatever other sign without bothering about the content of the message and the effects it may possibly have, we look at the *sign in itself*.

---

[2] We tacitly assume that S_1 too arises from some earlier interpretation process.
[3] In Chapter 3, we will pay attention to the different types of objects and especially interpretants distinguished.

2. If we analyze in what way the sign conveys something about something else, we look at the relation between the sign in itself and its *object*.[4]

3. If we want to find out in what way a sign realizes its effects, our primary interest is not the interpreter, but the possible effects of the sign on the interpreter, or, to put it in other words, we are interested in the relation between the sign and its *interpretant*(s).

The three perspectives on the sign are not symmetrical. It is possible to deal with the sign regarded in itself without paying attention to its relations with object and interpretant, but not the inverse. If we do focus on the relation of the sign to itself, we analyze the sign only as having the possibility to function as a sign. It is also possible to pay attention to the relation between sign and object without paying attention to the relation between sign and interpretant, but again, not the reverse. In this case we analyze the sign as having the possibility to actually function as a sign by conveying information about some object. It is only when we also take into account the relation with its interpretant that we analyze the sign as a real or effectual sign. But if we analyze the sign as a real sign, we have to take into account what is involved. So, it is not possible to analyze the effects a sign realizes without taking into account the relation it has with its object and the sign regarded in itself, as it is not possible to analyze the relation between sign and object without paying attention to the sign in itself. This asymmetry follows from the categorical underpinnings of the Peircean sign model and it dictates the sequence of the exposition (see Appendix A).

After we describe how to understand the sign in itself and its relations with its object and interpretant, we will, in the next chapter, gradually develop a model of interpretation. Note that the term *sign* regrettably has a twofold meaning by now. On the one hand it signifies the sign regarded in itself, on the other it embraces the composite whole of sign, relation with object and relation with interpretant (cf. the ambiguity of 'light' pointed out in the Introduction).

1.2 The sign in itself

At the very first moment that Peter, the head of IT, looks at the note he will recognize that something is inscribed, but he will not at this instant be able to recognize what it is. The note and the inscription at this moment appear as a collection of *qualities*. If he does not manage to make any sense of the note, that is if he does not recognize that something is written on it, to him the note will turn into a scrap of paper that may as well be discarded. So, qualities make signs possible. But the head does recognize this scribble. That is, he sees a familiar *form* in the distribution of qualities that constitute this *singular*

---

[4]Please mark that we are working with a very general meaning of the term object. It even embraces figments, objectives and intended objects that at the moment do not really exist as with the blueprint of a building not build yet, a mythical figure or an idea of justice not yet realized in the way people behave.

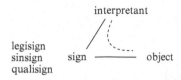

Figure 1.3: The three aspects of the sign regarded in itself

inscription. In psycholinguistics this problem is dealt with under the heading sign recognition processes.

It is by the form that we recognize the sentence, but it is by the instance that the form is expressed. So, without form there is no recognition and without instance there is no possibility of getting acquainted with the form. A sign regarded in itself involves *Qualities* that are cast in a *Form* that is *Instantiated*.

In Peircean terms: **Qualisigns** come into actual existence in a **Sin**(gular) **sign** (Token). Different singular expressions of the same sign (**Sinsigns**) are recognized as such because all they are instances of the same **Legisign** (Type).

An example may clarify the above distinctions. Are spoken and written sentences, containing the same words (in the same order), instances of the same Form or Legisign or not? That depends on the situation. For the head of IT it makes no difference whether the question is in writing (qualisigns of vision) or sound (qualisigns of hearing) as long as he recognizes the same words. For a graphical designer or an actress it may make a difference. But if it makes a difference, the goal, the object to be communicated, must be different.

As soon as the head of IT is able to reproduce the question –without being aware of what is communicated– he has grasped the sign as it is in itself. As long as it is not clear what it is that the sign communicates about its object, we are only dealing with a possible sign, i.e., a sign without a message and without any effect besides the possibility to copy it in instances. The three aspects of the sign regarded in itself are displayed in Fig. 1.3 and summarized in Table 1.1.

1.3   The sign in relation to its object

When the head of IT recognizes that the note contains a sentence in familiar language, he will be able to read the sentence in order to find out what is conveyed about the object(s) of the message. First of all it is necessary to determine the way in which the object is given by the sign. We have, according to the semiotic theory, three principally different ways in which the sign can be related to its object. In Fig. 1.4 the possible relations are depicted.

A sign has an **iconic relation** with its object if the sign represents by means of a similarity. Anything that has a similarity with something can be used as a sign for that something in order to express the characteristic shared. The strength of signs iconically related to their object is that they convey something, the weakness is that iconicity by itself does not determine an object to which it relates, it leaves open, so to speak, the world of objects to which it is applicable.

Qualisign (quality)

It is impossible to present a qualisign, it needs an instance for its embodiment; just imagine your whole consciousness consisting of the sensation of one color, that is the closest approximation of a qualisign possible. On the other hand we are immersed in qualities; it is the stuff of the world as we *know* it: color, touch, taste, sound and smell are the basic categories into which we humans divide the qualities of our experience.

Sinsign (instance, actual event, token)

With "help, help, Help, help, Help" we have 5 existing singular signs of the same legisign. The emphasis here is on existence.

Legisign (law, habit, type)

It is impossible to present a legisign directly since it can only be found in its instances. It is the *law* that governs that similar instances are taken as instances of the same form. The emphasis here is on the habit governing the decision that some instantiated qualities are of a certain type.

Table 1.1: Sign regarded in itself

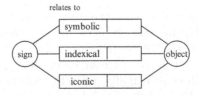

Figure 1.4: The three ways in which sign and object can be related to each other

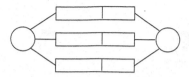

Figure 1.5: A sign with an iconic relation between itself and its possible objects

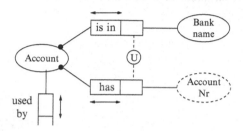

Figure 1.6: The dashed oval: an indexical, symbolic relation between sign and object

Let's remove the symbols from Fig. 1.4 and reproduce the more purely iconic part of the sign in Fig. 1.5 in order to make this clear.

If we confine ourselves to Object Role Modeling (ORM) notation[5] it will be clear that the iconic sign of Fig. 1.5 can be used to express all relations that comply with this form. If we step outside of ORM more possibilities emerge. For instance the diagram may be used as a blueprint for an airport interface by means of which a passenger can look up the travelling scheme for flights between two airports (circles) and gets the times of departure and arrival within an appropriate span of time (rectangles).

But it also will be clear that as long as the icon is not amended in such a way that it is applied to specific cases, the icon only has the *possibility* to function as a sign that contains information about objects, but actually does not function thus. In order to coordinate the relations stated with real objects we are in need of a different type of relation, a relation that points out to what (sets of) object(s) the iconic sign is assumed to apply. That is where the indexical relation comes in. In Fig. 1.6 we give ORM notation for a first impression of the role of the indexical relation.

It is the dashed oval that most clearly relates the model to the universe we want to model. However, since a model stands in a representational relation to its presumed objects, a physical, or pure, indexical relation is beyond reach and we have to settle for a symbolic indexical relation. Relating the model to the universe we communicate about with the help of icons is the function of the (symbolic) index.

A sign has an **indexical relation** with its object if it directs the attention

---

[5]More on ORM notation can be found in (Halpin, 1998/2006).

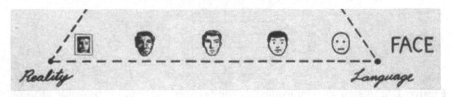

Figure 1.7: The continuum of icons and symbols. More iconic (left), more symbolic (right)

 "There"

Figure 1.8: The continuum of indexes and symbols. Note that iconic elements are involved as soon as we deal with indexes

to an object without conveying any information about it, besides its here and now existence (cf. a pointer to the object).

In its purest from the indexical relation consists in a physical connection between sign and object. The imprint[6] of a foot in sand is a pure index that some creature has been present at that spot. Note by the way that the footprint with regard to its form is a pure icon that may convey what kind of creature it is.

Like icons, most indexes do not have a pure relation with their object. The arrow on your route planner, although it is positioned by physical means (indexicality) on the street map (iconic relation with the roads you drive on), needs knowledge about the conventions of the mapping system in order to be interpreted as indicating your position on the road. With ORM the connection is even more conventional. So, it is best to look at icons and indexes as being located somewhere on a continuum between pure (physical) and conventional (see Fig. 1.7[7] and Fig. 1.8). Here *conventional* means: in need of knowledge of the projection rules used. Before we can dwell on this we have to introduce the symbolic relation between sign and object. An example of a sign symbolically related with its object is provided in Fig. 1.9.

A sign has a **symbolic relation** with its object if the relation can only be established by means of mastery of the rules that govern the relation between sign and object. This characteristic clearly applies to the question given in Fig. 1.9. If we do not know that it is a sentence, the scribble can only function as an index of its producer. Another way to express this is to state that a symbol signifies

---

[6]Merriam-Webster gives for imprint: "to mark by or as if by pressure".
[7]Reproduced with permission by the author from (McCloud, 1994).

```
Peter,
    Do we have to evaluate the model of the personnel administration?
Best,
Bernard
```

Figure 1.9: A purely symbolic relation between sign and object

and/or denotes by means of conventions. However, since symbols depend on conventions for their interpretation they are in need of iconic elements in order to convey something and in need of indexical elements in order to relate what is conveyed with the universe we discourse about.

In the question of Fig. 1.9 the expressions *Peter*, *model*, and *personnel administration* have an indexical function. But in this context the identification is weak and can only be made stronger by adding indexes that are more unambiguously related to the universe of discourse. For example, by providing the surname of Peter or his social security number and the country that number is used in. For Bernard and Peter we assume that, since they have collateral experience with the objects named, they will be able to complete the symbolic signs with the indexes and icons needed in order to understand the message. For us, the situation differs. This points to the fact that in symbolic signs indexes and icons are involved that must be known in order to understand the sign. With regard to the expression *Peter*, the icon involved can be an image of Peter.

In the question of our example the symbolic icons *of the* relate the model to the department meant and *evaluate* specifies the operation of which it is asked whether it has to be performed. On top of that we have to deal with the mixed iconic, indexical character of the weakly identified model. Attached to the word 'model' in this context is, so we assume, the possibility that the interpreting actor is able to dredge up an icon of a model of the desired characteristics. But before we deal with processes of interpretation, we first have to become acquainted with the different relations that can be distinguished between sign and interpretant.

To now we have not added much to what is commonly supposed to be going on in our dealings with signs, besides maybe the close connection that is established with the sensory realm and the ordered way of working. A comparison with some terms used in logic will make this clear.

(Symbolic) iconicity is comparable with the predicate in Aristotelian logic[8] or with the function in predicate logic; it contains what is to be conveyed about the subject. (Symbolic) indexicality is comparable with the subject or argument. It does not contain any information about the subject, but specifies instead the object about which the (symbolic) iconic part of the sign conveys its information. Note that most indexical parts of signs are not pure indexes since a pure indexical relation is a relation of contiguity (the foot and the imprint in the

---

[8]Cf. propositions of the form "S is P" where S stands for the subject and P for the predicate.

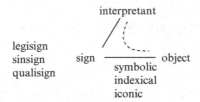

Figure 1.10: The three aspects of the sign–object relation added

Iconic relation (likeness)
A relation solely based on a similarity between characters expressed by the sign and characters of the object. It conveys something but does not denote any object.

Indexical relation (connection)
A relation based on a physical connection between the sign and its object. It does denote an object, but does not convey anything about it.

Symbolic relation (convention)
A relation between sign and object established by convention. Symbols have an indexical (*this, that*), iconic (*man, model*) or mixed function (*the man over there*). In the understanding of symbolic expressions both indices and icons are involved. In a sense the translation of our example sentence into an ORM scheme (Fig. 1.5) comes down to the extraction of relevant indexical and iconic elements from the sentence.

Table 1.2: Relations between sign and object

sand). Also note that the ORM diagram is not a pure icon since the conventions pertaining to the notation must be known in order to grasp the relations presented. The three aspects of the sign–object relation are shown in Fig. 1.10 and summarized in table 1.2.

N.B. In ORM notation the objects have an indexical symbolic relation with the objects of the depicted Universe of Discourse (UoD) and roles have an iconic symbolic relation with the way in which objects in the UoD are related to each other. The (entity) label is the closest possible approximation to a pure index. Since the modeled objects are not part of the model, a pure indexical relation with the depicted objects is not possible in the model. The model itself is thus of an iconic, symbolic character.

1.4 The sign in relation to its interpretant

Later, when we shift our attention from signs to processes of sign interpretation we will find out that signs 'generate' different kinds of interpretants or significative effects. For the moment we concentrate on the three modes in which a sign may address its interpretant sign. The modes, Term-like, Propositional and

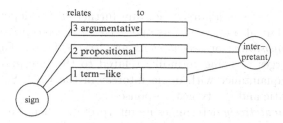

Figure 1.11: The three ways in which the sign offers its services to the interpretant

Argumentative, are distinguished by the way in which they govern our response possibilities. Or, as Peirce observes:

> [...] the difference between the Term, the Proposition, and the Argument, is by no means a difference of complexity, and does not so much consist in structure as in the services they are severally intended to perform. (CP 4.572)

Those services are raising an idea, stating a fact and convincing by reason, respectively. We will start with the term-like relation. See also Fig. 1.11.

Suppose that while you are walking on the street you find a note that you take up out of curiosity. The only words you find on the note are:

```
have to evaluate the model
```

There is not much you can do with this message in the proposed context. It conveys something, since we learned that supposedly there is a model of which it seems to be stated that it has to be evaluated. But that can be quite deceptive. Maybe we found a line that is meant to be part of a play, a question, or a school English assignment, etc. The message is about as informative as a word randomly selected in a dictionary. If a sign is related to its interpretant in this way, the object, thus also the interpretant, are left as they may be. The mode of address is *term-like* or *rhematic*. We may also formulate it negatively: if we remove the denotative force of the subject of a proposition or the informative content of the predicate, we are left with a blindly pointing term that just states existence or with a term that only proposes some character(s). A typical response to a term or rhematic sign is the exclamation: 'Oh'.

A *propositional* address of the actor that realizes an interpretant is already more engaging. The following sentence states some fact about the realm of objects.

```
Peter is head of IT.
```

Compared to a term-like sign the propositional sign definitely has a more determinate effect on the interpreting system without however prescribing the exact nature of the effect besides the invitation to judge the truth value of facts or assumed states of affairs. Since any further effects depend not only on the proposition but also on the goals operative in the receptive actor, typical responses to *propositions* or *dicent signs* are 'true', 'false'. But note that a proposition emerges as being term-like related to the interpretant for actors that have no acquaintance with or no interest in the UoD. So, for those the address is rhematic and the typical response is: 'Oh'.

A sign *argumentatively* determines its interpretant when the sign realizes its effect through compulsion by reason. In other words, if we accept the premises and we accept the rule of inference by which a conclusion is drawn from these premises, we will be ready to accept the conclusion.

What makes arguments quite confusing is that they need not be urged in full, but often only show themselves in fragments. A man tells his wife: "I am going to dry the laundry in the garden." The wife is offering an argument when she replies with: "It is raining." The premise "Laundry does not dry in rain" is hidden but effectively present, as is the conclusion.

Another complication arises when we realize that the distinction we made above between interpreting system on the one hand and interpretant on the other opens up the possibility of interpretants being part of different interpretative systems that form part of an encompassing organization that itself can be looked as an actor. For instance, questions, being requests for answers that serve a purpose, can be looked at as propositions that invoke reactions, or as being part of an argument in an encompassing actor on behalf of which the utterer and respondent act. Our sentence provides an example.

```
Dear Peter,
    Do we have to evaluate the model of the personnel administration with all
    the members of the personnel department before we decide to realize it in
    its current form or can we work with representatives of that department
    in order to validate the model?
Best,
Bernard
```

If we abstract from the human actors the question Bernard poses and the eventual reasoned answer of Peter together constitute an argumentative sign uttered by the organization regarded as the actor (i.e., the company as an 'individual').

From this we can conclude with Peirce that:

> An argument is a sign that tends to work on the interpreting actor through his[9] own self control. (cf. CP 4.538)

The three aspects of the sign–interpretant relation are depicted in Fig. 1.12 and summarized in Table 1.3.

1.4.1 Comparable terms

In the columns in Table 1.4 we provide the roughly equivalent terms in information science, logic and semiotics. Calling the turnstile (tourniquet) and the

---

[9]*its*, since not only man, but every dynamic sign is potentially an actor (see sect. 3.2).

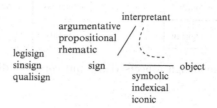

Figure 1.12: The three aspects of the sign–interpretant relation added

Term (qualitative possibility)
A sign that for its interpreter is neither true nor false, it just raises an idea.

Proposition (actual existence)
A sign that by its interpreter is taken as a statement of fact that can be true or false.

Argument (proposition)
A sign that for its interpreter states a relation of reason – as if it were a sign of the state of the universe to which it refers, in which the premises are taken for granted. (cf. CP 8.337)

Table 1.3: Relations between sign and interpretant

information science	logic	semiotics
1. Data	Term	Rheme
2. Knowledge	Proposition	Dicent
3. Information	Argument	Delome

Table 1.4: An overview of equivalent terms (the term information is used to indicate a knowledge increment)

rheme	dicent	argument		qualitative possibility	actual existence	proposition
icon	index	symbol		likeness	connection	convention
qualisign	sinsign	legisign		quality	actual event	rule

Figure 1.13: The nine sign aspects (left) and corresponding mundane terms (right)

		categorical aspect		
		1st	2nd	3rd
category	3	1 rhematic	2 propositional	3 argumentative
	2	1 iconic	2 indexical	3 symbolic
	1	1 qualisign	2 sinsign	3 legisign

Figure 1.14: From sign aspects to sign types

forced routing that ends at the pay-desk in a shop an argument, stretches the meaning of the term argument for some tastes too much. Calling it, after Peirce, a delome is a good, albeit not current, alternative. In this vein, a tourniquet is a rheme and a tourniquet conceived as being in a specific shop a dicent.[10]

An overview of all nine Peircean sign aspects is given in Fig. 1.13. Notice the difference in use between rhematic, propositional and argumentative on the one hand and rheme, proposition and argument on the other. In the first manner of use the emphasis is on the service rendered by the relational *sign aspect*, in the second it is as if we are talking about types of signs by means of a pars pro toto use of an aspect. For more on this see Appendix B.

1.5 A sign type as a combination of the three types of relation

Now that we have seen what modalities are possible for the relation of the sign (1) with itself, (2) with its object and (3) with its interpretant, it is of some interest to find out how those relations and relational modalities combine as *sign types*. In Fig. 1.14 the terms are summarized in a table.

Since a sign, in order to effectuate its representative possibilities, must have characters of its own, a relation with its objects, and a relation with its

---

[10]In a letter to Lady Welby (Oct 12, 1904) Peirce writes: "In regard to its relation to its signified interpretant, a sign is either a Rheme, a Dicent or an Argument. This corresponds to the old division Term, Proposition, & Argument, modified so as to be applicable to signs generally" (Hardwick, 1978), p. 33. The motive given, i.e., the extension of the scope of the terms beyond the domain of logic, urged Peirce in 1905 to be even more explicit, hence he suggested the terms Seme, Pheme and Delome (cf. CP 4.538).

interpretants, it follows that each sign will, at least, score in each of the categories discerned in the table (rows) on one of the categorical aspects (columns). Not all combinations are possible. Since the relations between the aspects from different categories are asymmetrical, we end up with 10 different basic sign types (see also Appendix A).

Included in CP. 2.254–2.263 is a description by Peirce of all 10 sign types and some of their interrelations and dependencies are given. In Appendix B the whole fragment with some amendments is given. It is steep reading, but also a good opportunity to get somewhat more familiar with the way in which the terms are put to use.

The important conclusion of this section is that in any actual process of semiosis, the only sign type that implies a reaction is the *argumentative sign*. Note that in an argumentative sign *all* other, less developed sign aspects are involved.

Chapter 2

From signs to interpretants

In the previous chapter the most general properties of signs were introduced. In this chapter the focus will shift from presenting a list of the most general sign aspects to an analysis of what happens in the process of interpretation, that is, to what can be said about the process in which a sign brings an interpretant into the same relation to its object as the sign itself stands.

As a start the sign definition of the last chapter will be looked at in greater detail. We will ask what it may mean that the interpretant is brought into the *same* triadic relation with the object as the sign itself stands. It will be shown that, depending on the sense in which 'same' is taken –strong or weak– two interpretations of the definition are possible. The strong interpretation of sameness only covers the copying of the representamen into the receptive system; it is when we use the weak interpretation that we can deal with the information that is conveyed by the sign. This differentiation of possible effects of the sign calls for a differentiation of interpretants. The focus of this chapter is on the different interpretants distinguished by Peirce.

2.1   Strong and weak sameness

Now that we have at our disposal the sign aspects that can be discerned, the time has come to take a more detailed look at the sign definition provided in the last chapter (see also Fig. 2.1).

> A *Sign*, or *Representamen*, is a First which stands in such a genuine triadic relation to a Second, called its *Object*, as to be capable of determining a Third, called its *Interpretant*, to assume the **same** triadic relation to its Object in which it stands itself to the same Object [...] (CP 2.274; bold added by the authors)

What, it may be asked, does the word *same* mean in the above definition? If same is taken in the strongest sense possible, the conclusion must be that a score of a sign and its resulting interpretant on all involved sign aspects remains

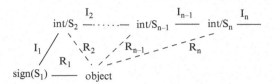

Figure 2.1: Diagram of the 1903 definition of a sign. As stated in Chapter 1, each instance of int/S_i ($1\leq i\leq n$) represents a sign as an interpretant-that-becomes-a-sign by actualizing its relational capability I_i; and that, as a consequence, stands in a relation R_i to its object. That relation to the object is 'the same'. So, R_1, R_2, ..., R_n are the same, in short R, and I_1, I_2, ..., I_n are the same, in short I

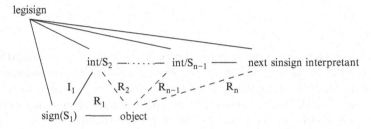

Figure 2.2: All interpretants have the same relation to the object as the sign has. Note that in this figure, as opposed to Fig. 2.1, the emphasis is put on the sign in itself. This is expressed by a shift from sign (or int/S) to sinsign interpretant. Qualisigns are assumed to be involved but not represented

the same in **form** and **content**. But then a sign can never grow in information and only the copy function is covered by the definition. If this is the case the diagram of Fig. 2.1 must imply that every interpretant becoming a sign for a new interpretant is a new sinsign (cf. instance) and that the whole range is governed by one legisign (cf. rule) in principle. This situation is depicted in Fig. 2.2.

In sign interpretation this copying must be involved, otherwise signs could not affect our life. Without copying the sign would not make any impression. In Sect. 2.2 this process of 'taking in' the sign (from S_i to S_{i+1}, in Fig. 2.2) is described in terms of different kinds of interpretants. But this copying of signs (which from the point of view of interpretation can be looked at as the apprehension of the sign as an object) alone does not go very far in explaining the ways in which signs work; they must be capable of having effects that exceed the transfer of instances, they must be able to reveal more than their own form and on top of that they must be able to grow in information. This calls for a weakening of the meaning of same. Is it to be taken as same in form, but not always in content? Or is it better to say that the relation must remain triadic, but that the form as well as the content may change in the process? In order to be better able to deal with this question we will have to study the way in which a sign achieves its informational effects. To that end Peirce distinguished still more kinds of interpretants. These will be presented in Sect. 2.3. Note that the sign aspect – sign type distinction ought to re-emerge as a distinction between interpretant aspects and interpretant types.

2.2 The interpretation of the sign taken in itself

Let's concentrate on human sign interpretation and ask what it takes to be able to get a new instance of a sign without bothering about its meaning. Suppose you are a member of the personnel department that is part of the company Peter and Bernard work for. One day you find a note on your desk with the following sentence written on it:

Do we have to evaluate the model for the personnel administration?

Our analysis starts at the moment you see the note, take it up and direct your eyes towards the surface the sentence is written upon. What happens in the split second before you have an idea of the meaning of the sentence, what modifications of mind occur? Note that the mind, as the domain we are working in, makes the question different from the same question from a neurological perspective. We are not following the tract of the sense involved (in this case the visual), we start at the moment the sign knocks at the door of the mind (cf. impression). It is also important to remark that the following analysis is not psychological. We do not investigate the workings of the human mind, we are not interested in response times, in effects of psychical pressures or personality traits on sign processing; we investigate the behavior of signs on the most general level possible.

When you have turned your eyes towards the note and look at the surface, your mind is affected by the qualities of the representamen you are facing. The sign produces an imprint that triggers a feeling in your mind. This feeling is aroused by the complexity of the manifold of impressions that arise in your mind when facing the sentence.[1] This feeling of complexity regarded in itself is the purely subjective accompaniment of being confronted with a manifold that asks for analysis (cf. a 'primordial soup'). It instigates us to try to make sense of what we are confronted with. This first significative effect of the sentence on the note Peirce termed an *emotional interpretant*.

If anything further follows from the sign this happens through the mediation of the emotional interpretant and it will involve an effort. The involvement of an effort is probably the reason why Peirce named those interpretants energetic. Two such interpretants follow from the emotional interpretant. Both are characterized by being of the nature of a single act. The first, the *mental energetic interpretant*, takes the emotional interpretant after its form. It is a one time occurrence (sinsign) of an iconic nature (the form of an imprint), with the emphasis on iconic. The second, the *physical energetic interpretant*, takes the form as an occurrence. It must be a single act and as such have a form, but here the

---

[1]Cf. CP 1.554

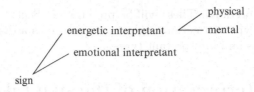

Figure 2.3: Interpretant aspects governing strong sameness between sign and interpretant

emphasis is on the occurrence (temporal aspect of the imprint), not the form. So, the sinsign aspect is predominant in the physical energetic interpretant.[2]

In the model of cognitive information processing introduced in this book we differentiate both interpretants more sharply, leaving for the mental interpretant just the iconicity apart from its one time occurrence, and for the physical interpretant only the one time occurrence and we assume that both must be present simultaneously. Thus we arrive at the point that a copy of the sentence, without the recognition that it is a copy, is generated by your mind.

To summarize, in the first stage the feeling, aroused by a manifold of unanalyzed qualities that is knocking at the door of your mind, instigates you to seek a resolution for an experience of uneasiness. In the second stage that which caused the feeling appears as a one time form (mental energetic interpretant) that impresses itself as a single occurrence in your mind/brain (physical energetic interpretant).[3] In Fig. 2.3 and in Table 2.1 a schema is provided for the interpretant aspects dealt with thus far.

As remarked above, up until this point the sign revealed nothing but its own shape, still without the recognition that the shape present to the mind is similar to the instance of the form of the sentence on the note. Any further significative effect a sign may have falls within the range of the logical interpretant. Since the logical interpretant covers more than the apprehension of the sign as an object we will proceed to the next paragraph.

2.3   The interpretation of what a sign reveals

In Chapter 3 we will have to introduce three kinds of interpretant that were not recognized by Peirce. One of these is the interpretant counterpart of the legisign. Since it is in the interest of the reader to keep a clear distinction

---

[2]It must be noted that our interpretation does not follow fluently from the sources. In (Peirce, C.S, 1931-58) the *energetic interpretant* only occurs five times. These occurrences can very easily be interpreted in a different way. We are of the opinion that if Peirce had considered linking the different sign aspects with the interpretant aspects or, in other words, if he had been more specific with regard to the distinction between interpretant aspects and interpretant types, he would have been more specific with regard to the definition of the energetic interpretants.

[3]For those interested in support from a neurological perspective see (Ramachandran & Hirstein, 1997).

Emotional Interpretant
A subjective element of thought, a **feeling** as it occurs at a specific moment, indicating the presence of a manifold of impressions that need to be brought to unity.

Energetic Interpretant
The name for the class of interpretant aspects that rule the copying of the external sign into your mind.
Energetic Mental Interpretant
The one time **form** the qualities appear in.

Energetic Physical Interpretant
The one time **imprint** of the form in the mind/nervous system. Or, to put it in other words, the recognition of the co-occurrence of the form and your mind.

Table 2.1: Interpretant aspects in the copy sign stage

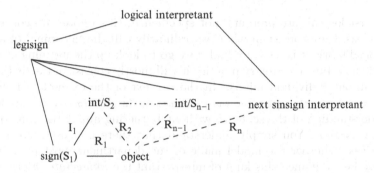

Figure 2.4: The logical interpretant and its relation to the iconic sinsign or energetic (mental and physical) interpretant on the one hand and the legisign on the other. The qualisign and emotional interpretant are assumed but not given

between what Peirce developed and what is added later, we will proceed as if the sentence written on the note already is recognized as an instance (sinsign) of a type (legisign) and thus can be meaningful to you as a sentence and not just as some erratic pattern of lines. Our starting point is depicted in Fig. 2.4.

What is the way in which the sentence, at this point consisting of the configuration of a mental and a physical interpretant and their associated legisign, develops its meaning in your mind? A first and very informal treatment is provided by the following quote taken from Peirce.[4]

In the next step of thought, those first *logical interpretants* stimulate us to various voluntary performances in the inner world. We imagine ourselves in various situations and animated by various motives; and we proceed to trace out the alternative lines of conduct which the conjectures would leave open to us. We are, moreover, led, by the same inward activity, to remark different ways in which

---

[4] Written around 1906–07.

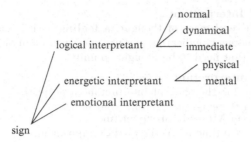

Figure 2.5: Schema with Peircean interpretants and their class names

our conjectures could be slightly modified. The logical interpretant must, therefore, be in a relatively future tense. (CP 5.481; italics added by the authors).

The first logical interpretants, not specified in this quote, are concepts or general ideas; they consist in what we ordinarily call the 'meaning' of a term. In the social fabric it is what we find if we go to look up the meaning of a word in a dictionary, but in ordinary practice it will mostly consist in the dictionaries we have in our individual minds. In the context of the example sentence, `Do we have to evaluate the model for the personnel administration?`, it comes down to your understanding of the sentence without bothering about the consequences of what is stated. You simply understand that there is a question in which someone asks whether the model made of the department must be validated. Elsewhere Peirce named this kind of interpretant the *immediate interpretant*.

Next you start doing what is stated in the quote above. You realize that the department meant is your department, that the question is directed to you and that an answer is expected. As a consequence you start thinking about the possible effects of the question on your working life. You start thinking about the real consequences of an affirmative answer and compare them with the effects of a negative. You are in short making up your mind in order to decide what this question means in your situation at this moment. Maybe you find it difficult to decide on your course of action. This may result in an evasive movement and a search for other types of response. You may even wonder why the note was delivered to your desk in the first place. Was it a recognition of ability and a honest question for approval or a law-inspired move in the process that leads to your dismissal? Or you may notice that no addressee is given and no sender indicated and decide first to find out what is the status of the message. However, whatever response you choose, you respond on the basis of the meaning the sentence on this occasion has for you and not on the basis of the meaning of the sentence in general. Both the specific response and the specific meaning the sentence has for you on this occasion are, ambiguously, named by Peirce the *dynamical interpretant*. In the next chapter we will disambiguate this term.

Logical Interpretant
The name for the class of interpretant types distinguished in the meaning evolution stage.

    Immediate Interpretant
    The **meaning** of the sign **in general**.

Dynamical Interpretant
1. The **meaning** that the sign gets **on a specific occasion** of sign interpretation in a specific interpreting system. Henceforth this interpretant is to be called a dynamical interpretant.
2 The **specific response** by an interpreting system triggered by the dynamical interpretant, but governed by the normal interpretant. Henceforth this interpretant is to be called a Dynamical Interpretant Response (DIR).

Normal Interpretant
The **dynamics that governs** the **response** to a sign on a special occasion and the **habit(s)** involved **as an evolving tendency**.

Table 2.2: Interpretant aspects and the resulting interpretant type in the meaning evolution stage

Now, suppose you have chosen a line of action and you responded in a certain way to the question. That response will probably have consequences and you will have to face the consequences. If the consequences are negative, you will probably choose a different response next time you face a similar question and if the consequences were according to or above expectations you will develop a propensity to act in the same way in future cases. Whatever the realized value, the response in combination with the reaction to it are part of a *process* in which a habit is formed that rules the way in which you will respond in future cases. In other words, your response tends to normalize in the long run. Peirce indicates this process with the term *normal interpretant*. Events of this process are approximations of the terminating normal interpretant also called the *final interpretant*. The Peircean interpretants and their class names are recapitulated in Fig. 2.5 and Table 2.2.

Chapter 3

A semiotic account of interpretation processes

In this chapter we will flesh out the consequences of the assumption that it makes no sense to distinguish aspects of a sign if those aspects do not play a role in the process of interpretation that leads to the generation of a new sign that must, by definition, have the same sign aspects as the original sign. That interpretational process is described by Peirce in terms of different kinds of interpretants. So, as a first step the different sign aspects will be matched with the different interpretant aspects. It will be shown in Sect. 3.1 that some sign aspects are not covered by interpretant aspects. If, as we assumed, it makes no sense to distinguish aspects of a sign if those aspects do not play a role in the process of interpretation, we need to find a way to introduce them. In Sect. 3.2, we propose the semiotic sheet as a means to focus on specific processes of interpretation by interpreting systems. In Sect. 3.3 we will introduce corresponding interpretant aspects for the remaining sign aspects.

3.1 Matching sign aspects with interpretant aspects

In Chapter 1 nine sign aspects were introduced and in Chapter 2 six kinds of interpretants. Figure 3.1 summarizes the results.[1] Note that the names *interpretant, energetic interpretant* and *logical interpretant* only serve as class names. We left them because in secondary literature and in applications of semiotics they may be used.

A basic rule of semiotics states that an interpretant sign only relates to its object through the sign of which it is an interpretant, and never directly. So, any mismatch between sign aspects and interpretant aspects cannot be resolved

---

[1]This arrangement was first presented by van Driel (1993).

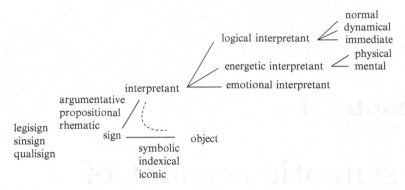

Figure 3.1: Sign aspects and interpretant types

by an appeal to a direct relation between interpretant and object. Having said this, can we match the terms and if so how?

At first sight the emotional interpretant does not match with the qualisign because a qualisign, as the name already indicates, has signifying possibilities due to the quality it has, while an emotional interpretant is a feeling that cries for resolution in the face of unanalyzed impressions. If, however, we realize that qualisigns can only be found in their realization in instances and never in themselves, the feeling indicating the presence of qualities that seek to make themselves known appears as a reasonable substitute for the qualisign aspect. Assumed by the notion *emotional interpretant* are the qualia in their unanalyzed form. Filling in a field in a web application may serve as an example. The 'mind' of the application (interpreting system) extends to your screen. You scribe characters on this interface. But until you hit the enter key, it does not matter to the system that something is written. After hitting the key the first action the system performs is the acceptance of input in order to determine the input type in a subsequent stage, i.e., is the input of the right type? The relation between the feeling and the impressions in their unanalyzed form is like the relation between the enter key and the input. In both cases the demand is: if possible, make sense of the input!

The mental energetic interpretant, regarded as the modification of the inner world, can directly be matched with the icon aspect, since it consists in giving shape to the unanalyzed impressions. The physical energetic interpretant, regarded as *existence*, can equally easily be matched with the sinsign aspect. All in all, by now we have a match between a sinsign and icon in which qualities are realized and organized in a form on the one hand, and an energetic physical and mental interpretant as a one time occurring shape in which the impressions become organized on the other. In terms of the field-to-be-filled example this moment in the process of interpretation is equal to making up the format of the input (the token) and the acceptance of it in working memory without at that point having judged whether the input is of a valid type.

With the members of the class of logical interpretants the issue of the transfer and/or evolution of meaning gets addressed. For the counterpart of the immediate interpretant, we have two candidates, the symbol aspect and the rheme aspect. The immediate interpretant is determined as the meaning of the sign in general or, what comes to the same thing, the meaning of the sign as it is revealed in the right understanding of the sign itself. A symbolic relation is defined as a conventional relation between sign and object. This rules out the symbol since the immediate interpretant is not specific about the objects to which the sign relates. A rhematic relation between sign and interpretant is defined as a relation in which the sign leaves it to the interpreter to relate it to an object, it just raises an idea. So, this must be the counterpart of an immediate interpretant. In the example, the immediate interpretant can be looked at as the input regarded in isolation from the application into which it is scribed.

The dynamical interpretant has its proxy in the propositional relation between sign and interpretant. This must be so because a sign with a propositional relation between sign and interpretant communicates a fact that can be judged according to its truth value, while the dynamical interpretant indicates the meaning the sign has here and now for the interpreter. In the context of the web form application the dynamical interpretant consists in that state of the application that arises just before the 'submit order' button (cf. return key) is hit and the check on the validity of the input (format) and on the completeness of obligatory fields is completed. It is the acceptance by the application of the order placed (items, order no.) by a specific person (name, address, customer no.) with a specific credit card account.

The Dynamic Interpretant Response (DIR) is a response to the sign. It is not just an interpretant aspect, but a full-blown interpretant (sign) type. This response is governed by the normal interpretant. So, the normal interpretant must be the interpretant equivalent of the argument. As the dynamical interpretant is subsumed under the habit contained in the normal interpretant and yields a DIR as its conclusion, the propositional relation between sign and interpretant only yields a response if the proposition becomes embedded in an argument. In the web form application the dynamical interpretant (the order) is subjected to several rules that govern the response of the system to the order. One of the first rules could be:

> If the address exists and the credit card account is valid, transfer the order to the delivery department. (Assuming that the check on availability is performed in the pre-order stage.)

This rule together with the validated dynamical interpretant will result in the actual sending of the order form to the delivery department. The actual sending of the order is the DIR. The rule, together with the two types of dynamical interpretant (the dynamical interpretant and the DIR), belongs to the normal interpretant. We can't say they make up the normal interpretant, because the normal interpretant is the tendency with a normalized response as its limit, while this is just one event in that tendency.

Figure 3.2: The proposition P→Q in Existential Graph notation

For three sign aspects we have no interpretant aspects as their counterpart, these are the legisign, the index and the symbol aspects. In Sect. 3.3 we will introduce their interpretant counterparts after the introduction of a special type of sign, a sign capable of sign processing and information growth, in Sect. 3.2.

3.2   Semiotic sheets

Although Peirce always carefully distinguished the interpreter from the different interpretants, he never brought them into an explicit, systematic relation in his writings on semiotics. Since he explicitly regarded man as a sign this is rather curious. In this paragraph we will repair the omission by transferring an idea (the *sheet of assertion*) he developed in his graphical system of logic (the Existential Graphs, see Fig. 3.2)[2] to semiotics.

Peirce introduces the sheet of assertion thus:

> It is agreed that a certain sheet, or blackboard, shall, under the name of The Sheet of Assertion, be considered as representing the universe of discourse, and as asserting whatever is taken for granted between the graphist and the interpreter to be true of that universe. The sheet of assertion is, therefore, a graph. (CP 4.396, 1903)

The term *graph* is used by Peirce solely in the context of discussions on logic. The sheet of assertion is a graph on which graphs are scribed. A graph is defined as

> [...] the propositional expression in the System of Existential Graphs of any possible state of the universe. (CP 4.395)

In semiotic terms a graph is a sign of the type symbolic, propositional legisign. But in semiotics we are not interested in only one type of sign; we are interested in all types of sign. And, on top of that, we are not only interested in the dialogue between a graphist and an interpreter on a sheet that is placed between both; we are also interested in the interpretative/responsive processes that take place in the graphist and the interpreter themselves.

---

[2]The Existential Graphs consists of three parts. The Alpha part is isomorphic to the propositional calculus, the Beta part to first order logic and the Gamma part to normal modal logic.

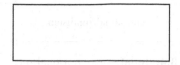

Figure 3.3: A blank semiotic sheet

A semiotic sheet(S_S)[3] is a means to represent any sign that is able to *interpret* and *respond* to signs. Being a sign, conceived as a sheet on which signs inscribe themselves, it has different modalities. Since the modalities can be applied recursively we do not claim to provide an exhaustive account in what follows. The modalities are: the Possible (P), the Actual (A) and the Lawful (L). In its P-modality (S_S^P) the sheet is conceived to contain whatever is inscribed and potentially can be used if a sign offers itself for interpretation. In its A-modality (S_S^A) the sheet is conceived to be in the state it is in at the moment a sign inscribes itself. In its L-modality (S_S^L) the sheet contains the habitually inscribed goals and the habits[4] that govern the production of interpretants on the occasion of a sign offering itself for interpretation.

Semiotic sheets may be subdivided into different types according to their ability to deal with signs for which no habits of interpretation are present. At one extreme of the continuum are S_S that always respond on unknown input with a DIR that communicates the termination of interpretation: these are rigid or closed systems. At the other extreme are S_S that are capable of producing new habits of and goals for interpretation even when these are contradictory on a more general level with existing habits and goals: these are open systems due to their ability to learn. Typical examples of the latter are organizations, interest groups and man. A typical example of the former is the web application that handles orders.[5]

3.3   Sign processing on semiotic sheets

Let us start with a cautionary remark before proceeding. In the following treatment the way of working is from the input to the responding DIR in an ordered way. In input driven information processing this is the regular way. In man however familiarity with certain aspects of our environment and expectation may cause selective perception and the production of DIRs on expectation. For instance: when confronted with a computer the habits of interpretation can be expected to differ significantly between a professional who sees his tool and a

---

[3]In the following S_S will be used to refer to the singular as well as to the plural form of semiotic sheet.

[4]For the importance of goal orientation see (van Breemen, Sarbo, & van der Weide, 2007).

[5]Note that in contradistinction to a mere calculator the web application stores the input that occasioned a DIR and uses the stored information, if needed, on subsequent occasions. This marks the difference between a clever tool like a calculator and a S_S or information system.

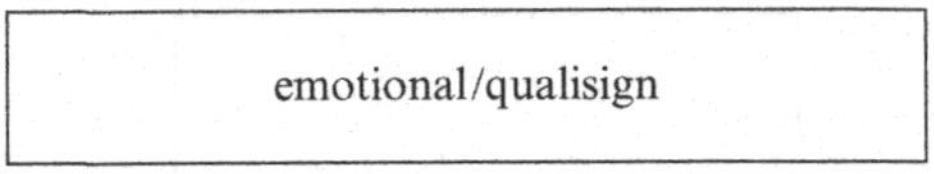

```
┌─────────────────────────────────────────┐
│                                         │
│           emotional/qualisign           │
│                                         │
└─────────────────────────────────────────┘
```

Figure 3.4: Input: the emotional interpretant

child who sees a potentiality to play, or between a retailer and a recycle special-ist (selective perception). Children that have an inclination to read 'top down'[6] and misread the number of a word (plural, singular) early in the sentence will as a rule systematically repeat the same mistake later in the sentence. This is an example of selective perception resulting in the production of DIRs on expectation.

At the start of Sect. 3.1 we remarked that the mismatch between the number of sign aspects and interpretant aspects cannot be resolved by an appeal to a contribution of the object because a basic rule of Peircean semiotics states that knowledge of an object is always mediated by signs and never direct. If the mismatch cannot be resolved by an appeal to a contribution of sign or object, the only remaining source is the S_S. In this section it will be shown that it is possible to introduce the three missing interpretant aspects by an appeal to the contribution of a S_S.

Figure 3.3 represents the S_S in an actual state (S_S^A), which at this moment is blank due to its not being confronted with a sign. It is supposed to contain the S_S^P and S_S^L, the contents of which can only have effects in acts of interpretation.

The moment a sign inscribes itself in a S_S^A, interpretation arises. The first effect of the interaction between the S_S and the sign is the production of an immediate interpretant. The immediate interpretant is the recognition of the fact that the sheet was in a certain state and now is in another state, a state in which some unanalyzed multitude of impressions asks for resolution.

Figure 3.4 represents the S_S in an actual state, being confronted with a sign. Considered as a *feeling*, this state is what it is independent of anything else. Considered as an *element of thought*, this state is assumed to consist in what was present in the previous state and the unanalyzed multitude of impressions aroused by a sign. Their collection as a whole (cf. input) is not sorted out at this point.

If this feeling is to have any further significative effects these effects must be mediated by the two energetic interpretants, the mental and the physical. Figure 3.5 represents the sorting out of the impressions in a *form*, the mental interpretant (iconic), as an *occurrence*, the physical interpretant, that happens now on this particular sheet (sinsign). The physical interpretant does not add any information besides the acknowledgment of the fact that the sheet and the form are co-existent. The mental interpretant at this moment is also not conveying information (although it contains the possibility to do so later on); it is just the presence of a form that was not present on the sheet in the state before.

---

[6]Top down readers read what they expect to see which may diverge from what is written.

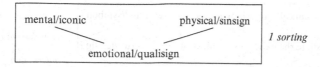

Figure 3.5: Sorting out: the mental and physical interpretants

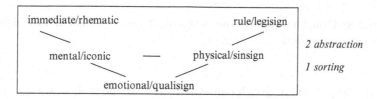

Figure 3.6: Abstracting: the rule and the immediate interpretant

Figure 3.6 represents the dual direction in which the process evolves. For each direction both elements of the first stage are required. The dependency is expressed by the horizontal line. The difference is determined by the element stressed. The **mental** *(energetic) interpretant* results in the immediate interpretant (rhematic). Through the rheme *all possible* forms of the sign can be explored, but it takes multiple processes to do so. The forms presented in Fig. 3.7 may serve as an example. Note that not only the vase and the faces belong to the class of all possible forms since the figure can also be looked at as a distribution of black and white.

With the **physical** *(energetic) interpretant* the stress is on the *instantiation* of the form. If the form is repeated on the same S_S the result is a growing familiarity and a rule of *interpretation* (legisign) arises. Once this rule is established, a new instance will be recognized as an instance of the form. The rule or legisign must be assumed to be given as a possibility in the immediate interpretant. But note that in an act of interpretation only one of the possible legisigns can realize itself, although in the rheme all possible legisigns are given. We see either the vase form or the faces form and are thus dealing with two different rule-physical-mental interpretant combinations. Since interpretation can be looked at from a 'bottom up' or data-driven and a 'top down' or anticipatory perspective, it makes sense to add here the top down way of looking at this

Figure 3.7: Different possible rhemes and legisigns are associated with this mental interpretant

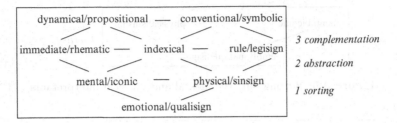

Figure 3.8: Complementation: the indexical, the conventional and the dynamical interpretant aspects

matter. In a top down approach one would say that the immediate interpretant mediates the form to the instance as an actual occurrence and that the rule mediates the instance to the form as a member of a class of instances. This is a very tricky point in thinking about the process of interpretation for several reasons:

1. It is very easy and tempting to switch from what happens in the perceptual process at a given instant to the sign that is on the sheet without noticing it. In the sign the two forms are present, but in the percept only one shows up.

2. The form is ambiguous, but once one of the possible forms becomes the percept, the associated symbol is retrieved; it will be either 'faces' or 'vase'. So, it is not ambiguity of meaning but of form (for ambiguity of meaning see the 'bank' example below).

3. Ultimately it is this stage on which we base the step from percepts of the mind to signs as the source of percepts just because there are percepts that we cannot think away, that therefore must be aroused by something that exists independent of our individual mind. Here the sign itself is the object of the percept (sign).

This interpretant aspect (cf. rule), not recognized by Peirce, may be looked at as a contribution of the sheet to the interpretational process, but notice that in the end it is the sign itself that enables the sheet to contribute in this way by repeatedly offering itself for interpretation.

Figure 3.8 represents the way in which the meaning of the sign unfolds on this occasion and on this sheet. In actual practice, if we are looking at one run of the process, only one interpretation follows out of the multitude of possible interpretations. In theory we have to deal with the way in which the different possibilities arise.

As a first approach we ask you to look at the left (middle) diagonal that runs from physical interpretant up to the dynamical interpretant and compare this diagonal with the one below and the one above, from the perspective of the different modalities of the sheet. The diagonal in the middle expresses the actuality of the process, the one at the bottom all possibilities offered by the sign

Figure 3.9: Different symbols attached to a legisign (source: Merriam-Webster's 11th Collegiate Dictionary)

that may become actual and even habitual, and the one at the top expresses the habits attached to what actually goes on in the brain. The latter determines the real effect a sign shall have on future states of the mind/brain and eventually, through exertions of the will, on the world. But the habits can only exert their different influences on specific occasions, that is to say, if they are connected with the actual sign and the possibilities offered by that sign. In order to express these connections a new interpretant aspect must be introduced. We call it the connective interpretant or *context* (pointer), but will use in the schema the term indexical interpretant or index(ical) for brevity's sake and because it is the corresponding sign aspect. The connective interpretant expresses the contiguity of all interpretation moments involved by tying subsequent stages of interpretation to what has happened thus far and by enabling the sheet to furnish whatever is needed in subsequent stages. It is through the indexicality that lower stages are always involved in the higher!

The rule (legisign) will normally have habitual meanings associated with it. In a dictionary the different meanings are given. See Fig. 3.9 in which, on the left hand side, one legisign is given and, on the right hand side, the different meanings of the legisign for one of its syntactical roles. On a sheet only one of these possibilities will be realized at a time, which is the possibility that through the mediation of the index gets associated with the legisign on a specific sheet. Note that different sheets may have different meanings associated with the same legisign, cf. "going to the bank" will have a preferred habitual meaning on the sheet of the financial specialist that differs significantly from the one on the sheet of a fisherman (ambiguity of *subject*), just as the meaning of "driving fast" on the sheet of a racing driver is opposed to that on the sheet of an average driver (ambiguity of *predicate*).

Peirce did not introduce an interpretant for this moment in the interpretational process. So, we introduce the *conventional interpretant*. It is the interpretant aspect that corresponds to the symbolic sign aspect.

Note that the conventional meaning that gets attached to the legisign on a specific occasion is still the meaning in general. It is not the meaning on a specific occasion with a specific purpose. It is in short not the contextualized meaning, but rather the involvement of the context in the effect of the legisign aspect. Contextualization is expressed on the other side of the model. The index

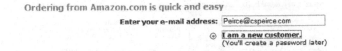

Figure 3.10: Contextualization performed in the dynamical interpretant

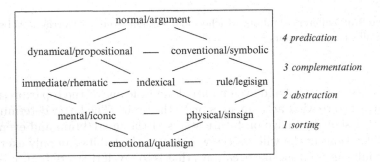

Figure 3.11: Predication: the normal interpretant delivering a DIR

mediates the immediate interpretant to a dynamical interpretant aspect which expresses the meaning the sign gets on a specific sheet in specific circumstances. It is important to note that through the index the legisign aspect is also involved in this interpretation moment.

In Fig. 3.10 a screen shot is made from one moment in the order sequence of Amazon. The string "Peirce@cspeirce.com" in the e-mail address field is a legisign with as its conventional meaning "the e-mail address of a person called Peirce". In its regular context, the order sequence as run on a server of Amazon, the previous state of the S_S^A is primed in such a way that the S_S^A leaves little room for ambiguity in the dynamical interpretant (the named customer is at this point in the process of ordering the articles on the associated order form), but the string out of this context (on another S_S^A) can be contextualized in different ways. We, knowing that Ch.S. Peirce died in 1914, was a famous philosopher, mathematician, etc., may think there is somebody with the same name. You may take the string in this context as part of an example and story to be told, but you could also surmise that there is a website to be found at `cspeirce.com`

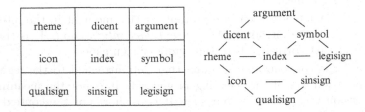

Figure 3.12: Static (left) and dynamic (right) interpretation of sign aspects

that is devoted to the semiotician. What you take the string to mean without any further action being taken, is what you pick out of all the different contexts in which the string may be put. This, however, does not mean that you are supposed to cycle through the possibilities; it only means that in each run of the process only one of them is taken.

Figure 3.11 represents the finalization of the interpretation of the sign that offered itself. In a strict sense the node of the normal interpretant represents the state change of the S_S^A from its previous state to its current state resulting from a sign inscribed in the S_S^A. If the symbol is compatible with the dynamical interpretant aspect a state of belief terminates the state of doubt that instigated us to resolve the unanalyzed impressions. In that state of belief all interpretation moments are assumed to be involved.

To summarize, there are nine interpretant aspects corresponding to the nine sign aspects. The difference between static classification and dynamic interpretation is illustrated by Fig. 3.12 in the left- and right-hand side diagrams, respectively.

3.3.1 Towards a theory of interpretation

In the process of generating a new sign, which possibly includes transformation and enrichment, the sign aspects appear as moments in the process of interpretation. This ideally implies that through interpretation increasingly better approximations of the import of the sign are realized. In this process, information pertaining to the sign is explicated in each interpretation moment, for otherwise subsequent interpretation moments would not be more than a mere re-generation of already existing states. As this growth of information involves a contribution by the interpreting system itself and assuming there is a single sign offering itself for interpretation, we need a shift of view and must consider the sign (S) to be an *effect*, affecting the interpreting system occurring in a *state*. As the interpretation, representing the system's reaction on the input, steadily develops, it can occasion the 'generation' of further interpretation moments that themselves may be regarded as signs. Such a process is schematically illustrated in Fig. 3.13.

In order to keep a clear distinction between the sign and the interpretant perspective we term these interpretation moments interpretant aspects, or simply, following Peirce, interpretants. By prefixing the term interpretant with an adjective we are able to distinguish the different characteristic contributions to the development of the import of a sign.

The individual interpretation events change the state of the interpreting system. In Fig. 3.13, this is indicated by the sequence of states $\sigma = <\sigma_1, \ldots, \sigma_k>$, for $1 \leq k$. We use the convention that in state σ_j ($1 \leq j \leq k$), the interpreting system is involved in the generation of I_j, the interpretant of S_j. O designates the shared, common object of S_j for $1 \leq j \leq k$. The triadic relation (S_j, O, I_j), or the next state of the interpreting system functions as a potential sign in a subsequent interpretation event.

For instance, $\sigma_2 = (S_1, O, I_1)$ is interpreted as S_2. Note that k may stand

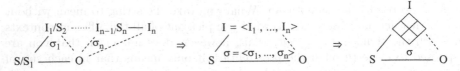

Figure 3.13: Interpretation depicted as a series of events (left) and a single event (middle), paraphrased as an instance of the processing schema (right). I_j, S_j, σ_j for $1 \leq j \leq k$ ($1 \leq k$) stand for interpretants, signs, and states, respectively; O is the shared, common object of $S_1, S_2, \ldots, S_k$. The symbol "/" expresses the possibility of a change of view from the result of a former to the start of a subsequent interpretation process. This enables I_j to be looked at from two perspectives as the interpretant generated in σ_j and, as a representation of the next state, as a potential sign. Angle parentheses are used for a series interpreted as a single entity

for any natural number, as the set of states define a non-strictly monotonic ordering of increasingly better approximations of the meaning of S for a given interpreter.[7]

On the basis of this model, nine classes of interpretant aspects can be defined, in conformity with the nine classes of sign aspects. Among these nine interpretants, six are due to Peirce himself, and three are derived from the assumption that, given the fact that according to the sign definition an interpretant becomes a sign itself, it is sensible to assume that all nine sign aspects discerned have to reappear in the process of interpretation. The coordination of sign aspects with the different interpretants only proved possible after the introduction of the assumption that interpretation must involve an interaction between an observer (interpreting system) and a sign (representamen) (Farkas & Sarbo, 2000).

3.3.2   The case of the candy

A sketch example may summarize how the process works according to the model. The interpretation moments are indicated by their stage and numbered accordingly (1)-(4). Let's assume the sign is the verb 'halt'. It enters the S_S as a series of feelings (emotional interpretant).

(1) The feelings get sorted out as an icon (mental interpretant) and settle as a singularity or a sinsign (physical interpretant).

(2) Since it is a familiar iconic singularity a legisign arises (rule). Up to this point the copy function is executed: a new sinsign of the word "halt" is generated. Since it is a singular icon out of any context at this moment, a rheme (immediate interpretant) arises.

---

[7] For k>9, there must be states that are *degenerately* represented. In such states there is no increase in the approximation of S. We do not come any closer to the generation of all sign aspects.

Figure 3.14: Anticipatory information processing

(3) Assuming there is a strong habit that is connected to the legisign, by means of that connection a conventional meaning is retrieved and the sign is interpreted as a request to stop (convention). But, of course, at this point it also could mean that someone limps or that some actor is rehearsing. These possibilities are contained in the rheme. If, later on, the strong convention proves wrong, a new run of the process may retrieve those possibilities. Doubt is time consuming after all. Through the connection with what is contained in the S_S about the present situation ("Who has to stop? I am not moving."), the conventional meaning gets embedded in an understanding of the situation at hand (dynamical interpretant).

(4) This dynamical interpretant is, again through a connection with what is contained in the S_S, placed under a rule of habit that covers this kind of case and a response (DIR) is generated (normal interpretant). Since experience with the effect of different types of response will be fed back in the mechanism, successful responses tend to strengthen interpretation habits (final interpretant). But also note that if the S_S is in the state of expecting a sign, a 'top down' response speeds up the process considerably by action on expectation (see Fig. 3.14[8]); the child in the candy store says in that particular voice "Mom, [...]" and gets "No!" as an answer before being able to finish.

This closes the semiotic analysis of our model of interpretation. In the next part we will proceed with a cognitive account of the model. The dependency between interpretant aspects (see Fig. 3.11) as well as sign aspects (see Fig. 3.12) defines a relational structure. The goal of interpretation is to establish a *consistent* evaluation of the positions of this structure. This can be achieved in any order such as bottom-up, top-down or by using a mixed strategy. As the first or matching mode interpretation of the appearing sign is priming the interpreting

---

[8]This drawing and the drawings in Chapter 7 are designed in the style of (Korcsmáros, 1985).

system,[9] analysis mode interpretation is most likely to proceed top-down, by exploiting the possibilities offered by the index.[10]

We will not pursue this line of optimization and, in order to enable a comparison of the different accounts of our model of interpretation, in the remainder of this book we will assume a bottom-up flow of information.

---

[9]Only if a consistent dependency structure cannot be established by matching, analysis mode interpetation will be offered to the sign.

[10]William James' distinction between associative thinking and reasoning is akin to our distinction between matching mode and analysis mode. In associative thinking the flow of thought proceeds uncontrolled; it yields the results it does. Reasoning controls and may inhibit spontaneous responses, it helps us out in novel situations; it requires inspection of the relations between ideas. Cf. (James, 1890/1983) Vol. 2, Chapter 22. If reasoning has achieved its goal by finding a satisfactory result, a habit is established that controls the associative stream of thought. The habit can be modeled as information processing. Capturing the reasoning that results in a habit is far more complicated.

Part II

Modeling cognitive information processing

In conformity with our assumption that knowledge arises from the observation of phenomena by means of signs, in this part we introduce a model for human information processing that is based on an analysis of properties of cognitive activity and signification. By offering a 'naive' logical interpretation of our model we establish a link between the interpretation moments we distinguish and Peirce's sign aspects. This yields a twofold result. On the one hand it enables us to understand Peirce's classification of sign aspects as a process, on the other hand it enables us to understand our model of cognitive activity as a procedure underlying meaningful interpretation.

Chapter 4

A world of signs

Knowledge is intimately related to signs. In this chapter we elaborate on this relation by considering an important property of phenomena, duality, and its consequences for an ontological definition of signs. The main result of this chapter is the definition of a process model of cognitive activity ('naive' knowledge representation).

4.1 The nature of observation

What are phenomena? What do observations consist of? Webster's Dictionary gives for 'phenomenon': appearance, or immediate object of awareness in experience. Earlier we suggested that observations always involve the element of an *interaction* between two entities: the phenomenon *observed* and the *observer*. Because both entities are part of the 'real' world (i.e., nature), it follows that observations, and so, knowledge must emerge from interactions between phenomena. Furthermore we suggested that knowledge arises through interpretation by the observer. An act of interpretation is an *event*, which may yield a result that may vary from an immediate response such as a *translation* (brute reaction) to complex answers involving additional reasoning. This broad understanding of interpretative acts will be maintained in this chapter only. In the rest of this book, we will mainly deal with interpretative processes in which additional reasoning is involved.

To summarize, we will assume that knowledge ultimately emerges from interactions that reveal themselves as events in our experience of change. The condition for change is what we call *duality*, for no change can occur unless there are two independent qualities. For the sake of clarity, a distinction is made between interaction, change and event. Though these three concepts are intimately related, the first, *interaction*, refers to what is assumed to occur, independently from any experience, the second, *change*, refers to the duality of what is involved in an interaction, and the third, *event*, refers to the interaction and change as experienced, that is, to a phenomenon. Because interaction

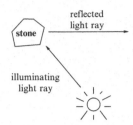

Figure 4.1: A sample interaction

requires duality, and events require interaction, the three concepts are related to each other by a relation of subservience. Though the concept of *event* is the more complex, *duality* is the more fundamental.

4.1.1 Sample phenomena

The concept of a duality may be illustrated by the interaction between a stone and an illuminating light ray (see Fig. 4.1). Due to its light reflecting properties, the stone changes the illuminating light ray by modulating its properties (as the properties of the stone are changed by the light ray – but that aspect shall be left out of consideration). This change may appear as a sign of the interaction between stone and light ray, if it is interpreted as such.

Because the reflected light ray signifies the interaction between stone and light ray (which we may know from experience), we must look into the conditions for signification in order to understand how this is possible. In the current example, the interaction occurs between two entities, the stone and the illuminating light ray, which appear as *qualities*. Because the two qualities are in principle *independent*, an adequate signification of their interaction requires a quality capable of representing them both. We maintain that 'light' is such a quality. Indeed, any light phenomenon can be uniquely characterized by two independent qualities: frequency and intensity.[1] Note that light functions as a simple quality (*constituent*), in the interaction with the stone,[2] and it functions as a duality, when it is interpreted as a sign of the interaction with the stone. From this it follows that each one of interaction, change, and event is a duality, but which may also appear as a single phenomenon which is a quality.

A completely different illustration of duality may be syntactic language phenomena, for instance, the noun-phrase 'nice girls'. As a single phrase, it can be interpeted as a syntactically meaningful concept (a syntactic modification), defined by the interaction between the independent symbols, nice and girls, appearing as syntactic qualities, an adjective and a noun, respectively.

An interaction only occurs if the interacting qualities (constituents) are compatible. The stone and the light ray, in the above thought experiment are

---

[1] Which values of frequency and intensity may be associated with a certain phenomenon is not the issue here.

[2] Cf. the ambiguity of terminology (of light) mentioned in the Introduction.

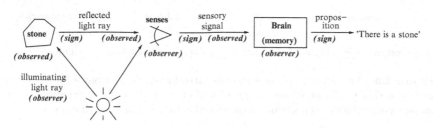

Figure 4.2: A sample sequence of interactions

capable of interaction since the stone possesses the quality of reflectiveness (of light) and the light ray has the potential that it can be subject to reflection. The compatibility involved in all interaction implies that the constituent qualities must have some shared, *common* property. For example, in the interaction between the stone and the light ray, both constituents can be interpreted as wave-type phenomena.[3] The properties of the constituents (frequency and intensity) can be used for a definition of the properties of the resulting phenomenon, the reflected light ray. By assuming that the stone is affecting the light, the reflected light may be interpreted as a *modulation* of the illuminating light ray by the stone.

Similarly, in our language example, girls and nice are compatible for a syntactic symbol interaction, as 'girls' may be interpreted as a noun having the potential to be modified by an adjective, and 'nice' as an adjective (syntactic modifier). The interaction between these two symbols as constituent qualities may 'generate' a new phenomenon: nice girls, representing girls (following the interaction) as a 'modulation' of girls[4] (preceding the interaction), due to nice.

4.1.2 Interactions

The example of the interaction between stone (observed) and light (observer)[5] is interesting, because the reflected light ray (sign) itself may become an observed phenomenon or a quality in a subsequent interaction with the eyes (the receptors of the retina). This interaction is depicted in Fig. 4.2 from the perspective of the eyes (observer). The eyes generate a sensory signal capable of representing the interaction between the reflected light ray and the eyes, and, transitively, the interaction between the stone and the illuminating light ray. That signal as a phenomenon (observed) may then interact with the brain (observer) which, by comparing the sensory signal with memory information about the stimulus,

---

[3]The stone through its reflectiveness.

[4]In the interaction, the combinatory potentials of nice and girls are satisfied. The consequences of the sequential character of language on the interpretation of language phenomena will be discussed in chapter 6.

[5] Note that the term *observer* is used in a much broader sense than usual. Light (quality) is undergoing the effect of the stone and responding to it. Hence, from the perspective of interpretation, it is observing the stone. The stone too can be looked at as an observer, but we will not follow that path.

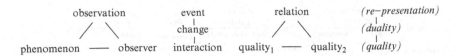

Figure 4.3: An overview of the concepts introduced. A horizontal line denotes an interaction, a diagonal one a representation, a vertical one a dependency or subservience relation. This convention will also be used in later diagrams

may eventually generate in the mind an observation (which is a sign) or its externalized equivalent, the sentence: 'There is a stone'.

As part of its observation, the eyes may 'compare' the quality of the reflected light ray with that of the background light ray perceived in a previous observation (the background light ray is indicated by the unlabeled arrow in Fig. 4.2). This enables the eyes to generate a sensory signal representing the reflected light as a modulation of the background light ray. That modulation can be recognized by the brain as a modulation of light due to an appearing stone or, briefly, as a stone. Note the similarity, in function, between sensory information due to the background light ray on the one hand, and memory information stored by the brain on the other.

The successive interaction and interpretation of qualities defines a *recognition process*, representing the observed input phenomenon as meaningful. This part of our book is an attempt to introduce such a process model for cognitive activity. In the next chapter we will instantiate our model for the two stages of cognitive information processing, which we call perception and cognition. In addition, we perform a logical analysis of our model and reveal the close relationship between the cognitive processual and logical concepts. Interactions between dual qualities that are signs will be called *sign interactions* .

4.1.3   The concept of *re*-presentation

An interaction is clearly a pre-requisite for its interpretation as a sign. But an interaction functions as a sign *if and only if* it is interpreted as such. Hence, the interpretation of an interaction of qualities is the other condition for sign recognition as a process.

In our theory of interpretation, events involve a duality between an observed phenomenon and an observer. When a phenomenon interacts with the observer, the representation by the observer of the event presented by nature is itself an event. The first event may be called nature's interpretation, the second the observer's. For example, the reflected light ray is nature's presentation of the stone-and-light-ray interaction (first event), the eyes are the observer and the sensory signal generated by the eyes functions as the observer's interpretation (second event).

Although the observed phenomenon as well as the observer are independent, and the event representing the (observed) phenomenon is 'conceived' by the observer, that conception is at least partly forced upon the observer by the

phenomenon	quality	duality
wave type	continuous stream	frequency–intensity
mechanical type	energy	distribution–intensity
chemical type	chemical bond	dilution–solubility
sign	representamen	form–content

Table 4.1: Sample dualities in 'natural' phenomena

interaction. Because the qualities of the two events must be related to each other by virtue of the interaction, we conclude that the observer is *re-presenting* the observed phenomenon. In sum, interactions in the 'external' world are represented by means of interactions in the 'internal' world of the interpreting system. As interactions in the 'real' world are dynamic, and knowledge must be a representation of such interactions, knowledge too must be dynamic: a process.

The concepts introduced so far are collected in Fig. 4.3. Table 4.1 contains sample dualities in 'natural' phenomena. Dilution and solubility refer to the independent qualities of the diluted substance on the one hand, and the liquid in which the substance is dissolved on the other. Not all pairs of qualities can be interpreted as a duality. For example, the two types of distribution of energy, potential and kinetic, are not independent, and therefore not dual. The examples of Table 4.1 are illustrations of types of phenomena, interpreted as signs. This relation is expressed by the terms in the last line. The quality underlying a phenomenon can be generalized in the concept of representamen,[6] 'carrying' form and content as dual qualities.

4.2   Towards a model of re-presentation

The fundamental assumption of our theory, that duality is involved in all signs, forms the basis for the definition of our process model of cognitive activity. An important property of all systems, including biological ones, is their potential to generate a response (*reaction*) to the input interaction (*action*). For example, if we observe smoke as a stimulus, then running away might be our reaction, representing our interpretation of smoke as a sign of danger. The 'goal' of cognitive processing is the generation of an *adequate* reaction to the input stimulus as an external effect. The external *effect* (stimulus) affects the interpreting system, occurring in some *state*. For instance, if the interpreting system is the brain, then a memory response is triggered by the input stimulus in the actual state of the brain (Squire et al., 1993). If the input stimulus *fits* in the memory response, more precisely, if each priming event, 'input', 'state', 'effect' and 'state-effect' (cf. Fig. 6) fits in the aroused memory response a reaction can be univocally generated. This is what we called 'matching' mode operation. If not, the input

---

[6]In computer science this is called information. Also according to that view, information (representamen) is *potential* knowledge (cf. data).

stimulus has to be analyzed, through matching with other possible memory responses until a fit is found. This so called 'analysis' mode operation will be the subject of the next section. Either way in our model we assume that the input interaction primes the interpreting system enabling it to access the appropriate memory information.

As any 'real' world entity (quality) can become an effect or a state, all phenomena can be considered as an interaction between independent qualities. It should be emphasized that there may be any number of qualities involved in an interaction, but according to the theory of this book these qualities are always distinguished by cognition into two collections (state and effect) and, consequently, are treated as single entities.[7] The generation of adequate reactions, on the basis of the above state–effect view of interpretation, brings us to the definition of a schema for information processing, which is the subject of the next section.

4.3 Processing schema

The input for interpretation consists in an interaction (cf. action) between an effect and a state. It is the change of this state by that effect that will be interpreted as an event. Following Harnad's theory of cognitive activity (Harnad, 1987), a model of 'analysis' mode interpretation of phenomena that can cope with the interpretation of change, can be introduced as follows.

By virtue of the change caused by the appearing stimulus, the input qualities are sampled by the senses in a percept (Solso, 1988). In a single operation, the brain compares[8] the current percept with the previous one, and this enables it to distinguish between two sorts of qualities/qualia (in short, *input*): one, which was there and remained there, which can be called a 'state'; and another, which, though it was not there, is there now, which can be called an 'effect'.

The change, signifying an interaction in the 'real' world, may be explained as follows. During input processing the stimulus may change, meaning that its current value and the value stored in the last percept are different. This may be interpreted by the brain as a change, mediating the present value of the stimulus to its actual significance. The reaction of an interpreting system is determined by the system's 'knowledge' of the properties of the external stimulus, and its experience with the results of earlier response strategies (habit). Such knowledge is an expression of the system's potential for *combining* with the input effect, depending on the system's state. These properties will be called the combinatory properties of the input qualia; they define the complementary *context* of the observation.

In complex biological systems, experience (knowledge) is concentrated in functional units such as the sensory, central, and motor sub-systems. The most

---

[7]In cognitive theory, the potential for treating a collection of qualities as a single entity is known as 'chunking'.

[8]The importance of comparison operations by the brain is also emphasized by Goldstone and Barsalou (1998).

important of these is the central system, which includes memory. The 'translation' from external stimuli to internal representation (qualia) is brought about by the sensory sub-system, which itself is an interpreting system, generating 'brute reactions' (translations). In this book, the role of the motor sub-system is ignored.

The primary task of cognitive processing is an interpretation of the external stimuli, by means of their combinatory properties (C). Since the input is assumed to consist of two types of qualia (state and effect) and their context, together appearing as a 'primordial soup' ($[q_1 \; q_2 \; C]$), the stages of recognition can be defined as follows (see also Fig. 4.4).

(1) The identification of the two types of qualia in the 'primordial soup';
   sorting: $[q_1]$, $[q_2]$, $[C]$.

(2) The separation of the collections of the two types of qualia;
   abstraction: q_1, q_2.

(3) The linking of the qualia with their combinatory properties;
   complementation: (q_1,C), (q_2,C).

(4) The establishment of a relation between the completed qualia;
   predication: (q_1,C)–(q_2,C).

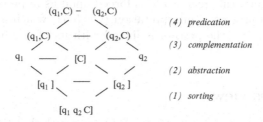

$$(q_1,C) - (q_2,C)$$

(4) predication

(3) complementation

(2) abstraction

(1) sorting

Figure 4.4: A schematic diagram of cognitive processing (q_1=state, q_2=effect, C=context). Square brackets are used to indicate that an entity is not yet interpreted as a sign; no bracketing or the usual bracket symbols indicate that some interpretation is already available. A horizontal line denotes an interaction between neighboring entities

Each of the above operations, all of which obtain relations on qualia comprising the 'primordial soup', can be represented by means of interactions between neighboring entities. Such entities are connected by a horizontal line, in Fig. 4.4. The only non-trivial operation is *abstraction*, in which the abstract input signs, q_1 and q_2, are generated by the separation of the qualia represented by $[q_1]$ (the state qualia in the context of all other qualia), from those represented by $[q_2]$ (the effect qualia in the context of all other qualia).[9]

The entire input or the 'universe of discourse' for cognitive processing consists of the input state and effect qualia, and the memory response (context)

---

[9] The term context is used ambiguously, in its potential ($[q_1 \; q_2 \; C]$) and its actual contribution ($[C]$) to information processing.

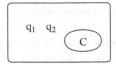

Figure 4.5: The entire input or the 'universe of discourse' for cognitive processing

triggered by them. We make a distinction between primitive and complex interpretative systems. In primitive interpreting systems, only capable of generating 'brute' reactions, the context is part of the state (q_1) in the 'primordial soup'. In such systems, complementation reduces to an empty operation and the entire process of interpretation to 'matching' (cf. Fig. 7). In complex systems, the context is separated from the input state and effect, as shown in Fig. 4.5. Through complementation the system analyzes the input and, by selecting one out of the possible interpretations, generates a reaction which may be adequate. Either way, in our model we assume that the input 'primordial soup' implies *all* information used in the interpretational process.

The model of cognitive processing depicted in Fig. 4.4 is compatible with the assumption laid down by the Peircean theory of perceptual judgments. According to this theory, the 'real' world is forced upon us in percepts (CP 2.142) and by means of a process of interpretation (CP 5.54) which is utterly beyond our control (CP 5.115), the percept is linked with its object in a (perceptual) judgment.

4.3.1   Process view

A process is considered to be any sequence of events such that (i) one event initiates the sequence and another terminates it, (ii) every event that contributes to the sequences yielding the terminating event is regarded as part of the process, and (iii) the terminating event governs the decision of which events make up the sequence (Debrock, Farkas, & Sarbo, 1999). The relation of the processing schema to the above three characteristics of a process can be summarized as follows. The interaction between the 'real' world phenomenon and the interpreting system on the one hand, and the perceptual judgment on the other correspond to the two events of the first characteristic, namely, the initiating and terminating events. The events generated by the interpretational process can be associated with the second characteristic. Finally, the teleological character of that process (the generation of an adequate response to the input stimulus) correspond to the governing property mentioned in the third characteristic. We will elaborate on this last point in Chapter 5. The dynamical character of 'real' world phenomena is re-presented by a process model of cognitive activity. Each 'real' world interaction is represented by a series of sign interactions in the model of the interpreting system. Such interactions, representing sign aspects, will be called *proto-signs* (Sarbo, 2006).

4.4 Input, memory and output representation

Before proceeding with an application of our processing schema, let us say a word about the representation of input and memory information.

We assume that the input for cognitive information processing consists of a collection of qualia. Following Harnad's theory of categorical perception, *qualia* arise from external stimuli/qualities through perception. The essence of his theory of categorical perception is that:

> [...] stimuli that are equally spaced on a physical continuum are perceived as if they belonged to one or another perceptual category, rather than appearing to vary continuously as a function of their physical values. (See (Harnad, 1987), p. 387)

An example of categorical perception is the speech frequency spectrum as it is subdivided into phoneme discriminations (e.g. formants). One of the possible mechanisms for categorical perception is selective attention, which is a mechanism used in cases in which categorization of certain stimuli has to be learned.

> If, through experience with human language or with animal calls, phonemes and call elements that differ only in the position of a parameter on a single physical continuum are perceived again and again, it is conceivable that their relative position on the continuum is learned. If only a few alternatives occur, their positions receive specific labels. (Idem, p. 323)

The existence of such parameters is the ground for the classification of phenomena. The assumption that a single physical continuum can be sufficient for the characterization of a domain of qualia is also adopted by this book. Following (Harnad, 1987) we shall maintain that qualia characterize human knowledge representation in all knowledge domains.

4.4.1 Memory representation

Besides input qualia, a second or complementary source of information used by the processing schema is information provided by the memory.

As the number of observations by the brain/mind is in principle unlimited, but the available storage capacity is finite, economical representation of memory information by the brain is required. This can be illustrated by our earlier example of the smoke (see Sect. 4.2). Smoke can be interpreted, among other things, as a warning of danger, but also as a sign of rising air or a thermal. In both cases the sign (smoke) mediates its object (fire) to its interpretant (either the symbolic sign of danger or the iconic sign of a thermal).

The fact that there may be different interpretants indicates that mediation will be *context* dependent. This is due to the activation of the brain: what is in its 'focus' and what is 'complementary'. We will return to the modeling issues of these distinctions in Chapter 5.

In conformity with our assumption that the use of qualia also characterizes the higher levels of information processing, we will assume that memory signs (memorized observations) and, in general, all input representations, including proto-signs, can be treated as qualia. The terms memory sign and memory qualia will be used interchangeably.

4.4.2 Natural representation

By virtue of its cognitive foundation, the processing schema may favorably be used in the development of human-computer interfaces. More specifically we conjecture that output generated by programs respecting the processing schema can be more efficiently processed as knowledge by the human user than information generated by programs that do not respect it. The essence of such 'natural' information processing can be illustrated with our earlier metaphor of apparent motion perception. If the pictures are presented correctly, eventually we may experience their entire series as conveying motion. If the presentation is not correct, for example, the pictures are in a wrong order or the difference between consecutive pictures is too big, adequate interpretation may still be possible, but it will be more difficult. In our view, an analogous 'correct' presentation of results produced by the computer may enable their 'natural' interpretation. In the context of human-computer interfaces this comes down to the conjecture that information processing respecting the nine types of relations of cognitive processing as well as their ordering, may *enhance* human interpretation of information generated by the computer.

4.4.3 Towards an experimental validation

Some evidence for a relation between human processing and the processing schema has been found in a couple of experiments conducted by the authors.

In the first experiment by Draskovic, Couwenberg and Sarbo (2010), 28 pupils of age 12 participated in mathematical problem solving. The pupils were individually asked to solve a difficult geometrical problem while thinking aloud. Their verbalizations were recorded and transcribed. Subsequently, verbal utterances were coded according to events of the processing schema. The results statistically show high congruence of concepts comprising verbal reports with interpretation moments specified in our model. Moreover, also the order of concept formation, as inferred from verbal reports, is congruent with the order of processing stages specified in our model.

In the second experiment we shifted our focus from individual processes to conceptualization by multiple participants (Klomp, 2008), (Sarbo, 2009). We considered problem elicitation by three clients guided by a professional elicitator at the software firm Sogeti Nederland. Two sessions each comprising 2 hours of verbal communication were recorded and transcribed. An analysis of a number of segments of the recorded communication shows some evidence for the development of a shared conceptualization by all participants. The events of this process are congruent with the processing schema introduced in this chapter.

Chapter 5

Perception and cognition

An adequate representation of the interaction experienced by the interpreting system requires that the two types of input qualia, state and effect, are interpreted in themselves as well as in relation to each other. The first requirement follows from the nature of input qualia that they may not precisely match memory information stored by the brain; the second is a consequence of the abstract character of memory signs, representing the general meaning of qualia occurring in earlier observations as abstract combinatory properties. The necessity for such a two-stage operation of cognitive information processing is acknowledged in this chapter by identifying two phases of cognitive activity, which we call perception and cognition.[1] It will be suggested that, although these stages are different, their models can be defined by isomorphic instances of the processing schema introduced in the previous chapter.[2]

The suggestion of a two phase model of information processing is also supported by cognitive research. According to (Ramachandran & Hirstein, 1997), basic properties of qualia are that they are irrevocable[3] (hence asking for perception); and that they do not always produce the same behavior to execute (hence requiring cognition). By virtue of their different characteristics, the degree of freedom of interpretation is different in the two stages. As the input qualia are forced upon the interpreting system, their interpretation is principally dictated by the external world (first stage). This is opposed to the interpretation of the qualia from the observer's point of view (second stage), which is mainly governed by the interpreting system itself.

Below we start with a process definition of perception and cognition. This is followed by a logical account of the processing schema, proving the completeness of the model of cognitive activity from the logical point of view. The chapter is closed by an example of the proposed two-stage model of information processing.

---

[1] Alternatively, cognition may be called conception.

[2] The assumption of common processing mechanisms underlying perception and conception is also suggested by Goldstone and Barsalou (1998), p. 232.

[3] "[One] cannot decide to start seeing the sunset as green, or feel pain as if it were an itch" (Ramachandran & Hirstein, 1997).

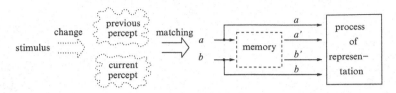

Figure 5.1: A schematic diagram of the input of perception. Triggered by a change, the actual value of the input stimulus is sampled. By comparing the current and previous percepts, the input for information processing is represented by a state (a), effect (b) and corresponding memory response signs (a', b')

5.1 Perception process

The 'goal' of the first process, *perception*, is the establishment of a relation between the input qualia and information stored in memory (the relation between the input qualia is of secondary importance in this process). In the end, an interpretation of the qualia in *themselves* is obtained. In accordance with the goal of this process, the context of perception ([C]), which is defined by the memory response triggered by the input qualia, points to information about the combinatory properties of the input qualia, independent from their actual relations.[4] Below, input state and effect qualia are indicated by a and b, respectively; those of the memory response by a' and b'. All four signs may refer to a type as well as to a collection of qualia. A schematic diagram of the input of perception is given in Fig. 5.1.[5]

Among the representations generated by perception, the most important one is step 4 (see Fig. 5.2). Following our earlier assumption, memory response signs (a', b') arise by means of input qualia (a, b) that trigger memory. Although we may distinguish memory response signs in two collections, which are independent, these signs have a shared meaning.[6] This is not only due to the existence of an interaction between the input qualia, but also to relations involved in the memory response. Note that the relations between a' and b' arise from earlier state and effect interactions that are stored in memory (cf. combinatory properties).

Depending on the activation of the memory, defining the state of the mind (brain) as an interpreting system, there may be qualia in the memory response having an intensity: (i) above or (ii) below threshold, referring to an input meaning which is in the brain's '*focus*' and which is only '*complementary*', respectively. A high intensity type (i) memory response signifies the recognition of the input as an *agreement* between the input and memory response: the input

---

[4]Experimental evidence for a mechanism in the brain for the generation of the context triggered by the input can be found in (Colgin et al., 2009).

[5]The conceptual model of this chapter is reworked into a more realistic model, in Appendix C. In that model, we do justice to the fact that the previous percept is part of memory and that the processes, perception and cognition, run simultaneously.

[6]In a neuro-physiological setting, a' and b' could be interpreted as the intensity and frequency of responding memory signals, respectively.

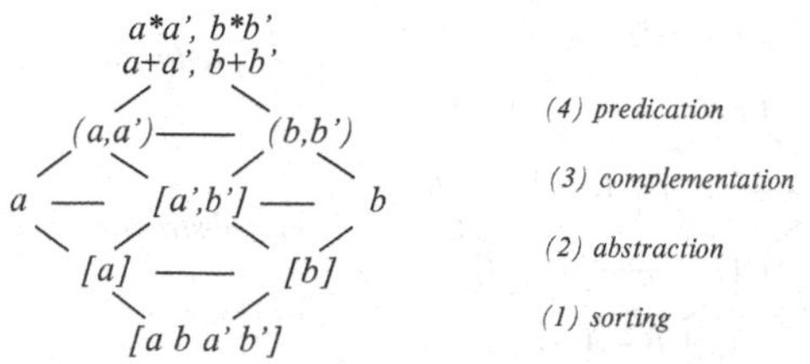

$$a*a', b*b'$$
$$a+a', b+b'$$

(a,a') —— (b,b')   (4) predication

a —— [a',b'] —— b   (3) complementation

[a] —— [b]   (2) abstraction

[a b a' b']   (1) sorting

Figure 5.2: A schematic diagram of perception as a process. The input signs appearing as a 'primordial soup' ($[a\ b\ a'\ b']$) are sorted ($[a], [b], [a',b']$), abstracted (a, b), complemented by the context $((a,a'), (b,b'))$ and, finally, combined in a single sign ($a*a', a+a', b*b', b+b'$) by means of predication

$a(b)$ is recognized or 'known' as $a'(b')$. A low intensity response of type (ii) refers to input recognition as a *possibility* only: the input $a(b)$ is not recognized or 'not known' as $a'(b')$. In this case, the memory response only represents a secondary or even less important aspect of the input qualia.

By indicating the first type of intensity relationship between input and memory response by a '$*$' symbol, and the second type by a '$+$', the signs of perception can be represented as: $a*a', a+a', b*b', b+b'$. For example, $a*a'$ is a representation of a positive identification of a by a'; as opposed to $a+a'$ which signifies the event of the identification of a possible meaning of a by a' (in other words, to a *denial* of a positive identification).

In the process model of perception (see Fig. 5.2), the four signs are represented by a single sign. The recognition of the difference between the four types of intensity relations is beyond the scope of this process (the ',' symbol separating the four signs above, is an expression of their synonymous interpretation as the final signs of perception; it is *this* perspective that makes them synonymous).

Note that, in the complementation operation (step 3), the input qualia are type-wise completed with memory information: a is completed with a', b with b', in conformity with the duality of input and memory signs, and the 'goal' of perception, which is the recognition of the input qualia in themselves (this explains why a is not completed with b', for example). Although information about memory response signs, whether they represent a meaning which is 'known' or 'not known' or, alternatively, focused or complementary, is already present in the context, however that information is not operational in the complementation sign interaction.

5.2 Cognition process

The second process, *cognition*, is an exact copy of the process of perception, except that the 'goal' of cognition is an interpretation of the relation between the input qualia, more specifically, the relation between the qualia that are in focus ($a*a', b*b'$), in the light of those that are complementary ($a+a', b+b'$) (now

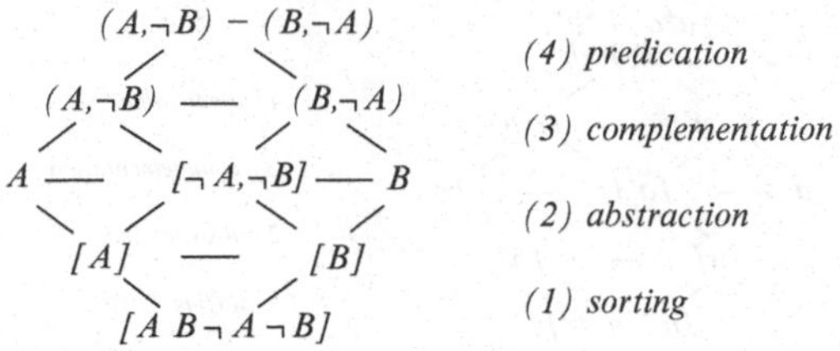

$$(A,\neg B) - (B,\neg A)$$

	(4) predication
(A,¬B) —— (B,¬A)	(3) complementation
A —— [¬A,¬B] —— B	(2) abstraction
[A] —— [B]	(1) sorting
[A B ¬A ¬B]	

Figure 5.3: A schematic diagram of cognition as a process. The input signs appearing as a 'primordial soup' ($[A\ B\ \neg A\ \neg B]$) are sorted ($[A]$, $[B]$, $[\neg A, \neg B]$), abstracted (A, B), complemented by the context (($A,\neg B$), ($B,\neg A$)) and, finally, combined in a single sign (($A,\neg B$)–($B,\neg A$)) by means of predication

it is the relation between input and memory that is of secondary importance). In accordance with cognition's 'goal', the context points to information about the complementary input qualia with respect to their actual relations. This means that, by combining the input of the cognition process with information activated in the context, the relation between A and B (and, similarly, the relation between a and b) may be disclosed.

Similar to perception as a process, in the process of cognition the input appears as a 'primordial soup', this time defined by the result of the process of perception. In fact, the difference between the four expressions ($a*a'$, $a+a'$, $b*b'$, $b+b'$) functions as a ground for the process of cognition. This is acknowledged in our model by introducing an initial re-presentation of the four relations generated by perception: $a*a'$ as A, $a+a'$ as $\neg A$, $b*b'$ as B, and $b+b'$ as $\neg B$. The presence or absence of a '$\neg$' symbol in an expression indicates whether the qualia signified are or are not in focus, i.e., identified (accordingly, '$\neg$' may be interpreted as a 'relative difference' operation with respect to the collection of a type of qualia, represented as a set). The instantiation of the processing schema for cognition is depicted in Fig. 5.3.

In the process of cognition the important interpretation moment is step 3 (complementation), in which the link between the input qualia and the context is established in accordance with cognition's 'goal' as well as with the duality of phenomena. This explains why there can be a relation between A and $\neg B$, and $\neg A$ and B, and why there is no relation between A and $\neg A$, or B and $\neg B$.[7] The cognition process is completed by establishing a relation between A and B, in step 4 (predication).

There are three relations, which correspond to the three types of interactions[8] between the input qualia. These relations may be characterized by means of the meaning of their constituents. From a computational stance, these interactions are relations (such relations are indicated below by a '–' symbol):

---

[7] A and $\neg A$ (but also B and $\neg B$) arise due to the same input trigger, indicating that the two signs are *not* independent.

[8] Their three types correspond to the three Peircean categories (see also Sect. 6.7.4).

(1) A–$\neg B$: A is 'known', but B is 'not known';
    the *complementation* of the input state ('actualization').

(2) B–$\neg A$: B is 'known', but A is 'not known';
    the *complementation* of the input effect ('refinement').

(3) $(A,\neg B)$–$(B,\neg A)$: both A and B are 'known';
    the *predication* of a relation between A and B ('proposition').

The fourth relation is not available for interpretation. Indeed, if neither A nor B is 'known', interpretation terminates, meaning that cognition as a process does not actually occur (the process did not reach its goal). Note the mediational function of context signs, in step 3. Through the correspondence between $\neg A$ and $\neg B$, that are triggered by the same input, the context *implicitly* determines the actual relation between A and B. The form of the relation is propositional since it explains the co-occurrence of this specific state with this specific effect. In a wider context, this explanation must be regarded as hypothetical. Note that, on the basis of (partial) information triggered by the input, in a single 'run' the processing schema obtains one interpretation of the relation between A and B. In general, different analyses may have to be considered in order to find an interpretation that complies with information 'known' by the interpreting system about the input qualia.

5.3   Logical analysis

The above interpretation of cognition illustrates, to some extent, the completeness of this process. This becomes even more clear from the logical analysis of the underlying processing schema. In this section we elaborate such an analysis, by making use of the model of cognition introduced in the previous section, but the results apply to the model of perception as well. We will proceed as follows. First, a logical expression will be assigned to each interpretation moment on the basis of common logical aspects. Second, operations will be introduced generating these expressions according to a procedure. Third, derivations will be presented, revealing the potential of these expressions to be generated by a Boolean logic.

The hidden agenda of this section is a tacit introduction of logical concepts into the process model of cognition. What makes the use of such concepts especially important is that they have a well-studied, precise meaning. In this section, the term logical is used as a reference to an *aspect* of an event or an expression, not to a formal mathematical concept. In the processing schema, the logical operations are defined only in terms of their neighboring elements (cf. horizontal lines). A specification of these operations as a rewriting system is beyond our goal.

An essential element of the logical interpretation of the process model of cognition is the abstraction of a common meaning for the two different types of input qualia (state and effect), which is the concept of a *logical variable*. By virtue of the duality of the input, the logical interpretation of cognition, as a process, requires the introduction of two variables. These will be denoted by A and B. The difference between the qualia that are in focus and those that are complementary is represented by the difference in their expression. Each of the two types of qualia is referred to by means of a logical variable which is either stated positively or negatively. Perceived state and effect qualia which are in focus are indicated by A and B, respectively; those which are complementary by $\neg A$ and $\neg B$. Note the use of '$\neg$' as a complementation operation on collections. For example, the complementary sub-collections of A-type qualia are denoted by A and $\neg A$ (the label A is used ambiguously). The relational operators introduced in the application of the processing schema for perception ('+' for possibility and '*' for agreement) are inherited by the process model of cognition and its interpretation as operations on expressions. The logical meaning of the expressions below are due to the meaning of a logical 'or' involved in the possibility meaning of '+', and the meaning of a logical 'and' in the agreement meaning of '*'.

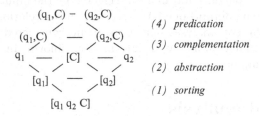

$$(q_1,C) - (q_2,C)$$

(4) predication

(3) complementation

(2) abstraction

(1) sorting

Figure 5.4: A schematic diagram of cognitive processing (recap)

In conformance to the above mapping of perceived state and effect qualia to logical variables, the logical expressions associated with the events of the cognitive process can be defined in the following way (the interpretation moments of cognitive processing are recapitulated in Fig. 5.4).

$[q_1]=A+B$, $[q_2]=A*B$: the expression of the simultaneous presence of the input qualia which are in focus, respectively, as a simple, possible co-existence $(A+B)$; and in the sense of agreement, as an actual co-occurrence $(A*B)$. As A and B are commonly interpreted as logical variables, the separate representation of either of the two types of input qualia contains a reference to both variables. However, we may only observe a state by virtue of an effect, but the occurrence of an effect entails the existence of a state. This difference between the two types of input qualia is expressed by means of the difference between their two types of relations, represented by the operators '+' and '*'.

$[C]=\neg A+\neg B$, $\neg A*\neg B$: the expression of the context as a co-existence $(\neg A+ \neg B)$ and as a co-occurrence relation $(\neg A*\neg B)$ of the complementary input qualia. A synonymous interpretation of these relations is an expression of their secondary (complementary) meaning, but also of the shared meaning of the simultaneously present qualia, represented by $\neg A$ and $\neg B$, comprising the context. Through this shared meaning the context *coordi-*

nates the interpretation of the two types of input qualia, represented by A and B.

$q_1 = A*\neg B$, $\neg A*B$: the expression of the abstract meaning of the focused input qualia, as constituents, irrespective of the actually co-occurring other type of input qualia. It is *this* perspective that makes the two logical signs synonymous (note the use of ',' in the definition of q_1 directly above, as a representation of this equivalence).

$q_2 = A*\neg B + \neg A*B$: the expression of the input as an abstract co-occurrence event, logically represented by a compatibility relation of the two types of abstract constituents of the input (which are now interpreted differently).

$(q_1, C) = A + \neg B$, $\neg A + B$: the expression of the abstract constituents (q_1) completed with information provided by the context ([C]). In other words, it expresses the 'actual' meaning of the input qualia (on this occasion and for this interpreting system) as constituents of the input phenomenon. For example, the actual meaning of A (perceived state) as a constituent, is signified by A itself and by $\neg B$, the complementary property connecting A with B (as the relation between A and B is not yet established, the B type qualia cannot contribute to the actual meaning of A, as a constituent). Looked at from the perspective of the logical interpretation itself, in context $\neg A*B$ is defined by the qualia completing this abstract meaning, i.e., A (completing $\neg A$) and $\neg B$ (completing B). As the two interpretations of A as an actual constituent are related to each other by the relation of co-existence, the logical meaning of (q_1, C) can be represented by $A + \neg B$. For the same reason, as in q_1, the two expressions of (q_1, C) are interpreted in the model as synonymous.

$(q_2, C) = A*B + \neg A*\neg B$: the expression of the abstract compatibility relation in context. This obtains the sign of the input as a characteristic or conventional property which appears as an event. That event can be looked at from two different points of view. Through the glass of the qualia which are in focus it can be represented as an event between A and B; from the stance of the complementary context it can be described as an event between $\neg A$ and $\neg B$. The two relations represent the interaction which is in the focus, respectively, positively and negatively. Alternatively, in the definition of (q_1, C) and (q_2, C) above, the complementary qualia are used to 'sort out' an interpretation from the range of meanings provided by the abstract signs, q_1 and q_2, that holds in context ([C]). In other words, the input is implicitly characterized by means of complementary information provided by the context. State qualia occurring in q_1 are represented by themselves $(A(B))$[9] and by their context $(\neg B(\neg A))$; and, similarly, effect qualia occurring in q_2 are represented by themselves $(A*B)$ and by their context $(\neg A*\neg B)$.[10]

---

[9] Remember that input qualia are commonly represented as variables.

[10] The occurrence of an effect entails the existence of a state (cf. the definition of [q_1] and [q_2] above). This simultaneity is represented by $A*B$ and $\neg A*\neg B$.

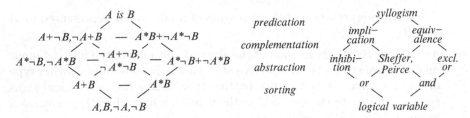

Figure 5.5: The logical expressions of cognitive processing (left) and the corresponding Boolean relations (right)

$(q_1,C)-(q_2,C)=A$ *is* B: the expression of the relation between the input qualia which are in focus, represented as a proposition.

The logical expressions assigned to the interpretation moments are presented in Fig. 5.5, on the left-hand side; the corresponding Boolean relations are displayed on the right-hand side of the same diagram. The logical signs, '0' and '1', which are omitted, can be defined as representations of a 'not-valid' and a 'valid' input, respectively.

Note in Fig. 5.5 the presence of *all* Boolean relations on two variables[11] as sign aspects, reinforcing our earlier conjecture concerning the completeness of the cognitive process. The results of the analysis above show that logical signs (and so, the concepts of cognition as a process) can be defined as relations (interactions) between *neighboring* signs that are in need of settlement. In Fig. 5.5 (on the left-hand side), such signs are connected with a horizontal line.

5.3.1 Semiotic analogy

That the formal computational and the intuitive interpretation of a sign are tightly related to each other must be clear from the above explanation of the logical relations of cognition. This dependency forms the basis of the semiotic interpretation of the nine types of relations, which can be explained as follows.

$[q_1 \, q_2 \, C]=A, B, \neg A, \neg B$: represents the appearing phenomenon as *qualities*.

$[q_1]=A+B$: represents that A and B, as constituents, are part of the input collection, as a whole. Hence they are similar to it. So, the representation of the input, as a constituency relation, expresses *likeness* with respect to the input, which is represented as 'primordial soup'.

$[q_2]=A*B$: represents that the aspect of *simultaneity* is a primary element of the input, as an appearance (event) that happens now.

$[C]=\neg A*\neg B, \neg A+\neg B$: represents that the relation between the input and the complementary context has the meaning of a *connection*.

---

[11]The Boolean relations as functions: $f_0=0$, $f_1=A*B$, $f_2=A*\neg B$, $f_3=A$, $f_4=\neg A*B$, $f_5=B$, $f_6=\neg A*B+A*\neg B$, $f_7=A+B$, $f_8=\neg A*\neg B$, $f_9=A*B+\neg A*\neg B$, $f_{10}=\neg B$, $f_{11}=A+\neg B$, $f_{12}=\neg A$, $f_{13}=\neg A+B$, $f_{14}=\neg A+\neg B$, $f_{15}=1$.

$q_1 = A * \neg B, \neg A * B$: represents that the abstract conception of the input is an expression of its being as a *qualitative possibility*.

$q_2 = A * \neg B + \neg A * B$: represents that the compatibility of the abstract meaning of the input qualia is expressive of a *rule*-like relation.

$(q_1, C) = A + \neg B, \neg A + B$: represents the abstract meaning of the constituents in context. It is a definition of the actual meaning of the input qualia, as something *existent*.

$(q_2, C) = A * B + \neg A * \neg B$: represents the interpretation of the abstract compatibility relation in context as a characteristic property; it presupposes the existence of a consensus or *convention*.

$(q_1, C) - (q_2, C) = A$ *is* B: represents that the assertion of a relation between the input qualia involves the formation of a *proposition* which is a hypothesis.

From this semiotic interpretation of the logical relations, the analogy with the Peircean classification of sign aspects (see Fig. 5.6 and also Fig. 1.13) follows trivially. Note the differences between the use of the term proposition as a fact, in (q_1, C), and as a premise in subsequent reasoning, in $(q_1, C) - (q_2, C)$.

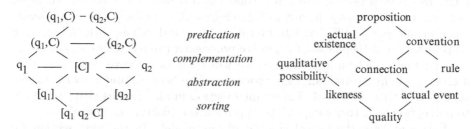

Figure 5.6: The interpretation moments (on the left) and corresponding semiotic aspects (on the right)

5.3.2 Towards 'naive' logic as a calculus

The classification of logical expressions depicted in Fig. 5.5 can be interpreted as a procedure, generating expressions from other expressions, repeatedly. It is defined by a series of operations on collections of qualia, in which the operands as well as the result of the operations are associated with a logical relation, syntactically represented by a Boolean expression. This *procedure* is what we call in this book '*naive*' logic (a full account of this logic may be found in Appendix D). Although a definition of 'naive' logic as a Boolean algebra is not part of this book, the possibility of Boolean interpretation of the processing schema may be illustrated by the close relationship between some of the expressions displayed in Fig. 5.5 and corresponding syntactically equivalent Boolean relations. For example, the expressions associated with q_2 can be defined by means of a relative difference operation ('\') on the expressions of $[q_1]$ and $[q_2]$, this time interpreted as Boolean relations: $(A+B) \backslash (A*B) = A * \neg B + B * \neg A$. The expressions associated with (q_1,C) and (q_2,C) can be defined as a Boolean negation operation (representing the complementary meaning of the context) on the expressions of q_1 and q_2 interpreted as Boolean relations, respectively: $\neg(A*\neg B)$, $\neg(\neg A*B)=$ $\neg A+B$, $A+\neg B$; $\neg(A*\neg B+\neg A*B)= A*B+\neg A*\neg B$.

The above close relationship between 'naive' and Boolean logic does not hold for the other expressions and 'naive' logical operations, however. From a more general perspective, Boolean logic can be said to differ from 'naive' logic in three aspects. The first is a uniform representation of the perceived qualia as a universe of discourse and the collections of qualia as logical variables (Boolean logic), not of those collections as state and effect ('naive' logic). The second is the interpretation of the logical operations as operations on sets (Boolean logic), not on collections ('naive' logic). The third is that Boolean logic, unlike 'naive' logic, introduces non-synonymous interpretations for cognitively synonymous expressions such as $A*\neg B$ and $\neg A*B$ (cf. Fig. 5.5).

There are also other, less important differences between the two systems. One of them is the possibility in Boolean logic to combine any number of variables and logical operations in a single expression. This is opposed to the limitations of 'naive' logic, which is a procedure only capable of establishing relations between two variables at a time and a realization of operations in an order that is dictated by the order of sign interactions in the processing schema. Another one is the different interpretation of logical values (*true/false*), as a representation of the status of cognitive processing ('naive' logic) and as a logical constant (Boolean logic). Later we will show that 'naive' logic may play a crucial role in natural language processing (see Sect. 6) and we will suggest that it may have a similarly important function in all domains that are 'close' to perception and, therefore, can be approached as natural or 'naive' too.

This completes the logical account of our model. In the next section we return to an exposition of the processing schema as a combinatory machinery.

5.4 Combinatory relations and properties

Earlier we mentioned (in Sect. 5.2) that we may observe an entity as a state, only by virtue of an appearing effect, but the occurrence of an effect always entails the existence of a state. This asymmetry between state and effect is the ground for a semiotic interpretation of the differences between the three types of relations recognized by cognitive processing. This can be exemplified for the process model of cognition, as follows (cf. Fig. 5.3).

(1) $A-\neg B$: A is a potential meaning, which is actualized by $\neg B$;

(2) $B-\neg A$: B, which is in principle self-sufficient, receives its full meaning from its association with $\neg A$;

(3) $(A,\neg B)-(B,\neg A)$: A and B, which both are self-sufficient, together generate a new meaning.[12]

---

[12] In line with the assumption that all interaction is between state and effect, the constituents of the three relations above show an analogous difference.

These (cognitive) relations can be interpreted as a representation of the three types of nexus between signs, which in turn correspond to the three Peircean categories. An example of the three types of relations in language syntax are a syntactic modification of a noun (e.g. by an adjective), a syntactic complementation of a verb (e.g. by a verb-complement), and a syntactic predication (subject and predicate forming a sentence), respectively. The important consequence of this transitive relation between cognition and the Peircean categories is the existence of a necessary and sufficient condition for ontological specifications, which are typically syntactical too, in particular those which are meant to be used in computer applications. The analysis of the meaning of the constituents, in the three types of relations, proves that the specification of the (combinatory) properties of qualia can be restricted to three cases. The specification of:

(1) the qualia in themselves;

(2) with respect to other qualia
    (i) which are complementing it or
    (ii) which they are complementing;

(3) with respect to other qualia, together with which they can generate a new meaning.[13]

This may be exemplified with the specification of smoke:

(1) in itself: a quale, having properties underlying its combinatory potential, such as a dark color, a density, etc.;

(2) in relation to another quale:
    (i) which is complementing it: e.g. blowing (as a smoke-producing effect) or
    (ii) which it is complementing: e.g. rising-from-the-chimney (as a state undergoing smoke production);

(3) as a self-sufficient sign: such as the subject of any-burning.

Note that the qualia of (1) function as the ground for the connections of (2), which in turn underlie the meaningful relations of (3). For example, smoke represented as rising-from-the-chimney involves the qualities of smoke as a certain dark color. In turn, smoke as the subject of any-burning involves the qualities of smoke as rising-from-the-chimney.

Such a specification will be called a trichotomic specification or, briefly, a *trichotomy*. By virtue of the dependency between the Peircean categories, in a trichotomy a more developed class involves a less developed one. By assuming that the three types of meanings can be recursively defined in each trichotomic class, we have in front of us the hierarchical schema of ontological specification suggested by the theory of this book. Trichotomies will be extensively studied in the model of 'naive' semantic-syntactic signs (see Sect. 6.7). In this book we assume that the qualia used in the examples are specifiable for the above

---

[13]Note that (1) allows a single interpretation, (2) provides two and (3) can be expanded to three meanings, which differ from each other in the answer to the question which of the qualia has a dominant function in the relation: either the one, or the other, or both.

three types of relation. Such a specification of qualia is an expression of the 'conditions' that a representation of (external) qualities by means of (internal) qualia must satisfy, as already indicated in the Introduction.

In sum, there are three types of relations between signs, in accordance with the three types of categories of phenomena. As each sign interaction introduced by the processing schema can be interpreted as an interaction between some state and some effect, the constituents of a sign interaction can be characterized as:

(1) a quality, which is a potential existence;

(2) a state, which appears by virtue of an effect;

(3) an effect, which implies the existence of a state.

The three Peircean categories are not independent of each other. Though thirdness is the most developed, it nevertheless requires secondness and firstness (the latter via the mediation of secondness). Analogous with the categorical relations, an effect can be said to contain a state and, transitively, a potential existence, which are involved. By means of the induced ordering of the dependency between the categories ('$<$') used as a polymorphic operation, the relation between the cognitive types can be abstracted as follows: $a<b$, $A<B$. For example, the interpretation of a quale as an effect (b) implies the possibility of its interpretation as a state (a). The ordering of qualia as well as relations on qualia (cf. interpretation moments) will be extensively used later in our approach for meaningful summarization, in Chapter 9.

5.5   An extended example

The running example of this chapter is the interpretation of the phenomenon 'smoke' as the sign of 'danger'. Assume, that you have been watching for some time a dark cloud of smoke above a roof, and suddenly you 'see' that the cloud is rising upward and that fire is burning on the roof. In addition let us assume that you are focussing on the smoke and appearing burning, which are determinate, but your observation of the roof and the rising air is vague. Below we use **boldface** for input qualia; sans-serif for memory qualia; memory response signs that are in focus are underlined and comments are preceded by a '%' sign. For instance, danger and thermal are memory response signs triggered by the input qualia **burning** and **rising-air**, respectively. Interpretation moments will be referred to by means of their Boolean expressions. A trichotomic specification of qualia is not required for our example, therefore is omitted.

The input qualia of the perception process are defined as follows.

$$
\begin{array}{llll}
a & = & \textbf{smoke, roof} & a' = \underline{\text{smoke}}, \text{roof} \\
b & = & \textbf{burning, rising-air} & b' = \underline{\text{danger}}, \text{thermal}
\end{array}
$$

In words, the qualities of the dark cloud of smoke (**smoke**) above the roof (**roof**) are associated with smoke and possibly also with roof, and the suddenly observed

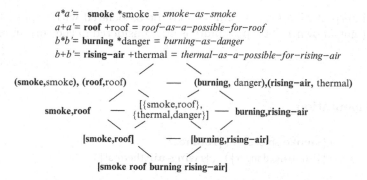

Figure 5.7: Expressions generated by the process of perception (for reasons of economy, memory response signs are omitted in the input position). Braces are used for a collection of qualia of some type (state or effect)

qualia of the burning fire on the roof (**burning**) and of the cloud rising upward (**rising-air**) with danger and possibly also with thermal.

5.5.1 Perception

The perception process begins with the operations *sorting* and *abstraction*, which can be defined as follows. An overview of the expressions generated by this process is given in Fig. 5.7.

Sorting

$[a]$ = **smoke, roof** % in the presence of **burning** and **rising-air**
$[b]$ = **burning, rising-air** % co-occurring with **smoke** and **roof**

Abstraction

a = **smoke, roof** % independently from the input effects
b = **burning, rising-air** % independently from the input states

In the subsequent operation, (i) the abstract input representations are interpreted in context (*complementation*) and (ii) the resulting expressions are merged in a single term (*predication*). In (i) the abstract representations of the input are completed with (prototypical) information of the memory response. In the current example we assume that **smoke** is 'known' as smoke, representing anything 'smoke-like' such as the steam of a locomotive or even a picture of smoke, and **roof** (that is not in the focus of the mind) is associated with roof, referring to some roof-like form which is 'not-known' as a roof. Similarly, **burning** (b) is associated with the habitual meaning of danger (b'), and **rising-air** (b) with that of thermal (b').

Note that a single input quale may simultaneously trigger memory response, both in the sense of agreement and in the sense of possibility. For instance, in

another interpretation process, **smoke** may be associated with smoke ('known')
and roof ('not-known'). This possibility is not considered in the current example,
however.

Complementation

$$(a,a') \quad = \quad (\{\text{smoke,smoke}\}), (\{\text{roof,roof}\})$$
$$(b,b') \quad = \quad (\{\text{burning,danger}\}), (\{\text{rising-air,thermal}\})$$

Predication

$a*a'$	=	**smoke***smoke	% **smoke** known as smoke
$a+a'$	=	**roof**+roof	% roof as a candidate for **roof**
$b*b'$	=	**burning***danger	% **burning** known as danger
$b+b'$	=	**rising-air**+thermal	% thermal as a candidate for **rising-air**

5.5.2 Cognition

The cognition process proceeds with the final expressions generated by perception, dealt with as input qualia. An overview of all expressions generated by
this process of cognition can be found in Fig. 5.8.

A	=	$a*a'$	=	**smoke***smoke	=	*smoke*
$\neg A$	=	$a+a'$	=	**roof**+roof	=	*roof-like-form*
B	=	$b*b'$	=	**burning***danger	=	*burning-as-danger*
$\neg B$	=	$b+b'$	=	**rising-air**+thermal	=	*rising-hot-air*

Sorting

$A+B$	=	*smoke*+*burning-as-danger*	% or in short
	=	*a-certain-form*	
$A*B$	=	*smoke***burning-as-danger*	% or in short
	=	*an-appearing-event*	

At this stage of interpretation the input qualia are 'known' as possible constituents ($A+B$) and as a co-occurring that is happening now ($A*B$). However,
it may not be known yet that, in context, *smoke* can be propositionally related
to *burning-as-danger*, and so, the fire fighters should be called as soon as possible.
That level of interpretation may be reached later.

5.5 An extended example

Abstraction

$A*\neg B$ =   *smoke*rising-hot-air*
            % smoke in relation to any rising-like motion,
            % e.g. smoke may ascend, whirl, etc.

$\neg A*B$ =   *roof-like-form*burning-as-danger*
            % dangerous burning in relation to anything roof-like,
            % e.g. ubiquitous, fierce, etc.

A synonymous interpretation of these expressions may be conceived as *a-possible-for-danger-etc.* (such as the burning and smoke produced by a cigarette, a roof, a torch). See also Sect. 5.3.

$A*\neg B+\neg A*B$
     = *smoke*rising-hot-air + roof-like-form*burning-as-danger*   % or in short
     = *smoke-formation*

Smoke ($A*\neg B$) can be associated with the property 'rising hot air', and *burning-as-danger* ($\neg A*B$) with the subject of this effect: a 'dangerous burning of a roof'. The compatibility of these expressions enables the observed phenomenon to be looked at in two different ways, from the points of view of *smoke* and *burning*. This is the habitual aspect included in this co-occurrence of the appearing qualia of smoke and burning.

Complementation

A representation of the input as a sign of an actually existent object may be obtained by an interpretation of the earlier abstract input representations in context. The context expressions are:

$\neg A+\neg B$ =   *roof-like-form+rising-hot-air*
            % some roof and some rising hot air in the background

$\neg A*\neg B$ =   *roof-like-form*rising-hot-air*
            % rising hot air above the roof in the background

A synonymous interpretation of these expressions may be generated by unifying them in the phrase: *fire-above-the-roof.*

     Complementation may yield a representation of the input as a possible co-occurrence of qualia of *burning-as-danger* (B) and those of some *roof-like-form* state ($\neg A$), and a similar co-occurrence of qualia of *smoke* (A) and those of a kind of *rising-hot-air* effect ($\neg B$).

$\neg A+B$ =   *roof-like-form+burning-as-danger*   % this dangerous burning
$A+\neg B$ =   *smoke+rising-hot-air*   % this rising smoke

A synonymous interpretation of the above expressions may yield *this-smoke-is-a-sign-of-danger*, representing the subject of the observed phenomenon. *Complementation* may also obtain a representation of the input as a characteristic or conventional property:

81

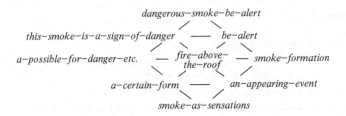

Figure 5.8: Expressions generated by the process of cognition

$A*B+\neg A*\neg B$

   $=$ smoke*burning-as-danger+ roof-like-form*rising-hot-air   % or in short

   $=$ be-alert

This property or predicate, involving a relation between the qualia of the appearing smoke and danger, and between those of the rising hot air and their location on the roof, characterizes the input as the subject of the observation. This relation between subject and predicate can be important, either because we are familiar with its habitual meaning (we may be aware of an adequate reaction that we learned from observations of similar phenomena) or because something or somebody is drawing our attention to it, and we learn its importance now. This is expressed by *predication*, in which the expressions of the subject and predicate are merged into a judgment which is a hypothesis (proposition):

A *is* B $=$ *this-smoke is a-sign-of-burning-as-danger*   % or in short

           $=$ *dangerous-smoke-be-alert*

An alternative representation of the above proposition may be generated by means of reasoning. For example, if we have memory information about smoke (sign) that it may refer to fire (object), then we may deduce that it is fire that smoke signifies as dangerous. If, furthermore, lexical information suggests that 'dangerous smoke' implies the existence of danger,[14] which in turn is related to asking for help, eventually we may generate a reaction by shouting: *Run!*

5.6   Related research

A framework which is remotely related to the one presented in this work, is the theory of Nonagons (Guerri, 2000), which was introduced originally as a support to guarantee the completeness of architectural design.

Nonagons are also based on Peirce's signs and a recursive expansion of his nonadic classification. There is however an important difference between the two approaches with regard to the interpretation of a sign: in the Nonagon approach as an entity which emphasizes its character as a single unit; in our model

---

[14]Effect qualia enable their interpretation as a state.

as an entity which stresses the inherent duality implied by authentic semiosis.[15]
A practical advantage of the latter view lies in its capacity to define the nine
classes as a product of (dual) trichotomies, thereby potentially simplifying the
specification task. An example, illustrating the benefits of a trichotomic specification of qualia in text summarization, will be given in Chapter 9.

---

[15]Both models depart from a triadic definition of signs, but the difference in goals served
puts a different emphasis on the properties of signs. In this work it is maintained that full
understanding of semiosis is only possible when the different perspectives are combined.

Part III

Applications

The aim of the next chapters is to *show* that our theory can meet the requirements for knowledge representation set earlier. A formal proof is not possible as knowledge is not some 'thing' that can be captured in formal rules. Factors that play a role in this matter, amongst others, are the habitual character of knowledge that is notoriously difficult to specify, and the real possibility of the existence of as yet unknown phenomena (including those related to our cognitive potential), implying that knowledge representation can never be considered to be complete. What can be done however is to test whether the theory proposed in this book can be applied to the modeling of phenomena in different knowledge domains. We will call a model of a domain natural if the concepts suggested by the theory form a subset of the 'naive' or natural concepts of the domain, known from experience. Although a test is weaker than a formal proof, the introduction of natural models for a number of domains may increase our confidence that our theory can be applied to any domain and, on top of that, it can be applied in a uniform fashion.

As part of this program, in Chapter 6 we show that the processing schema introduced in Sect. 4.3 can be applied to natural language processing. To this end we develop a knowledge representation for the domain of 'naive' morphosyntactic, syntactic, and semantic-syntactic signs.[16] In Chapter 7 we will extend our focus by introducing models for the domain of 'naive' reasoning symbols and, in Chapter 8, for the domain of 'naive' mathematical symbols. Finally, in Chapter 9, we hint at the theoretical possibilities of our model of knowledge representation for meaningful text summarization.

An important result of Part III is a definition of a sequential version of the processing schema, enabling complex and simple phenomena to be interpreted in an identical fashion.

---

[16] See Sect.6.7.

Chapter 6

Language signs

Natural language consists of symbols that are signs (Jakobson, 1980). What makes language processing especially interesting as a test case for the theory of this book is that interactions between language symbols can be interpreted as relations between *lexically* defined combinatory properties (Debrock et al., 1999). As language appears 'naturally' in our experience, the introduction of a 'naive' model for language processing may enable us to answer the intriguing question: What is 'natural' in natural language?

An application of our process model to the domain of language symbols, and in general to any knowledge domain, asks for a definition of the properties of input qualia. Natural language is one of the few domains for which such definitions are already made, as is witnessed by the various lexicons specifying combinatory properties of symbols. As a full scale specification of such properties is beyond our scope, a systematic comparison with traditional language modeling is omitted.

Natural language processing is sequential, implying that language phenomena can be complex and may contain nested phenomena. In order to get hold of this complexity of language, in this chapter we equip the processing schema (cf. Sect. 4.3) with facilities that enable it to interpret series of language symbols as single entities. Symbols occurring in series can be interpreted either as independent phenomena or as qualia of an encompassing language phenomenon, for example, the sentence. In this chapter we concern ourselves with the second interpretation, which is also the more natural one, as in our everyday experience of language subsequent input symbols appear so fast that an interpretation of their individual meaning cannot be realized; as a rule we directly interpret the constituents with respect to their contribution to the import of the entire series. This implies that in the interpretation of series of language signs the preceding signs, at each later step, can be conceived to be involved as proto-signs.[1]

The focus of this chapter is on the introduction of a model for the domain of 'naive' syntactic, morpho-syntactic and semantic-syntactic symbols. The

---

[1] Proto-signs are a procedural equivalent of sign aspects (see Sect. 4.3).

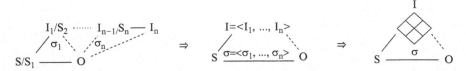

Figure 6.1: Interpretation of simple phenomena (recapitulated from Fig. 3.13)

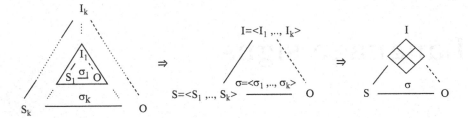

Figure 6.2: A schematic view of the interpretation of complex phenomena depicted as a series of nested phenomena (left) and a single phenomenon (middle), paraphrased as an instance of the processing schema (right). For $1 \leq i \leq k$, S_i are input signs, having O as their shared object; σ_i are states of the S_S. In σ_i, the interpretant of the change due to S_i is represented by I_i. For $1 \leq i \leq k$, the triadic relations (S_i, O, I_i), depicted by a triangle, represent an instance of the interpretation process as shown in Fig. 6.1. Angle parentheses are used for a series interpreted as a single entity

language of illustration will be English. The word classes used in the definitions are restricted to the major types such as verbs, nouns, adjectives and adverbs. In conformity with the examples of earlier chapters, lexically defined language signs (cf. memory signs) and signs generated by the interpretation process are given in sans-serif and *slanted* fonts, respectively.

Below we begin with the introduction of a theory of interpretation for complex phenomena. This is followed by a definition of models for syntactic and morpho-syntactic symbol processing which show a number of similarities. The development of a model for semantic-syntactic signs is postponed until Sect. 6.7.

6.1 Modeling complex phenomena

We call a phenomenon *complex* if it contains nested phenomena. The interpretation of complex phenomena (S) requires the processing of phenomena that are nested in them. Examples of complex phenomena are sentences. Input symbols (e.g. words) stand for the sentence (O) they are part of and signify it from a certain point of view. As a rule, nested phenomena can be interpreted as primary constituents of the complex they are part of, hence as signs having the complex (O) as their object. The similarity between Figs. 6.1 and 6.2 shows that the processing of simple and complex signs can be modeled identically. This implies that the model is *scalable*.

Let us assume that the interpreting system (S_S) is involved in the processing of a complex sign $S:=<S_1,\ldots,S_k>$ (see Fig. 6.2). In conformity with the process view of sign interpretation, introduced in Sect. 3.3.1, in state σ_i ($1\leq i\leq k$) the S_S is involved in the generation of I_i, representing the change due to S_i, and the generation of the next state, (S_i,O,I_i). The processing of S can be modeled by means of nested interpretation events, representing the change due to subsequent input signs (S_i) by proto-signs, in the interpretation of the entire series (S). As a consequence of nesting, σ_i contains all earlier interpretants, I_j for $1\leq j\leq i$. As each σ_i can be represented by an instance of the processing schema, each state can be defined as a series of interpretation moments, as shown in Fig. 6.1. In contrast to the limited number of different sign aspects and interpretation moments, complex phenomena may consist of any number of nested signs. How interpretation of complex phenomena can be modeled by a single instance of the processing schema is the subject of the next section.

6.1.1 Properties of sequential sign processing

In the processing of a sequence of input signs, $S=<S_1,\ldots,S_k>$, each state σ_i ($1\leq i\leq k$) is defined by a collection of proto-signs, that can be interpreted as qualia (see Sect. 4.4.1). As for the modeling of the processing of a single input sign, this means that the previous and current input percepts can be defined by the proto-signs included in σ_i or the actual state of the S_S (S_S^A), and the qualia of the next input sign (S_i), respectively. As the current and previous percepts are different, if only by virtue of their different temporal properties, the condition for an interaction is satisfied. Because the proto-signs included in σ_i are uniquely marked by their sign aspect, the next state of the S_S can be defined by a change of σ_i, brought about by the interaction of the S_S with S_i as a qualisign. This requires S_i to be interpreted as a combinatory potential with respect to the sign aspects or positions of the processing schema, specifying the positions in which S_i can establish a relation with another sign.

Below we assume that less developed interpretation events are generated before more developed ones (cf. economical representation). Although in theory the term *proto*-sign is associated with interpretation moments, introduced in our process model in order to make a distinction between signs to be interpreted and signs that comprise the process of interpretation, below, because it is a relative distinction, for the sake of simplicity we omit the prefix. Having said this, we define our model of sequential sign processing, as follows.

For the sake of convenience we suppose the qualisign position on the S_S to be empty at the moment the first input sign offers itself for interpretation. This enables us to represent the appearing first sign in the qualisign position. The interaction between the subsequent input sign and the already existing proto-sign representation in the qualisign position forces the latter to be represented

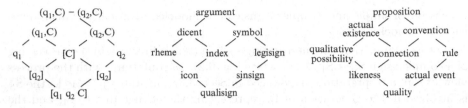

Figure 6.3: Interpretation moments (left), corresponding sign aspects (middle) and their mundane terms (right)

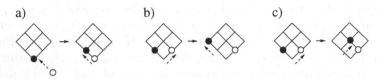

Figure 6.4: Sample coercion sign interactions. A '•' indicates an already existing sign, a '○' an appearing new one; a '→' designates a state transition of the S_S. Dashed arrows are used for representing traces of sign interpretation

by a more developed sign,[2] which can be either in the icon ($[q_1]$) or the sinsign position ($[q_2]$). Such a sign interaction between an existing sign and an appearing sign, triggering a representation of the already existing sign by a more developed one,[3] is called a *coercion*. See Fig. 6.4(a), for coercion into the icon position. As $[q_1]$ and $[q_2]$ are representations of the same 'primordial soup' but the input signs are in principle independent of each other, in sequential sign processing the icon and sinsign positions cannot be simultaneously realized in any state of the S_S^A. This means that the generation of input representations in the icon and sinsign positions will trigger further interpretation events (cf. Sect. 3.2). If there is a sign in the icon or sinsign positions, it will become represented by a sign in the rheme (q_1), index ($[C]$) or legisign positions (q_2). See Fig. 6.4(b), for the rheme position.

In sequential sign processing, we may not know in advance whether an appearing input sign conveys information which is in focus or is complementary. In our model we assume that each input sign represents information which is in focus, and only if this hypothesis fails[4] we assume the conveyed information is complementary and can be represented in the index position. Since for each input sign, a validation of the above hypothesis is preceded by a representation of an input sign in the icon or sinsign positions, its representation in the index position can always be generated through a coercion operation. See Fig. 6.4(c).

The generation of a sign in the rheme or legisign positions may trigger further sign interactions. Besides as coercion, sign interactions can be classified as

---

[2] In conformity with the assumption that qualisigns are independent by definition.

[3] The dependencies between the different sign aspects of Peirce's classification define an induced partial ordering with the qualisign aspect as bottom element.

[4] Interpretation may fail if the entire input cannot be represented by a single sign.

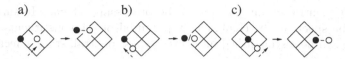

Figure 6.5: Sample genuine binding (a), accumulation (b), and degenerate binding (c) symbol interactions. Dashed arrows represent traces of sign interpretation. Infix '/' and '−' symbols are used for a representation of the result of accumulation and binding operations, respectively

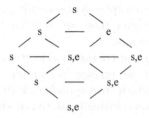

Figure 6.6: The positions of the processing schema as constituent states (s) and effects (e) in syntactic sign interactions. The final representation of the input qualia, as a state, can be interpreted as a quality (state or effect) in an encompassing interpretation process

binding and *accumulation* operations. In a binding, the position of the resulting representation of a sign interaction is higher in the processing schema than the position of the signs in the interaction (cf. constituent signs). See Fig. 6.5(a) for the dicent position. This is opposed to an accumulation, in which the position of the representation of the sign interaction and the position of one of the interacting signs is identical. See Fig. 6.5(b) for the rheme position. In our model we allow sign interactions to be represented degenerately. In that case, the position of the representation of a sign interaction is equivalent to the position of one of the constituent signs. See Fig. 6.5(c) for the legisign position.

Looking at accumulation and coercion from the perspective of degenerate representation, the two operations can be considered to be degenerate versions of a binding (note that both coercion and accumulation satisfy the condition for a non-strictly monotonic representation of increasingly better approximations of the final input sign). The importance of degenerate representation is due to its potential for enabling positions of the processing schema to be re-used, thereby allowing processing of input series of any length.

Relations between neighboring signs in the processing schema are representations of an interaction between signs interpreted as a state and an effect. An account of the processing schema from this perspective is given in Fig. 6.6. Following our analysis of sequential sign processing, signs are relationally neutral in the qualisign, icon and sinsign positions, as well as in the argument position (in the last by virtue of our assumption concerning the completeness of sign interpretation as a process). By virtue of the possibility of coercion operations, signs can be neutral in any position of the processing schema. In sum, from a relational perspective, the combinatory potential of the constituents of a sign interaction can be distinguished into three types: neutral, state, effect.

6.2   Towards a model of language signs

The above model of sequential sign processing can easily be adapted to language parsing. For instance, in syntactic language phenomena the input qualia are defined by the occurring morpho-syntactically finished signs such as words; in morpho-syntactic phenomena they are defined by the occurring morpho-syntactic entities such as lexemes.

Analogously to our model of cognitive activity, the proposed model of language processing consists of two phases: *perception*, linking the input qualities with memory information (which corresponds to lexical analysis), and *cognition*, establishing a relation between lexically analyzed signs (which corresponds to parsing).

Although there are more similarities between the morpho-syntactic and syntactic domains of signs, and this holds for semantic-syntactic signs as well, a simultaneous development of their models would be too ambitious. In the next section we restrict our focus to an analysis of syntactic symbols. We return to morpho-syntactic signs in Sect. 6.6, and consider semantic-syntactic symbol processing in Sect. 6.7. We will look into the similarities of the process models of these domains in Sect. 6.8.

6.3   Syntactic signs

Roughly speaking, in syntactic phenomena nominals, appearing as a state, undergo effects due to non-nominals. Examples are syntactic modification and predication of nouns by means of adjectives and verbs, respectively. Which existing representations (proto-signs) are affected by an appearing input symbol, that is, how the state of the interpreting system is eventually changed, can be derived from the interactions triggered by the input symbol. Such series of interactions and representation events will be called an *evaluation moment*.

Because of its minor importance for the goals of this chapter, a definition of the process of perception (lexical analysis) is omitted. We assume that input language symbols are represented by their lexical combinatory properties.

In our model of syntactic signs[5] we will assume that input nominal entities are defined as nouns, and input non-nominal symbols as verbs, adjectives, adverbs and certain prepositional phrases.[6] A classification of basic syntactic concepts and their dependencies is depicted in Fig. 6.7, on the left-hand side. The reader may compare the syntactic meaning of these concepts with the corresponding sign aspects, in Fig. 1.13.

---

[5] As our focus is on 'naive' language processing, the 'naive' prefix can be omitted.

[6] Non-nominal entities signifying an appearing new property are interpreted as effects.

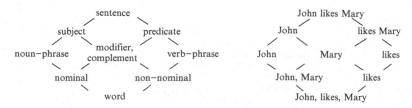

Figure 6.7: A classification of basic syntactic concepts (on the left), and proto-signs of the sample utterance 'John likes Mary' (on the right)

For example, words, nominals and noun-phrases can be associated with sign aspects of a syntactic quality, a syntactic constituent (cf. likeness) and a potential for a syntactic relation (cf. qualitative possibility), respectively. On the right-hand side of Fig. 6.7, the reader may find an analogous classification of syntactic entities and relations involved in the utterance: 'John likes Mary'.

6.3.1 Relational needs

Following the model of sequential sign processing introduced in Sect. 6.1.1 and the traditional interpretation of syntactic relations as interactions between an active and a passive element such as a modifier and modified, the three types of constituents of a syntactic sign interaction can be characterized as: (1) a *neutral* entity which is a potential existence, (2) a *passive* state which appears by virtue of an effect and (3) an *active* effect which assumes the existence of a state. In short, the three types of a relational need are called n-, p- and a-need.

From a relational perspective, the three types of bindings can be described as follows. A *coercion* satisfies an n-need, conceptually; an *accumulation* merges two relational needs of the same type into a single need; a (genuine) *binding* satisfies a pair of a- and p-needs. Combinatory needs that are fulfilled are removed.

Language symbols can be formally defined by a *set*, consisting of references to the types of syntactic interactions the symbol can be involved in as a constituent. Such a set, defining the symbol's *relational potential*, consists of combinatory properties referring to sign aspects (for reasons of economy, sign aspects are abbreviated by a four-letter name). For example, the syntactic relational potential of likes can be defined by the set: $\{n_{sins}, p_{legi}, a_{legi}, a_{symb}\}$, expressing the potential of likes (1) to appear as an effect (n_{sins}), (2) to undergo modification by another symbol, e.g. an adverb (p_{legi}), or bind with a verb-complement, e.g. a noun (a_{legi}), and (3) to predicate the subject of the sentence (a_{symb}).

A language symbol is called *A-type*, if its relational potential only consists of p- and n-needs; otherwise it is called *B-type*. A-type symbols stand for 'things', B-type symbols represent 'events'.

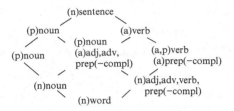

Figure 6.8: A classification of the types of word classes used, on the basis of their relational properties

6.4 Towards a formal model

In Fig. 6.8 we summarize the relational potential of syntactic symbols for the major types of word classes. Constituent input symbols, interpreted as qualisigns, are defined as follows:

$A=$ noun

$B=$ verb, adjective, adverb, preposition(-complement)

where 'complement' can be a noun, verb, adjective or adverb (a precise definition of 'preposition-complement' symbols is postponed until Sect. 6.6). In accordance with the asymmetry between state and effect, we assume that lexically defined syntactic a-needs always have to be satisfied; p-needs are optional. As syntactic symbols usually possess p- and n-needs in all positions of the processing schema, in the examples a definition of the relational potential of a symbol can be restricted to a specification of its a-needs. For instance, the definition of likes in Sect. 6.3.1 can be simplified as: {*legi, symb*}.[7] Dot symbols are defined as generic A- *and* B-type signs that are incompatible for a binding with another symbol. Dot symbols can trigger a 'realization' of pending syntactic sign interactions. In our model we assume that the series of input symbols is closed by a constant number of dot symbols.[8]

In English, the relational potential of syntactic symbols can be classified as follows. A-type symbols can have a relational potential in the (1) icon, (2) rheme or index and (3) dicent positions; B-type symbols in the (1) sinsign, (2) legisign or index and (3) symbol sign positions. The category-related dependency between A- and B-type symbols can favorably be used for modeling modification phenomena such as 'runs quickly'. Although both runs and quickly are B-type, in their interaction the a-need of quickly (index) is satisfied by the p-need of the effect type symbol runs (legisign), this time interpreted as a state. Object complementation phenomena (Quirk, Greenbaum, Leech, & Svartvik, 1985), for example, 'painted black' can be modeled analogously.

---

[7]A preliminary version of a lexicon for syntactic symbols used in the examples can be found in Appendix F.

[8]This restriction is necessary in order to keep the complexity of the model linear. See (Sarbo & Farkas, 2002). Formally, the processing schema can be modeled by a two-level grammar: a first, context-free s-grammar (Sippu & Soisalon-Soininen, 1988) is augmented with set-valued features for expressing agreement between constituents.

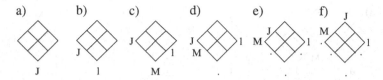

Figure 6.9: A failing syntactic analysis of 'John likes Mary'. As in (f), a final input representation is already available, but J (argument position) does not stand for the entire input, parsing fails. Note that each state (except the initial state) contains information about interpretations introduced in previous states. For instance, (b) includes information about the representation of J, in the qualisign position

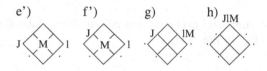

Figure 6.10: A successful syntactic analysis of 'John likes Mary', following backtracking to stage (d), in Fig. 6.9. The unit element of backtracking is defined by an evaluation moment (cf. Sect. 6.3). Evaluation moments, representing a change triggered by an input symbol, are depicted by a single 'diamond'

6.4.1 An example

This section contains a syntactic analysis of a most simple example: 'John likes Mary' (in short 'J I M'). See also Fig. 6.9. In this and later diagrams, states of the S_S^A are referred to by subsequent letters of the alphabet given in parentheses. In Fig. 6.9(a), the appearing first symbol, J (A-type), is interpreted as a qualisign. As the input symbols are in principle independent and partake in the syntactic phenomenon expressed by the entire sentence, the appearing next symbol, I (B-type), forces the parser to reconsider the earlier interpretation of J (qualisign) and represent it via coercion, in (b), as a constituent (icon) of the entire input.

In (c), the appearance of M (A-type) has similar consequences on the interpretation of I (qualisign) and, transitively so, on the interpretation of J (icon). The latter is a consequence of a feature of sequential sign processing, that input representations in the icon and sinsign positions are incompatible for a binding, except in a 'negative' sense, through their relative difference, via coercion (cf. *abstraction*). For this reason, J has to be represented again, this time as an abstract term or a possible for the subject of the sentence (rheme). The subsequently appearing dot symbol, in (d), triggers the representation of M (icon) by a more developed sign. By following the same strategy as in the case of J, parsing will eventually fail, as it will not be possible to represent the entire input by a single (sentence) sign. The failure will make the parser backtrack[9]

---

[9]We assume nondeterminism to be implemented by backtracking (Aho & Ullman, 1972).

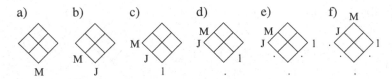

Figure 6.11: A failing syntactic analysis of 'Mary, John likes'

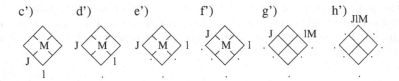

Figure 6.12: A successful syntactic analysis of 'Mary, John likes', after back-tracking to stage (b), in Fig. 6.11

until the first choice-point providing another alternative.[10] Such a choice-point is (d), enabling M (icon) to be represented as a complementary sign (index). This is illustrated in Fig. 6.9(e'). A representation of M in the index position is possible due to the existence of I (legisign), anticipating M as a complement.

6.4.2 Complementary syntactic signs

The analysis depicted in Fig. 6.9 already illustrates to some extent how the parsing process may reveal whether an input symbol is referring to the complementary context of a language phenomenon. Input symbols can be interpreted as context signs, if they posses an a-need in the index position. Examples of such symbols are adjectives, adverbs and prepositional phrases. A sign (S) having a p-need in the index position can be represented as an index sign for two reasons: if there is a sign in the legisign position (a-need) anticipating S (p-need) in the index position; or, if any interpretation of S fails, and a suitable legisign symbol will arise in a subsequent interpretation event. An illustrative example of the latter is the utterance: 'Mary, John likes'. The first analysis assuming M (A-type) to be the subject of the sentence fails (see Fig. 6.11), as the argument sign (M) does not represent the entire input (there are pending relational needs in this analysis). As a result, the interpretation process backtracks to step (b), which is the first choice-point[11] providing a successful alternative. Syntactic parsing can be resumed by coercing M to the index position (see Fig. 6.12), in conformity with the potential of noun symbols to function as syntactic complements of verbs such as likes, which appears in the next interpretation moment.

---

[10]Note that this laborious procedure is a consequence of the assumed bottom-up flow of information.

[11]Note, in Fig. 6.11, that step (c) does not provide another alternative for parsing. The coercion of J to the index position would force M to be represented as the syntactic subject, which assumption has already been tried and rejected.

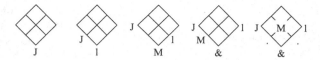

Figure 6.13: An analysis of John likes Mary and Kim (until the coordinator)

6.4.3   Nested analysis

Nested phenomena frequently occur in language. In accordance with our earlier assumption that in the observation of a phenomenon the entire input is defined by a single collection of state and effect qualia (cf. 'primordial soup'), in our model we assume that syntactic phenomena are always defined by a *contiguous* series of input symbols. Nested phenomena such as subordinate clauses and complex phrases are degenerately represented as input symbols (qualia) in the encompassing nesting phenomenon. Interpretation of nested phenomena can be modeled by means of recursive parsing. As the number of the types of nested syntactic phenomena is finite, the potential of language symbols for starting and/or ending such a series can be modeled as a syntactic relational need, as usual. Besides nesting, recursive parsing can be useful for an analysis of multiple modification and complementation phenomena as well.

6.5   Coordination phenomena

The above framework can successfully be applied to the modeling of coordination phenomena. The kernel of such an algorithm can be defined as follows.

Interpretation of syntactic coordination phenomena can be distinguished into three phases. In the first phase, input symbols preceding the coordinator are analyzed. In the second phase, first, signs generated in the first phase are saved (e.g. on a stack), their relational needs are remembered in the positions of the processing schema, as 'traces'. This is followed by an analysis of a series of subsequent input symbols, as a nested phenomenon. In the course of this analysis, actually generated signs and saved signs corresponding to identical positions are coordinated (this may involve an inheritance of syntactic properties). In the last phase, saved representations that are not coordinated, are restored. Save operations can be preceded and restore operations can be followed by elaboration of pending sign interactions. The number of such interactions is limited by the number of simultaneously existing signs in the processing schema and the size of their set of relational needs, which are both finite (Sarbo & Farkas, 2004).

Parsing of a sample coordination structure is illustrated in Fig. 6.13–Fig. 6.15 (saved representations are given in parentheses). The analysis depicted in Fig. 6.15 assumes that, preceding coordination, representations generated by the interpretation process, displayed in Fig. 6.13, undergo an additional coercion operation: M is coerced to the index position. Note, in Fig. 6.14, the use of 'trace' information about the *a*-need of I (legisign), in the coercion of K (icon)

Figure 6.14: Coordination (alternative #1). Save and restore operations are represented by the addition and removal of a pair of parentheses symbols, respectively)

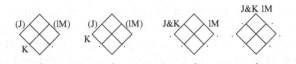

Figure 6.15: Coordination (alternative #2)

to a syntactic complement of I (index). The sentence 'John likes Mary and Kim' is not ambiguous, but it can be, if it is used for the utterance 'John likes Mary and Kim (too)'. See Fig. 6.15.[12]

This closes our treatment of syntactic phenomena. Interested readers may find analysis of examples taken from actual language use, in Appendix E.

6.6 Morpho-syntactic signs

A model for 'naive' morpho-syntactic signs can be defined analogously to our model of 'naive' syntactic signs. Morpho-syntactic symbol processing deserves our attention if only in order to show how certain prepositional phrases ('prep-compl') can be interpreted as syntactic input symbols. This section might also be interesting for another reason, as it provides another example of how in domain modeling the nine Peircean sign aspects can be used as 'pigeonholes'.

In the model of this chapter we assume the dependency between the syntactic and morpho-syntactic domains to be hierarchical: syntactic input signs ('words') arise from morpho-syntactically finished signs. Moreover, morpho-syntactical sign interactions can be interpreted as 'generators' of syntactic properties. Although syntactic and morpho-syntactic signs can have identical linguistic representations, their relational needs in the two domains are different.

Morpho-syntactic signs can be characterized as follows. Proposition signs (argument position) are representations of the input as morpho-syntactically finished symbols. In conformity with the 'flat' structure of morpho-syntactic symbols, arising from adjacent input entities by means of 'gluing' them together, we assume that signs in the morpho-syntactic dicent and symbol positions are incompatible for a binding hence are in principle finished too. Indeed, these

---

[12]In this analysis, preceding coordination, J is coerced to the dicent position; the complementation of I by M is represented by IM in the symbol position.

positions exhibit essentially different properties. Morpho-syntactic signs in the symbol position such as adjectives have the *conventional* property that they are adjacent to their syntactic complement, on 'surface level'. Besides adjectives, also adverbs and certain prepositional phrases in the symbol position represent morpho-syntactically finished signs, ready to function as B-type syntactic symbols. Morpho-syntactic symbols in the dicent position such as nouns and verbs, which are in lack of the above property, represent the input as an *actually existent*, that is, as a morpho-syntactically finished sign, having the potential to function as an A-type syntactic symbol.

Morpho-syntactic rheme, index and legisign symbols exhibit the aspect of a qualitative possibility, a connection, and a rule, respectively. Rheme signs, such as nouns and verbs, are an expression of a range of possibilities underlying morpho-syntactic dicent signs. Legisign symbols, for example, prep(-compl), are an expression of a *rule* involved in morpho-syntactic complementation structures. Index symbols, for instance, articles and morpho-syntactic complements, can furnish rheme signs with referential properties or alternatively legisign symbols with morpho-syntactic complement(s).

In conformity with the goal of morpho-syntactic symbol interpretation, which is the generation of 'words' for a subsequent syntactic analysis, morpho-syntactic rheme, index and legisign symbols can be involved in the generation of *syntactic* relational needs. For example, morpho-syntactic complementation of girl (rheme) by the (index) is furnishing 'the girl' with a syntactic p-need in the rheme position; complementation of with (legisign) by a fork (index) is assigning 'with a fork' the a-need of adverb-like syntactic signs in the legisign position.

Morpho-syntactic icon and sinsign symbols arise through *sorting* from input symbols appearing in the qualisign position. Interactions between icon and sinsign symbols can be represented by morpho-syntactic signs in the rheme, index and legisign positions. In English, such icon and sinsign symbols are typically written as one word. For example, an interaction between the verb walk (icon) and the participle affix -ed (sinsign) is represented by the sign walked (index) having adjective-like syntactic properties.

A classification of the morpho-syntactic symbol classes used, on the basis of their lexical relational properties, is displayed in Fig. 6.16. At first sight this diagram seems to enable morpho-syntactic icon and sinsign symbols to establish a binding, but this is not the case. In our model, affixation is interpreted as a *nested* phenomenon. A specification of affixation phenomena can be simplified by allowing *predication* –occurring in the nested phenomenon– to overlap with *abstraction* occurring in the encompassing nesting phenomenon.[13] See Fig. 6.17.

The relational potential of morpho-syntactic input symbols (qualisign position) can be specified as follows:

$A=$ noun, verb, adjective, adverb
$B=$ preposition, article, particle, affix

Space symbols ('$\sqcup$') are interpreted as generic A- *and* B-type signs that are unable to genuinely bind with another sign. Space symbols can combine

---

[13] Abstraction is the first genuine interaction in the processing schema.

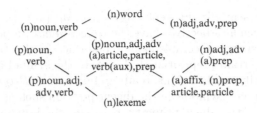

Figure 6.16: A classification of the major types of morpho-syntactic symbol classes used, on the basis of their relational properties

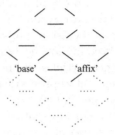

Figure 6.17: Overlapping sign interactions in affixation phenomena

with other signs through accumulation, and can be subject to coercion operations, however. Appearing space symbols can trigger a 'realization' of pending morpho-syntactical symbol interactions. Contrary to syntactic sign interpretation, our model of morpho-syntactic symbol processing does not make use of recursive parsing (except in the case of affixation phenomena), as a consequence of the 'flat' structure of English morpho-syntactic symbols.

An analysis of the morpho-syntactic phenomenon, 'John ␣ like -s ␣ Mary', is depicted in Fig. 6.18 (the parsing of the embedded affixation phenomenon 'like -s' and the processing of accumulated space symbols are omitted). In our model we allow interpretation moments (see Sect. 6.3) corresponding to subsequent morpho-syntactically finished signs to be merged. Morpho-syntactic parsing of article symbols is illustrated by an analysis of the string 'the beautiful Queen'. See Fig. 6.19. This example shows that, in our model, article symbols can become immediate neighbors of their references.

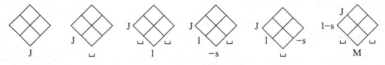

Figure 6.18: An initial segment of the morpho-syntactic analysis of the string 'John like -s Mary'

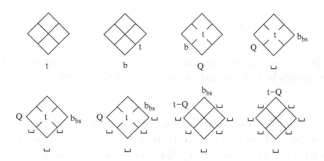

Figure 6.19: A morpho-syntactic analysis of 'the beautiful Queen' (in short t b Q; bs='base-degree'; inter-word space symbols are omitted)

6.7 Semantic-syntactic signs

Language symbols that fall outside the domain traditionally acknowledged as syntactic, but that nevertheless can be treated as syntactic-like are called in this book semantic-syntactic or, simply, semantic symbols.

A distinguishing property of semantic signs is that they can more aptly capture the diversity of 'real' world phenomena than logical or syntactic symbols. For example, 'a girl' and 'the girl' can identically be interpreted as noun-phrases. From a semantic perspective the two symbols are different, however, by virtue of their different referential properties.

Analogously to the 'naive' logical interpretation of the processing schema in Sect. 5.3, in our model of semantic-syntactic signs we capitalize on the asymmetry between the ontological status of state and effect (cf. Sect. 5.4). Theoretically, there can be any number of different states that are in principle *independent*. Following our model, however, states appear due to an effect, which enables a state to appear due to any number of effects (on different occasions). The existence of a shared state is a necessary condition for effects to be *compared* with each other. On a more basic level, comparison is enabled by the assumed homogeneous representation of states and effects as collections of qualia.

Semantic symbols are signs, that involve an interaction between dual qualia (cf. Sect. 4.2). In our model we assume that semantic state and effect qualia can be represented by means of *discrete* and *continuous* types of values, respectively.

Like other signs, semantic symbols can be classified categorically, enabling semantic state and effect symbols to be distinguished according to an order relation ('<'). For instance, a<the, by virtue of the different referential properties of the two semantic state symbols, which are an *indefinite reference* or a reference of a symbol to itself ('a') and a *definite reference* or a relation with another symbol through selection ('the'). From a categorical point of view, the first reference exhibits the aspect of firstness, the other the aspect of secondness.

Effect symbols can be categorically classified as well, on the basis of their involved state. For instance, 'is' and 'do' expressing an effect of *existence* (of an entity in itself) and *modification* (changing the state of another entity),

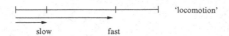

Figure 6.20: A continuous domain representation of 'locomotion' effects; slow and fast are symbolic indexes indicating different measures

respectively, define the induced ordering: is<do. Another example of an ordering are the syntactic relational needs and, in general, relational needs of any kind, ordered according to the category of their involved relations: $n<p<a$.[14]

Besides a categorical ordering, semantic effects can be ordered according to their values as well. Semantic signs corresponding to a single domain of effects can be ordered according to their measures. For instance, slow<fast, in the domain of 'locomotion'-effects (see Fig. 6.20).

6.7.1 Lexical definition

As opposed to (morpho-)syntactic symbols, a lexical definition of semantic combinatory properties may not be available. However, as a consequence of the possibility to apply the Peircean categorical schema recursively to itself, a lexical specification can always be assumed to exist (see Sect. 5.4). So, in general, while in actual practice a specification of qualia may not be available, it can be systematically developed in *any* domain, including the domain of semantic signs as well.

6.7.2 Memory representation revisited

The proposed representation of semantic signs as discrete values (state) and measures of a continuous domain (effect) sets additional conditions for the representation of memory information. Unlike (morpho-)syntactic symbol processing in which input symbols may trigger a small collection of neurons containing abstract information about relational needs, in semantic symbol processing we assume the number of responding neurons to be high. Put differently, we assume that semantic symbols may not possess generalized, abstract combinatory properties, but their relational properties refer to different values in each responding neuron. For instance, in a syntactic interpretation, the symbol 'chair' may trigger a single neuron representing the abstract relational needs of 'nouns'. This is opposed to a semantic interpretation of the same symbol, involving a number of responding neurons representing qualia of earlier observations of chairs, such as their number of legs, color, shape, etc. Although those semantic qualia can be different, they are related to each other. This property can be used for a representation of semantic signs, as follows.

As an interpretation of input qualia as a state or an effect only depends on the occurrence of those qualia in the previous and current percepts, it follows

---

[14]We assume that syntactic relational needs arise through generalization (cf. learning) from semantic state–effect relations.

that input qualities (stimulus) can equally be represented by a state or an effect sign. However, from the principle of economy it follows that memory representation by the brain must be *homogeneous*. In conformity with these conditions we assume that state and effect type memory signs arise from identical memory information, through *different* interpretations. The above view is acknowledged in our model, by representing memory signs by an *average value* (a') and a *dense domain* (b') of qualia.[15] Memory qualia, being obtained from neurons responding to an input stimulus, must have similar values. The above representation of semantic memory signs can be beneficial from the point of view of efficiency as well. As the processing speed of the brain is limited, an individual analysis of memory qualia may not be viable. The use of a shared representation abstracted from a collection of responding neurons can significantly improve the efficiency. Such a dynamic, semantic representation is different from a static, syntactic one. Whereas the first can change with a changing memory content, the latter must be invariant.

By virtue of the involved abstraction, the suggested representation of a' and b' semantic signs can be called *prototypical*. Dense domains can be modeled, amongst others, by a chain-ordering of a collection of qualia (Birkhoff & Bartee, 1970). Such sets can favorably be used for deciding if a value precedes or succeeds another value in the chain, simply by means of a comparison operation.

The benefits of a homogeneous memory representation of qualia can be illustrated with the potential of memory qualia of 'run' to be interpreted as a nominal state (a') or a verbal effect (b'). Note that in our model the input of cognitive activity is assumed to be homogeneous as well. Input percepts (cf. previous and current percept) are defined by 'static' collections of sampled qualities. It is due to the interpretation of these percepts that we conceive the involved information as state and effect qualia.

In our process model of perception (cf. Sect. 5.1), we capitalize on the above definition of memory signs, as follows. In *complementation*, input a- and b-type qualia are rendered as instances of a prototypical state (a') and effect (b'), respectively. As a' is indicates an average value of qualia triggered by the input state, a can be used for the generation of a proposition about these qualia, which is the meaning of (a, a'). This is opposed to the interpretation of b as a measure of a continuous domain (b') of memorized effects, which is the meaning of (b, b').

A dense domain representation of effect qualia (cf. Fig. 6.20) assumes the existence of monotonic functions mapping a domain (b') to a linearly ordered set of values. If these values can be associated with a symbolic representation, the domain is called a '*scale*'. A measure (b) of a domain (b') can be represented by a *relative* value, defined by the distance of b from the smallest value or *zero point* of b'. Conceptually, the zero point of a domain is defined by the threshold value of the sensory perception of the sort of qualities involved.

The proposed representation of memory signs enables a flexible use of language symbols. As input qualia can be associated with different average values

---

[15] Which definition of an average is used, e.g. an arithmetical mean or a weighted average, is not the issue here. Dense domains are a representation of a continuous, ordered collection of elements.

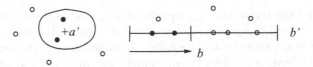

Figure 6.21: An average value (left) and a dense domain representation of memory qualia (right). '•' and '○' represent values (in an n-dimensional space) of responding and not-responding neurons to an input trigger, respectively; b indicates a measure in the effect domain b'; the average value ('+') of responding neurons triggered by a is labelled a'

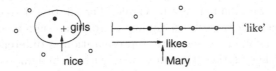

Figure 6.22: A representation of 'nice girls' (left) and 'likes Mary' (right)

and measures, symbolic representations of memory information can be efficiently re-used. For example, the measure represented by the symbol 'fast' can refer to locomotion by a race car, or by a rabbit, in the domains of 'race-car-speed' and 'rabbit-run-speed', respectively, in spite of the obvious differences between the absolute values of their speed. Similarly, the average value 'chair', prototypically representing a class of objects that one can sit on, may furnish any perceived chair-like object (state) with general properties of chairs observed earlier.

A measure of an effect can be referred to by different symbols. In our model of language symbols we make beneficial use of this facility. For instance, in a semantic analysis of the sentence 'John likes Mary', the verb likes refers to a certain measure of 'like'-effects. Linking Mary with that measure enables the verb-phrase 'likes Mary', to be represented by a measure of 'like'-effects: "Mary-likes". In an analogous representation of modification phenomena, for example, 'nice girls', the adjective nice can be linked with the average value associated with the nominal girls. See Fig. 6.22.

Blueprints of a computational model of the processing schema respecting the memory representation introduced in this section can be found in Appendix C.

6.7.3 'Naive' semantic sign processing

The average values and measures assigned to the input qualia by perception ($a*a'$, $a+a'$, $b*b'$, $b+b'$) are involved in the input of the subsequent cognition process (A, B, $\neg A$, $\neg B$) as well. More specifically, A and $\neg A$ involve an average value, B and $\neg B$ involve a measure of a sort of effect. As a consequence of the dependency between the Peircean sign aspects, these elements are involved in all more developed representations as well.

Because of the similarity between semantic and syntactic symbol processing (cf. Sect. 6.4), a definition of the semantic cognition process is omitted.

Syntactic and semantic symbol processing can be different, however. For instance, syntactic dicent signs can be a representation of the subject, semantic dicent signs that of the 'patient' or 'agent' of the predicate of the sentence. As, in the examples, the semantic terminology is restricted to a small subset, semantic-syntactic concepts can be introduced 'on the fly'.

The close relationship between syntactic and semantic symbol processing is an assumption maintained by traditional language modeling as well. According to this view, semantic input structures can be built upon or developed in parallel with syntactic ones. Following the theory of this work, the two types of interpretations are developed independently. Their results are merged in a single representation by means of structural coordination. The isomorphism between the models indicates the possibility of a simultaneous processing of syntactic and semantic information by the brain/mind. Experimental evidence supporting simultaneous processing can be found in (Hagoort, Hald, Bastiaansen, & Petersson, 2004).[16]

6.7.4 Trichotomic specification

We assume that combinatory properties of semantic symbols can be specified on a categorical basis, by means of trichotomies (see Sect. 6.7). Whereas syntactic symbols typically can be characterized by a relatively small set of properties, a specification of semantic symbols may require a vast number of such values. Although semantic symbols too can be specified in terms of (semantic) n-, p- and a-needs, the diversity of semantic-syntactic phenomena demands a recursive classification of semantic combinatory properties. As a result, a hierarchical ontology of in principle arbitrary depth can be constructed. In sum, in trichotomic specifications, states and effects (the latter through their involved states) can be ordered categorically. In addition, effects of some sort can be ordered according to their value (cf. measure) as well.

6.7.5 Semantic-syntactic relational needs

In the arbitrary examples below, the category label of a symbol is given by an integer in parentheses. For instance, semantic rheme symbols (e.g. nouns), expressing a range of possible interpretations of the input state, can be classified as a possible existence(1), an actual reference(2), and a conventional function(3).[17] A recursive analysis of the second class above ('referential rheme symbols') reveals them as a general(1), an indefinite(2), and a definite reference(3). For example, girl(1), a girl(2), the girl(3). Similarly, semantic legisign symbols (e.g. verbs), expressing a habitual interpretation of the input effect, can be distinguished in an act of existence(1), a modification(2) and a transformation(3). For instance, is(1), covered with mud(2), disappeared(3). This ordering assumes

---

[16]In their paper the authors show by means of fMRI measurements that language-related ('syntactic') and world-related ('semantic') knowledge processing can be quasi-simultaneous in the brain.

[17]For example, a thematic function.

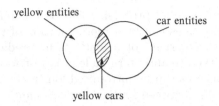

Figure 6.23: A sample intersective nomen-adjective relation

that 'covered with mud' refers to a property that can be removed, as opposed to 'disappeared' which refers to an irreversible change of some state.

Through their duality, index signs ($\neg A*\neg B$, $\neg A+\neg B$), representing the context of a phenomenon, have the potential to express a relation of 'conversion' (such as the relation between two sides of a coin). An example is the verb 'escape' ($\neg A*\neg B$) and its converse, the nominal 'running' ($\neg A+\neg B$): if we observe an escape event to occur then there can be somebody or something in a state of running. The existence of a conversion relation between signs assumes the existence of a common meaning element shared by them.

6.7.6 Psycholinguistic evidence

Evidence for a categorical ordering of semantic qualia and the use of semantic trichotomies in adjective-noun combinations has been experimentally shown by Draskovic, Pustejovsky and Schreuder (2001). The results of this study show that subjects distinguish such combinations into three categorically different types, called: intersective(1), subsective compatible(2), and subsective incompatible(3).

Intersective adjective–noun combinations represent something existing (cf. Sect. 5.4). An example is 'yellow car', referring to an object that is both yellow and is a car, intersectively:[18] yellow is a potential meaning, which is actualized by car (see Fig. 6.23).

Subsective compatible adjective–noun combinations include a link between two entities that are both meaningful. An example is 'interesting car'. There can be various cars around, and we can select a subset of them by pointing to certain cars through interesting.[19] See Fig. 6.24. The interpretation of car is restricted by means of interesting, complementing car's interpretation in a restrictive or 'negative' sense (cf. the 'naive' logical interpretation of *complementation* as a negation operation, in Sect. 5.3).

Subsective incompatible adjective-noun combinations include the aspect of a conventional use of some rule or habit. An example is 'fast car'. A car can be fast, because its interpretation includes the aspect of speed, which in turn

---

[18] Assume there are many things around, some of which are yellow. Then the utterance, "Show me a yellow one", can be meaningful.

[19] "Show me an interesting one" can only be interpreted if a collection of cars is already selected.

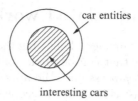

Figure 6.24: A sample subsective nomen-adjective relation

can be modified by fast in the intersective or subsective compatible sense of combination. Car and fast, which are both complete, together define the symbol 'fast car'.

The findings obtained in the experiments testing the semantic interpretation of the three types of combinations show the differences in terms of computational complexity, with intersective combinations being the simplest and the two subsective types being progressively more complex.

6.8 Merging knowledge from different domains

Since there are many different meaning aspects, ranging over different domains, and information processing by the brain is assumed to be efficient, language symbols are frequently used in an ambiguous fashion. For example, the symbol 'Mary' can signify the subject of a sentence (syntactically) and the agent of the predicate of the sentence (semantically).

From an analytical point of view, a synonymous interpretation of signs can be obtained through *coordination* (in the broad sense). An advantage of the uniform representation suggested in this book is that such an interpretation can be realized by means of *structural coordination*, merging expressions exhibiting identical meaning aspects into a single representation. In Chapter 9, we will use this potential of our model for the definition of a simple 'calculus' on signs, enabling text summarization. An example will be helpful.

Assume that in different sentences we encounter syntactic rheme signs: (i) girl, (ii) a girl, (iii) Mary.[20] Further assume that a semantic analysis reveals that these signs can be classified as referential rheme signs (cf. Sect. 6.7.5). Then, by making use of the trichotomy: general<indefinite<definite, the above signs can be ordered: girl<a girl<Mary. As, in a categorical order relation, a smaller element can be omitted in favor of its larger element, the signs in the rheme position can be summarized in a single sign: Mary.

---

[20] Here Mary is used as a reference to a familiar person, as opposed to the general reference involved in girl.

6.9   Summary and related work

What is 'natural' in natural language? Following the view taken in this chapter, it is the *types of distinctions* that can be made cognitively, the organization of their recognition events in a *process* and, the appearance or *'feeling'* of such a process as knowledge (the last is beyond the scope of this work).

The close relationship of our model with Peirce's semiotics may contribute to the robustness of our language model. More specifically, an occurrence of a new, as yet unknown language phenomenon may only require an adjustment of the lexicon; the parsing algorithm can be used invariantly. A systematic adjustment of the lexicon is possible by virtue of the use of trichotomic specification. In this way, we provide a more flexible approach to language modeling than traditional specification techniques using formal grammars, which are less easily adjustable. As the different sub-domains of language, as well as a 'naive' logical interpretation of symbols, can be modeled by means of isomorphic instances of the processing schema, we suggest that the proposed knowledge representation enables us to merge interpretations obtained in different domains into a single form, by means of *structural coordination*.

The language model of this chapter bears similarity to the dependency based formalisms of cognitive linguistics such as Word Grammar (Hudson, 1984). Word Grammar is a branch of Dependency Grammar in that it uses word–word dependencies as a determinant for linguistic structure. As a result it presents language as a network of knowledge that links concepts about words, such as their meaning (e.g. grammatical function), to the form, the word class, etc. Such grammars do not rely on phrasal categories. But the proposed language model is also remotely related to constituency based approaches, in that its types of rules define an induced triadic classification of language concepts which show some analogy to that of X-bar theory (Chomsky, 1975), (Cowper, 1992), (Pollard & Sag, 1994). The three concepts of X-bar theory, which are denoted by X, X', and X", are a representation of a lexical category, a relation, and a phrase, respectively. In turn, the three categories of X-bar theory correspond to the operations: *sorting*, *abstraction*, and *complementation*.

A fundamental difference between the above two approaches and the one presented in this chapter lies in the character of their rules. Contrary to cognitive linguistics, which aims at incorporating the conceptual categories of language in rules that are dictated by a formal theory, the rules of our language model are derived on the basis of an analysis of certain properties of cognitive activity and the processing of signs. The complexity of language parsing can be polynomial or even exponential (Aho & Ullman, 1972). The complexity of the processing schema is linear, which indicates that the proposed representation can be practical (Sarbo & Farkas, 2002).

Chapter 7

Reasoning signs

Reasoning consists of the derivation of conclusions from premises according to rules. The goal of this chapter is to introduce a model for 'naive' reasoning as a kind of sign recognition process. We base our approach on the Peircean analysis of the three major reasoning forms: abduction, deduction and induction. We show that besides 'naive' (mathematical) logic and natural language also 'naive' reasoning can be modeled by means of the processing schema (cf. Sect. 4.3). The results of this chapter reinforce our conjecture that all representations of human knowledge, be it low- or high-level, can be cast in a single type of process.

7.1 Logica Utens

In ordinary life everybody has a reasoning instinct or habits of reasoning by which he forms his opinion concerning many matters of great importance. We not only have a reasoning instinct but we also have an instinctive *theory of reasoning*, for every reasoner "has some general idea of what good reasoning is" (CP 2.186). According to Peirce, such an instinctive theory of reasoning, antecedent to any systematic study of the subject, constitutes our *logica utens* (cf. CP 2.189), the acritical and implicit or 'naive' logic of the common man. It is only because we do not possess a full stock of logical instincts to meet all occasions that we study the process of reasoning and inquire into the methods by which we can most efficiently advance our knowledge. The result of such a study is called *logica docens* (see CP 2.204). Thanks to our logica utens we are able to adequately respond in many instances. However, where our instinctive reasoning power begins to lose its self-confidence, as when we are confronted with extraordinary or unusual problems, we look to the help of our logica docens (see (Fann, 1970), pp. 38–39).[1]

---

[1] The distinction between 'utens' and 'docens' shows similarity with an assumption by (Schurger, Pereira, Treisman, & Cohen, 2010) that it is not a difference in states, but a difference in reproducibility that may mark the distinction between unconscious and conscious information processing.

Earlier in this book we suggested that our logica utens is co-existent with sign processing. In this chapter we work from the hypothesis that the logica docens stems from the implicit or 'naive' logic of the brain. More specifically, we propose that the information processing underlying our logica docens may also satisfy the conditions set for the processing schema.

7.1.1   The three modes of inference

Reasoning consists of making inferences. Thoughts are the ground for any inference and any thought is expressible in a proposition that can function as a premise. Following Peirce (see CP 2.508-2.514), the three fundamental modes of inference are to be characterized as follows:

> [...] Abduction is the process of forming an explanatory hypothesis.
> It is the only logical operation which introduces any new idea; for
> induction does nothing but determine a value, and deduction merely
> evolves the necessary consequences of a pure hypothesis. Deduction
> proves that something must be; Induction shows that something
> actually is operative. Abduction merely suggests that something
> may be. Its only justification is that from its suggestion deduction
> can draw a prediction which can be tested by induction, and that, if
> we are ever to learn anything or to understand phenomena at all, it
> must be by abduction that this is to be brought about. (CP 5.171)

The above characterization of the three modes of reasoning enables us to make a few interesting observations about their properties.

In *deduction* initially we know something, a hypothesis or belief. Next, we evolve part of what is involved in our belief and actualize it in a belief that is subordinate to, but also given by the belief we started with. From the point of view of our process model this 'increase' of knowledge consists of deducing information about the object in our focus, revealing part of its additional properties relevant to the case at hand.

In *induction* the ratio of a relation is determined. Induction is used to test whether an object does or does not satisfy a certain property. That we have knowledge about the property implies the existence of experience with like objects. Successful testing shows that our current object is similar to earlier ones. This similarity can be expressed by a value of a ratio, or equivalently, by a subset of an ordering induced by the objects. For example, if the property is 'locomotion', possible measures can be 'strolling', 'walking' and 'running'.

In *abduction* an explanatory hypothesis is generated. It is the only mode of inference that generates new ideas. Peirce defined abductive inference as follows:

> The surprising fact C is observed. But if A were true, C would be
> a matter of course. Hence, there is reason to suspect that A is true.
> (CP 5.189)

Such a process is inferential, because the hypothetical belief "is adopted for some reason, good or bad, and that reason, in being regarded as such, is regarded as lending the hypothesis some plausibility" (CP 2.511).

7.2 Towards a model for 'naive' reasoning

In order to show that human information processing involves all three inference modes, we revisit our memory model introduced in Sect. 6.7.2 and reveal its potential for representing perceptual judgments. As for the properties of perceptual judgments Peirce writes:

> Every judgment consists in referring a predicate to a subject. The predicate is thought, and the subject is only thought-of. The elements of the predicate are experiences or representations of experience. The subject is never experimental but only assumed. (Fisch, 1982), Vol. 1, p. 152

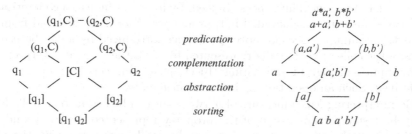

Figure 7.1: The processing schema (left) and the perception process (right)

Perceptual judgments are propositions about the world. It is an assumption of this book that such propositions arise through a process of sign interpretation. The relation between perceptual judgments on the one hand and our model of cognitive activity on the other can be made more precise by linking properties of perceptual judgments with interpretation moments of our processing schema. Below we analyse the perception process (see Fig. 7.1); an analysis of the process of cognition is postponed until the next section.

In the perception process, the interesting interpretation moments are the *complementation* events generating (q_1,C) and (q_2,C), in which the input state and effect are represented in context: as an actual existence (cf. subject) and a conventional property (cf. predicate) respectively. In the perception process the first is represented by (a,a'), the second by (b,b'). Both representations express the input as a concretisation of a prototypical memory sign. Following our definition of the processing schema, (a,a') arises from a (rheme) through *complementation* by a' (index). Memory response qualia, which are triggered by a, must be experienced hence 'thought'. Their average value representation by a' must refer to an object which is imagined or 'thought-of', and this property must hold for (a,a') as well. An example can be a visual perception of an oak which is a sapling (a). By linking the input (a) with memory information about prototypical properties of oak trees (a'), obtaining (a,a'), we may be able to interprete our input as 'a hardwood tree' or 'a timber tree', which is 'thought-of'.[2]

The proposed memory representation of effect qualia enables (b,b') to be interpreted as a characteristic property. Memory response qualia triggered by b must also be experienced, hence 'thought'. However, in conformity with the continuity involved in the generalization of those qualia in a continuous domain (see Sect. 6.7.2), b can always be interpreted as a measure of b', implying that (b,b') must be 'thought' as well. For instance, if we perceive the familiar sensation of acceleration ('thought'), e.g. during take off, we may interpret our sensation as a measure of acceleration effects, e.g. 'fast' or 'rapid', which are 'thought' as well.

7.2.1 Sign interactions and inferences

The above analysis enables us to draw the conclusion that *complementation* is closely related to logical inferences. Indeed, by interpreting a as a concretisation of a' two goals can be achieved. First, properties of a can be deduced from the context, obtaining a'; second, novel properties introduced by a can be used to enhance the collection of qualia represented by a'. Either way an interpretation of the input as a sign of an existing object, possessing certain properties, can be derived. Such an operation is similar to *deduction*.

By interpreting b as a measure of b' two goals can be attained as well. First, b can be tested for possession of the property represented by b'; second, the continuum of the effect domain of b' can be made more dense by the value represented by b. Such an event is similar to *induction*. It is by virtue of the continuity involved in the domain representation of effect qualia that the processing schema has this potential for inductive generalization. This means that *complementation* capitalizes on a property which is general by definition. Induction as a 'naive' reasoning operation does not teach us anything qualitatively new. This conforms with Peirce's view of inductive inference (cf. Sect. 7.1.1).

An analysis of the cognition process obtains similar results. The input, which consists of the final signs generated by the process of perception, involves discrete values $(A, \neg A)$ and measures of dense domains $(B, \neg B)$. These values and measures are inherited by all more developed input representations. For example, the index $(\neg A + \neg B, \neg A * \neg B)$ and legisign positions $(A * \neg B + \neg A * B)$ involve a possible co-occurrence of a measure of an effect and the value of a state.

Complementation of the legisign position by an index sign can be interpreted as follows. The measure (or sub-domain) of effects represented by the legisign is completed by the value indicated by the index. Such an enrichment of a domain of effects, introducing potentially new objects in relation to a measure

---

[2]The relation represented by (a,a') is commutative.

of an effect, is similar to induction. An example of 'naive' induction, this time in natural language, can be the complementation of 'give' (legisign) by 'a book' (index). The measure associated with 'give', as an effect in some domain, is linked with the value associated with 'a book'. According to our model, in a lexical specification such values ought to be classified in trichotomies.

Complementation of the rheme position by an index sign can be interpreted as completion (cf. modification) of the value represented by the rheme ($A*\neg B$, $\neg A*B$), by the value indicated by the index ($\neg A*\neg B$, $\neg A+\neg B$). More specifically, the value represented by $A*\neg B$ can be completed by the value referred to by $\neg A+\neg B$, and the value of a measure represented by $\neg A*B^3$ by the value indicated by $\neg A*\neg B$. Such a modification of a state is similar to *deduction*. An example, in natural language, can be the adjectival modification of 'girls' ($A*\neg B$) by 'nice' ($\neg A+\neg B$) obtaining 'nice girls', representing 'a-kind-of-girls' or a value of girls (rheme), completed by the value of a measure of the property, e.g. 'beauty', indicated by nice (index).[4]

The final stage, *predication*, represents the result of an interaction between signs in the dicent (cf. subject) and symbol positions (cf. predicate). As this result arises through analysis, not by matching (see Introduction), the resulting relation must be hypothetical. Note that a combination of *sorting* and *abstraction*, generating an abstract state (rheme) and effect (legisign) interpretation of the input, used as premises of a 'naive' deductive and inductive inference respectively, is similar to *abduction* (degenerately). In later diagrams, abduction involved in *sorting* is omitted.

7.3   An extended example

This section contains an illustration of 'naive' reasoning regarded as a kind of information processing. Our working example is an observation by a roe deer. We assume that the deer, walking in the forest, arrives at a location of her daily round, which is marked by a tree (see Fig. 7.2). At this location the route branches in two directions: one leading to her grassland, the other to her watering place. Every day the deer follows her route and habitually goes to the pasture if the sun is before zenith and to the watering place otherwise. In our example we will assume that the marking tree is the only provider of information about the location of the branching in the route and that the tree has no special marks.

We will develop an interpretation of the case in which the deer, arriving at her branching point before noon, decides to turn to the right, towards her habitual grassland.[5] The case is dealt with in a third person perspective. This explains the overload of meaning in the labels of qualia and generated representations.

---

[3]The state involved by this effect.

[4]Note that girls are in focus as opposed to nice, which is complementary and must be provided by the S_S.

[5]'To the right', 'to the pasture', 'to the grassland' are used interchangeably.

Figure 7.2: A roe deer looking at her marking tree

Below, in our analysis of the perception process, we only list the representations obtained in the initial and final stages. Those of the final stage act on behalf of their function as input qualia in a subsequent cognition process. We refer to interpretation moments by means of their 'naive' logical expressions. Synonymous representations can be labelled by identical symbols. Lacking a true lexicon, we have to trust in the reader's common sense knowledge with respect to the circumstances of the deer and the combinatory properties of the involved qualia. So, our input signs of the perception process are:[6]

a = **tree-somewhere**
a' = marking-tree-prototype
b = **shadow-on-the-left**
b' = branching-state-prototype

The input signs of the cognition process are:

A = $a*a'$ = *tree*
$\neg A$ = $a+a'$ = *tree-info*
B = $b*b'$ = *to-branch*
$\neg B$ = $b+b'$ = *branching-info*

The *tree* (A) represents a tree that potentially marks a branch in the route and *to-branch* (B) a branching need that appears as a property. A full scale specification of complementary memory response signs is beyond our goal. An example of other complementary memory response signs is tree-prototype (a'), which expresses prototypical information about trees.

The qualisigns of cognition can be explained as follows. The deer is looking at her marking tree at a certain location of her route (A). She may have additional information about trees ($\neg A$). Suddenly she perceives the shadow of the marking

---

[6]Note that a, b, a', b' may refer to a single object, as well as a collection of objects, ambiguously. For instance, **tree-somewhere** may stand for a number of perceived trees.

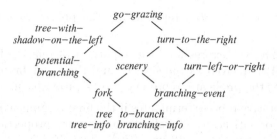

Figure 7.3: Interpretation moments in the case of the marking tree

tree. This is a potential sign for branching (B). She may have additional information about shadows, for instance about their orientation ($\neg B$).

A qualisign is an expression of the input as an uninterpreted, potentially meaningful sign. At this stage, the deer does not know that the perceived tree signifies a location of branching and, more importantly, she is not aware of the directions she could take. That level of understanding may arise later as a result of a process of interpretation, the stages of which are briefly explained below (see also Fig. 7.3).

$A+B=tree+to\text{-}branch=fork$: the expression of the perceived tree and appearing branching need as constituents of the input phenomenon.

$A*B=tree*to\text{-}branch=branching\text{-}event$: the expression of the simultaneous occurrence of the perceived tree and appearing branching need as an actual event.

$\neg A+\neg B, \neg A*\neg B=scenery$: the expression of the complementary qualia as the context of the perceived phenomenon, conveying information about additional properties of marking trees ($\neg A+\neg B$) and branching needs ($\neg A*\neg B$) such as the orientation of the shadow cast by the input tree.

$A*\neg B, \neg A*B=potential\text{-}branching$: the synonymous expression of the abstract meaning of the input marking tree ($A*\neg B$) and branching need ($\neg A*B$) as a range of possibilities.

$\neg A*B+A*\neg B=turn\text{-}left\text{-}or\text{-}right$: the expression of the compatibility of the abstract interpretation of the input marking tree ($A*\neg B$) and branching need ($\neg A*B$), representing the habitual meaning triggered by the perceived bifurcating path ('branching-at-a-marking-tree-to-the-left-or-right').

$\neg A+B, A+\neg B=tree\text{-}with\text{-}shadow\text{-}on\text{-}the\text{-}left$: the expression of the input as an act of branching at a certain location ($\neg A+B$), or alternatively, branching in the direction implied by *this* perceived tree ($A\rightarrow B$). The representation by $A+\neg B$ can be explained analogously. A synonymous interpretation of the two expressions immediately above is used as a representation of the subject of the input phenomenon.

$A*B+\neg A*\neg B=turn\text{-}to\text{-}the\text{-}right$: the expression of the input as a conventional property in context, which is 'turning' ($A*B$) 'in-a-direction-indicated-by-the-context' $(\neg A * \neg B)$, representing the predicate of the input phenomenon.

A is B=go-grazing: the expression of a hypothetical relation between the input tree (A) perceived as the subject and the input branching need (B) perceived as the predicate, represented by a proposition.

This interpretative process terminates if the final (argument) sign represents all input qualia or satisfies the involved combinatory properties in one of the possible ways. Interpretation will proceed however if during information processing the input stimulus changes, for instance when the deer gets a feeling of thirst. The difference between the new qualia and the deer's actual state, representing a change, may trigger further information processing. This possibility is not considered in our current example, however.

Assume that while the deer was away her marking tree was injured by a rabbit (see Fig. 7.4). How will she react when she arrives at the tree as usual?

Although the damaged tree cannot be interpreted as a potential marking tree (A), we assume that its interpretation as an appearing branching need (B) is still possible (if this were not possible either, no 'branching' would occur and the deer would proceed without noticing anything). Input information can be specified now as follows.

The input signs of the perception process are:

a = **damaged-tree-somewhere**
a' = tree-prototype
b = **shadow-on-the-left**
b' = branching-state-prototype

The input signs of the cognition process are:

$A = a * a' =$ *tree?*
$\neg A = a + a' =$ *tree-info*
$B = b * b' =$ *to-branch*
$\neg B = b + b' =$ *branching-info*

As for the perception process we assume that, in spite of the damage to the observed tree, the input triggers prototypical memory information about trees (a'). This enables *sorting*, in the subsequent cognition process (see Fig. 7.5), to invariantly represent the input qualia as constituents (*fork*) of the input interaction. However, suppose that, in the interpretation stage *abstraction*, the injury to the tree hinders its interpretation as a possible for a marking tree (*tree-like?*).

Although the input effect impels the deer to move ahead, to branch according to the orientation of the shadow, the perceived state cannot be interpreted as a tree at a branching (*branch-here?*), and her final hypothesis (*where-to-branch?*) does not activate the motor functions that accompany branching behavior. The deer is vacantly staring at the tree. This is what Peirce formulated as an observation of a "surprising fact C" or the condition for abductive reasoning (see Sect. 7.1.1).

Figure 7.4: The marking tree is damaged by a rabbit

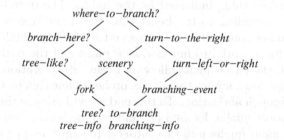

Figure 7.5: Interpretation moments of the damaged tree phenomenon

Figure 7.6: Injury conceptually removed from the tree

7.4 Towards a process model of abduction

We can easily help the deer in her desperate situation. For us her problem is almost trivial: The perceived tree does not match memory information about marking trees. If nevertheless we assume that the input tree could be a marking tree, we may prove our conjecture by abductively deriving that the tree has been damaged. By conceptually removing the injury from the perceived tree we may reveal qualia of a genuine tree, enabling an interpretation of the perceived damaged tree as a marking tree (see Fig. 7.6).

How can we put this strategy into action? The current input does not contain qualia of a marking tree. Let us assume that the daily growth of the observed tree, the natural increase or decrease of its leaves does not hinder its recognition as a marking tree. As the injury to the tree is not due to a natural cause that the deer would know from experience, the deer is unable to link the input qualia with memory information about marking trees and derive an interpretation through deductive or inductive reasoning.

The problematic concept is the rheme (*tree-like?*) which, due to lacking information about marking trees, cannot be complemented by information about the direction of branching indicated by the index. The deer has two options. Either she acts according to the belief that the input tree is not a marking tree or she assumes something has happened to the tree while she was away, depriving it of its potential to function as a marker of the path. As, following our assumption, the effect qualia allow an event interpretation while the state qualia do not, the deer may try to improve on her rheme sign by the introduction of new qualia through abduction. To this end we will assume that the two types of memory response qualia, focused (f) and complementary (c), can be used to distinguish the input qualia into two subsets. In sum:[7] $a=a_f+a_c$; $a'=a'_f+a'_c$.

In abductive reasoning, complementary memory information plays an essential role. In order to be able to 'see' the input in a way other way than it is perceived, we need information about phenomena similar to the actual

---

[7]Focused and complementary memory response signs are related to the input in the sense of agreement and possibility, respectively (cf. Sect. 6.7.2). We assume that the two subsets of a are defined by the two subsets of a', e.g. a_c is defined by the input qualia triggering a'_c.

one. Returning to our example, we assume that for a'_f =tree-prototype[8] there exists complementary memory information about marking trees,[9] for instance, a'_c =marking-tree-prototype. A definition of a_f and a_c is postponed until Sect. 7.5.

7.4.1 A revised schematic model of perception

Abductive reasoning can be modeled by interpreting the difference between a' and a as an effect, conceptually transforming a into a'. This way we may 'shift' our focus: we take a different look at our phenomenon. For instance, by removing input qualia that are not present in a prototypical representation of trees (e.g. qualia of injury) and by adding qualia that can be there in prototypical marking trees (e.g. a characteristic shadow), we may conceptually 'heal' the injured input tree and enable its interpretation as a marking tree. A more precise definition of this approach, requiring a minor revision of the schematic model of perception, can be given as follows.

In our earlier model (see Sect. 4.3) we assumed that the input of cognitive activity arises from percepts through comparison. Input state (a) and effect qualia (b) are defined by an intersection and a relative difference operation, respectively, on percepts represented by sets. Note that in the definition of effect qualia, the previous percept is always compared to the current one, in conformity with the assumed teleological character of cognitive activity, interpreting phenomena as transitions from a previous to a current percept, with the latter functioning as the 'goal'. Below we will suggest that this principle can be applied to model the generation of input qualia via abduction as well.

From a computational stance, a relative difference operation on a' and a can be computed with the same machinery as is used in the generation of input qualia for cognitive information processing: a- and a'-type qualia that are related to each other in the sense of agreement can be used for the definition of a new state (new-a); those related to each other in the sense of possibility, for the generation of a new effect (new-b).[10] In our definition below, for the operation intersection we use the symbol '$*$', for union '$+$', for relative difference '$\backslash$'[11]. All operations are performed on collections represented as sets. Note that a relation in the sense of agreement ('$*$') is only possible between collections of qualia that are in focus (a'_f, a_f); a relative difference operation ('$\backslash$') can be executed on all other combinations of the input qualia.

$$
\begin{aligned}
new\text{-}a &:= a'_f * a_f \\
new\text{-}b &:= a'_c \backslash a_f + a'_f \backslash a_c + a'_c \backslash a_c
\end{aligned}
$$

---

[8] Following our earlier assumption, the perceived damaged tree qualifies for a prototypical representation of trees.

[9] It must be so since the deer does possess information about marking trees, according to our earlier analysis, in Sect. 7.3.

[10] This definition capitalizes on our earlier assumption of a homogeneous representation of memory information by the brain (see also Sect. 6.7.2). a, a', b, b' being collections of qualia, their intersection and union can be defined by collections of qualia as well.

[11] $X \backslash Y := X * \neg Y$

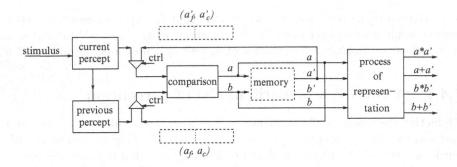

Figure 7.7: The revised schematic model of perception. The difference from the model depicted in Fig. 5.1 consists of the controlled feedback (ctrl) of a and a' to the comparison unit. The relative difference of a and a' can be used for an abduction of new qualia

We assume that new qualia generated by abduction are type-wise merged with existing input qualia. The rationale behind this strategy is that it enables the entire input state to be affected by the surmised new effects (new-b), transforming the previous state to a next or current state, which may be more suitable for interpretation.

The importance of the relative difference operations in the definition of new-b can be explained by means of our earlier metaphor of apparent motion perception. By considering the input (a_f) and memory response signs (a'_c) to be subsequent pictures of a film, their difference ($a'_c \setminus a_f$) can be interpreted as an effect, transforming the previous picture into the current one. A different illustration of abduction, in natural language, is the semantic phenomenon defined by the qualia a_f=**girl** and a'_c=**beauty**. The relative difference of **beauty** and **girl**, interpreted as an effect, new-b:=$beautiful$, can be used to transform 'girl' into 'beauty', thereby enabling an interpretation of **girl** as $beautiful$-$girl$ (new-a). Note that qualia involved in new-a always form a subset of a, by virtue of the agreement relation involved in the intersection operation ('$*$') defining new-a.

Abduction can be modeled by considering a and a' to be percepts, in the generation of input qualia for information processing. Note that a similar feedback of b and b' cannot be effective. Since b' is a dense domain, a meaningful difference between b and b' cannot be defined (b can always be interpreted as a measure or sub-domain of b').

In the revised schematic model of perception, depicted in Fig. 7.7, we assume that the content of the current percept is 'copied' to the previous percept after some delay following input sampling. A control signal (ctrl) is used to enable either the qualia of the feedback or those of the external stimulus to be processed in the generation of the input state (a) and effect (b). The two modes correspond to 'abduction' and 'normal' mode operation, respectively. Abduction mode operation may be activated, if normal mode information processing fails. The feedback of a and a' is represented by the expressions

(a_f, a_c) and (a'_f, a'_c), respectively. For qualia collections x, y, z, we define:
$x*(y,z)=x*y+x*z$; $(x,y)*z=x*z+y*z$; $\neg(x,y)=\neg x+\neg y$.

The above definition of abduction can be simplified as follows. An agreement relation can only be interpreted between qualia that are in focus. This explains why the last three terms in (i) and the first term in (ii) below can be replaced by the empty set.

$$
\begin{aligned}
new\text{-}a \quad &:= \quad a'*a \\
&= \quad (a'_f, a'_c)*(a_f, a_c) \\
&= \quad a'_f*a_f + a'_f*a_c + a'_c*a_f + a'_c*a_c \qquad \text{(i)} \\
&= \quad a'_f*a_f
\end{aligned}
$$

$$
\begin{aligned}
new\text{-}b \quad &:= \quad a'\backslash a \\
&= \quad (a'_f, a'_c)\backslash(a_f, a_c) \\
&= \quad (a'_f, a'_c)*(\neg a_f + \neg a_c) \\
&= \quad a'_f*\neg a_f + a'_f*\neg a_c + a'_c*\neg a_f + a'_c*\neg a_c \qquad \text{(ii)} \\
&= \quad a'_f\backslash a_c + a'_c\backslash a_f + a'_c\backslash a_c
\end{aligned}
$$

Through abduction, new qualia can be introduced and merged with already existing ones, thereby enabling an interpretation of the entire collection of input qualia as a (meaningful) sign. In the brain/mind, an analogous merging of qualia could be due to the brain's potential for maintaining input activation for a longer time.

Maintaining input activation enables the interpreting system to modify its input thus establishing a change that requires further processing. So instead of generating signals for the motor sub-system, the brain may control the activation of its executional functions and possibly even block them, thereby enabling prolonged information processing. For example, if we hear a shout: "Fire!", we will not run away if we can abductively infer that the sound is coming from the motion picture we are watching.

7.5 Sample abduction

Let us now return to our example of the injured tree. The input qualia, preceding abduction, can be recapitulated as follows (below, comments are indicated by a percent sign):

$$
\begin{aligned}
a \quad &= \quad \textbf{damaged-tree-somewhere} \quad \% \ a_f \\
a' \quad &= \quad \text{tree-prototype,} \quad \% \ a'_f \\
&\quad \ \ \text{marking-tree-prototype} \quad \% \ a'_c
\end{aligned}
$$

According to our revised schematic model of perception (see Fig. 7.7), the relative difference of **damaged-tree-somewhere**(a) and marking-tree-prototype(a') can be used for the generation of new effect qualia (*new-b*), transforming the perceived damaged tree to a marking tree, by means of conceptually removing the qualia of injury from the input state (a_f). The terms $a'_c\backslash a_f$, $a'_f\backslash a_c$, $a'_c\backslash a_c$, on the right-hand side in the definition of *new-b*, are introduced stepwise. We begin with the first term.

$$a'_c \setminus a_f \quad = \quad \text{marking-tree-prototype} \setminus \textbf{damaged-tree-somewhere}$$
$$= \quad \textit{tree-at-branching}$$

This value of *new-b* can be used as an effect completing the qualia of the perceived damaged tree by prototypical qualia of marking trees. The abducted new effect may trigger memory response, for example, b'=marking-tree-prototype.[12] This closes the first term. Let us now continue with the second term.

The input tree being damaged, there must exist complementary input qualia indicating its injured status, for instance, a_c=**injury**.[13] This quale too enables an abduction of new effects.

$$a'_f \setminus a_c \quad = \quad \text{tree-prototype} \setminus \textbf{injury}$$
$$= \quad \textit{tree-injury}$$

This value of *new-b* can be used as an effect removing the qualia of injury from the perceived injured tree, thereby conceptually 'healing' it and turning it into a sign of a (prototypical) genuine tree. The abducted new effect may trigger new memory response signs, for instance, b'=tree-injury-prototype. This closes the second term. In the current example we assume that the third term contributes to an effect that we already know:

$$a'_c \setminus a_c \quad = \quad \text{marking-tree-prototype} \setminus \textbf{injury}$$
$$= \quad \textit{tree-injury}$$

Besides effect qualia, new state qualia can also be generated through abduction.

$$new\text{-}a\text{:} \quad = \quad a'_f * a_f$$
$$= \quad \text{tree-prototype} * \textbf{damaged-tree-somewhere}$$
$$= \quad \textit{tree-at-branching}$$

The memory response (a'_f) triggered by the perceived tree (a_f) must contain information about branching, but it is unlikely that it contains information about tree damage (which is why the deer was unable to recognize the input as an injured genuine tree). This implies that *new-a* represents its object – the tree the deer is facing – through the glasses of her prototypical information about trees. The abducted new state (*tree-at-branching*),[14] defined by qualia involved in both the perceived and the 'thought' tree, represents a potential tree which, being damaged, must be incomplete, but its incompleteness is not re-presented. It is by virtue of this meaning – tree with supressed injury – involved in the abducted new state that the entire input can be interpreted as a marking tree.

In conformity with our revised schematic model of perception, we assume that abducted new qualia are type-wise merged with existing ones. Below, abducted new qualia are indicated by the subscript "*new*". Although some of the symbols, such as *tree-at-branching* and marking-tree-prototype, can be used ambiguously, their function is always clear from the context. The input for further information processing at this point can be recapitulated as follows.

---

[12]Note the ambiguous use of this symbol as an effect.

[13] Note that the qualia of injury have been there in the input stimulus all the time, but not interpreted so far (for example, 'chunked' in the collection represented by a_f).

[14]Note the ambiguous use of this symbol as a state.

The input signs of the perception process are:

a	=	**damaged-tree-somewhere**, *tree-at-branching$_{new}$*,	% a_f
		injury	% a_c
a'	=	tree-prototype,	% a'_f
		marking-tree-prototype	% a'_c
b	=	**shadow-on-the-left**,	
		tree-at-branching$_{new}$,	
		tree-injury$_{new}$	
b'	=	branching-state-prototype,	
		marking-tree-prototype$_{new}$,	
		tree-injury-prototype$_{new}$	

The input signs of the cognition process are:

A	=	tree?,	% **damaged-tree-somewhere**∗tree-prototype
		tree	% *tree-at-branching$_{new}$*∗tree-prototype
$\neg A$	=	*tree-info*	
B	=	injury,	% *tree-injury$_{new}$*∗tree-injury-prototype
		to-branch	% **shadow-on-the-left**∗branching-state-prototype
$\neg B$	=	*branching-info*	

Although the input still contains qualia of a damaged tree, the good news is that it also contains qualia of a genuine tree (a'_c). The abducted new qualia enable the generation of a new representation in the icon and sinsign positions:[15]

$A+B$	=	*tree?+injury*, *tree?+to-branch*, *tree+injury*, *tree+to-branch*
	=	*some-tree*
$A*B$	=	*wounding*

as well as the generation of a new rheme (details are omitted):

$A*\neg B$	=	*tree?∗branching-info*, *tree∗branching-info*,
$\neg A*B$	=	*tree-info∗to-branch*, *tree-info∗injury*

$A*\neg B$ represents the input as a 'tree-like' object remotely related to 'branching', $\neg A*B$ represents a potential 'branching act' in relation to an 'injured tree'. A synonymous interpretation of these signs, combining the meaning of an abstract tree involved in the first sign with the meaning of 'healing' involved in the second sign can be paraphrased as 'a-tree-that-has-been-damaged-though-has-the-potential-for-indicating-branching', or, in short, *damaged-tree* (see also Fig. 7.8). As $\neg A*B$ represents a nominal interpretation of branching as a range of possibilities, including its interpretation as a marking tree, and, in a similar vein, $A*\neg B$ represents an abstract interpretation of genuine trees, our earlier signs can arise again: The deer can go grazing at last (cf. Fig. 7.3).

Such a process, generating potentially more meaningful interpretation(s) of a phenomenon by the introduction of new qualia, is what we call *'naive' abduction*. Note the important role memory information plays in this type of sign interaction. If the abductively generated new propositional sign (argument

---

[15] Already existing signs, e.g. $A*B=branching-event$, are omitted in our presentation.

Figure 7.8: The generation of a new rheme sign

position) can be evaluated true, the involved input qualia can be used for the adjustment of existing habits. This potential of 'naive' abduction is beyond the scope of our book.[16]

Although the deer must be satisfied by now, the abducted new qualia enable further information processing. We will treat this issue on the basis of our earlier index sign, *scenery*, and the abducted new sinsign, *wounding*, and show how these signs can be used to generate a more meaningful interpretation of the complementary input qualia.

Through a shift of the deer's focus, via abduction, new complementary qualisigns and index signs can be introduced. The new sinsign (*wounding*) mediates between the new qualisigns and the existing index sign, thus it contributes to the generation of a new index sign, for example, *symptoms-of-bark-injury*. An adjustment of the index (cf. context) may trigger a revision in the sinsign position,[17] for instance, by incorporating 'bark injury' in its representation. This may trigger the generation of a new propositional sign and an introduction of corresponding effect qualia and memory response signs. As a result, new qualia can be introduced that are not directly related to the original input. This may enable an interpretation of events not present in the original phenomenon, such as stripping, carving and biting (by an animal). There can be many such events, but only those will be considered that are compatible with the existing rheme sign (*damaged-tree*). An example of such an event is the act of biting (by an animal). The introduction of effect qualia involved in that event may trigger a revised interpretation of the legisign (*damage-due-to-biting*) and index positions (*symptoms-of-bark-injury*), the latter by virtue of its reference to the bark of the input tree. Expressions generated by this process are depicted in Fig. 7.9.

7.6 Interpretation 'game'

An important result of abductive information processing is that the distorted final sign (*go-grazing*) can be 'repaired', allowing the deer to proceed as usual. This is not the only benefit of this process, however. By focusing on abductively

---

[16]Sign interpretation and habit formation can be considered to be orthogonal dimensions of knowledge. Thus the processing schema can be combined with any machine learning algorithm.

[17]An adjustment of the index triggers an adjustment in the qualisign position. Via abduction the appearing new qualia may introduce new effects (cf. *new-b*) as well.

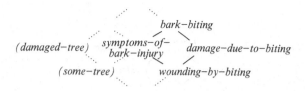

Figure 7.9: Representations arising through the abducted event, *wounding*. Existing ('frozen') representations that are unchanged are given in parentheses

generated new qualia, new memory response signs can be introduced, both focused and complementary. This is by virtue of the brain's potential to shift its focus, for example, due to a high intensity memory response, or an internally generated change (e.g. a saccadic movement of the eyes). Such an abductive process is akin to a 'game', in which new representations are generated and existing ones modified or revised. This game continues until a consistent instantiation of all positions of the processing schema is obtained. The 'goal' of 'naive' reasoning, including abduction, is the generation of such a collection of representations.

Interpretation as a 'game' can be illustrated by the generation of the revised sinsign, *wounding-by-biting*. By 'freezing' its earlier interpretation (*wounding*), new qualia extending the interpreter's focus can be looked for (e.g. *biting*). A condition set for abduction is that the new input qualia as well as their memory response must enable the already existing ('frozen') input interpretations.

The above strategy can be used to generate a revised legisign as well. Only those sinsign representations need to be considered that are compatible with the existing index sign, for instance, *wounding-by-biting*. The interaction of this sign with the existing icon sign, *some-tree*, can be interpreted as a compatible combination of the abstract effect 'biting' ($\neg A*B$) and an abstract state capable of enduring such an effect ($A*\neg B$). The resulting new legisign can be called *damage-due-to-biting*. Through complementation of this sign with background information provided by the index (*symptoms-of-bark-injury*), the rule-like meaning of the legisign is inductively generalized in the predicate of a hypothetical phenomenon: *bark-biting*. Analogous contextualization of the rheme (*damaged-tree*), by the index (*symptoms-of-bark-injury*) may obtain a deductive generalization of the rheme in the subject: *bark-bitten-tree* (see also Fig. 7.10).

7.6.1 The explorative nature of abduction

What happens if we put together the representations yielded by the above deductive and inductive generalizations? It can be shown that a combination of these signs can be interpreted as the propositional sign of a *nested* process: 'causation-of-damage-to-a-tree'. This sign, degenerately represented as a quale in a nesting phenomenon (e.g. the deer feels hunger), can be interpreted as contextual information for the generation of a predicate (*turn-to-the-right*). In linguistics such information is usually called a thematic relation.

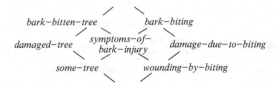

Figure 7.10: Representations of the sample nested phenomenon

The above example illustrates how complementary qualia can be generated by means of nested analysis. Natural language, for instance, makes beneficial use of this potential in the introduction of transitive forms for verbs. For example, if experience shows that 'damaged-tree-phenomena' frequently occur, this may motivate the introduction of a transitive form for 'branch' (*turn-left-or-right*) such as: 'branch+<direction>'.

As in an observation input qualia may not precisely match memory response qualia, the generation of an adequate response may not be possible. We can improve on this by abductively generating new qualia, enabling potentially more meaningful input interpretation(s). In our view, the 'core business' of abduction is the generation of such qualia, exploring the extension (a') and comprehension (b') of potential concepts.

7.7 Logica Docens

In this section we investigate the idea that our logica docens stems from our logica utens. Though a full account of this idea is beyond our goal, we briefly illustrate the dependency for syllogistic logic. The reason for a treatment of syllogistic logic instead of more recent systems that are better equipped for proof theory is a composition of two elements. First, the distinction between utens and docens is relative. Until the nineteenth century syllogistic logic was the dominant logica docens. Nowadays, one could say, it has become part of the utens studied with deductive systems as their docens. Second, a major motif behind the program of syllogistic logic is to distinguish valid analytical inferences from not valid ampliative inferences. With the association of deductive, abductive (or hypothetical) and inductive inferences with the first, second and third syllogistic figures, respectively, it pointed the way to the empirical cycle. See (CP 5.171), dated 1903, or (Popper, 1959).

We suggest that syllogistic reasoning can be modeled as sequences of sign interpretation similar to our treatment of natural language processing, except that the input qualia are now represented by logical premises. In particular we will show that the progression from premises to conclusion in each of the three[18] Aristotelian syllogistic figures (see Fig. 7.11) can be analyzed as sign interactions, each syllogistic figure bringing to the fore the peculiarities of a different

---

[18]The fourth syllogistic figure arises through a combination of the operations with which the second and third figures can be made out of the first. Hence it is reducible.

figure–1	figure–2	figure–3
X B	X C	C B
A X	A C	C X
A B	A X	X B

Figure 7.11: The three Aristotelian syllogistic figures or inference schemes

part of the processing schema. This implies the possibility that the different types of inference are developed from perceptual judgments as reifications implying particular perspectives on phenomena.

The syllogistic figures are distinguished by the distribution of the middle term. In figure-2 the middle term is in the predicate position in both premises, in figure-3 it is in the subject position. If we disregard the different moods of the figures and the demand of validity we obtain inference schemes that also cover ampliative or a posteriori reasoning. In the processing schema the inference schemes appear as events. Scheme-2: Initially we know A *is* C. From X *is* C we abductively conclude or surmise that A and X must have something in common, that is, A *is* X, too. This is similar to abduction. Scheme-3: Initially we know C *is* X. From C *is* B we conclude that B can be inductively generalized in X, that is, X *is* B holds too (X is more general than B). This is similar to induction. Finally, scheme-1 can be said to be similar to deduction, by virtue of its mediating term (X), propagating properties of the predicate (B) to the subject (A).

7.7.1 Structural analysis

Inferences consist of three propositions, functioning as case, rule and result. Following Peirce we will suggest that these functions can be associated with the minor and major premises, as well as the conclusion of an inference, respectively.

In deductive inferences, the conclusion (result) is drawn from the major (rule) and minor (case) premises. The mechanism of induction is fundamentally different. According to Peirce, the key to induction is that

> [. . .] by taking the conclusion [of induction; the authors] so reached as major premiss of a syllogism, and the proposition stating that such and such objects are taken from the class in question as the minor premiss, the other premiss of the induction will follow from them deductively. (CP 5.274)

In other words, induction must be an inference of the major premise of a syllogism, from the minor premise and the conclusion. Following this analysis, the three schemes of inference can be characterized as shown in Fig. 7.12.

From the point of view of its characteristic meaning, a premise can be 'general' or 'experienced'. This can be illustrated by means of scheme-1, as follows. Aristotle proved (Bochenski, 1961) that from Barbara (scheme-1) any other syllogism can be generated by means of two transformations, which he called

	deduction (1)	abduction (2)	induction (3)
major	rule	rule	result
minor	case	result	case
concl.	result	case	rule

Figure 7.12: A functional characterization of the three inference schemes

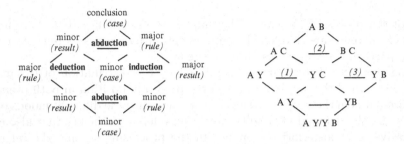

Figure 7.13: A syllogistic interpretation of the processing schema. 'Naive' reasoning is modeled by a sequential process, in which input premises (qualisign position) have either the form $A\ Y$ or $Y\ B$. As a consequence of merging the three syllogistic schemes into a single diagram, variables need to be renamed (cf. Fig. 7.11)

conversio[19] and *reductio ad impossibile*[20] (note that the focus of this section is on a structural analysis of the three figures; quantification and negation are left out of consideration). Aristotle assumed that any conclusion must be derived from a major and a minor premise.

But what are the origins of these premises? According to Peirce, some may come from experience, but since Barbara requires a universal premise and experience without cognition (and learning) cannot be universal, the original major premise cannot be derived from experience alone. Thus, Peirce concluded, only minor premises can come from experience, major premises have their truth in the brain (see (Fann, 1970), p. 13). In our model of 'naive' reasoning we assume that such general premises correspond to rules (cf. legisign) and abstractions (cf. rheme).

7.7.2 A classification of reasoning symbols

On the basis of our analysis above, a classification of 'naive' syllogistic concepts can be given as follows, see Fig. 7.13. In our mapping of premises to their function: *case, rule* and *result*, we make use of Aristotle's assumption that syllogistic terms represented by formal variables can be subject to renaming and that in inference the order of the premises is free. Argument expressions, representing a hypothesis, are modeled as *case*.

---

[19]SOME S is P $\Leftrightarrow$ SOME P is S.
[20]X,Y$\rightarrow$ Z $\Leftrightarrow$ NOT Z,X$\rightarrow$ NOT Y.

Figure 7.14: A classification of the three modes of 'naive' reasoning

The relation between the Aristotelian figures and the functions of the premises with Peirce's nine sign aspects is the following. Qualisigns, as well as their representations generated by *sorting* (cf. icon and sinsign) are experienced hence exhibit the character of a minor premise. As complementary qualia represent information which is experienced too,[21] symbols in the index position must involve the character of a minor premise (in conformity with their logical interpretation, synonymous index signs may arise through a relation of conversion as shown in Sect. 6.7.5). Representations obtained by *abstraction* have the character of a major premise in a deductive or inductive inference. In line with the similarity between 'naive' reasoning and 'naive' or natural language processing, *sorting* and *abstraction* can be interpreted as degenerate symbol interactions (cf. coercion, introduced in Sect. 6.1.1).

Symbols in the rheme position represent the input as a candidate for the subject, those in the legisign position represent the input as a habitual property involved in the predicate position. The general character of these signs justifies their interpretation as major premises. Symbols in the dicent position express a selection from the range of possibilities that is offered by the rheme. By virtue of its potential to represent the input as an actually existent object which is experienced, dicent signs involve the character of a minor premise. This is opposed to symbol signs which, by expressing the law-like property of the legisign in context, involve the aspect of a major premise.

This closes our analysis of 'naive' reasoning. An analysis of the three types of inferences, deduction, induction and abduction as reasoning methods is beyond our possibilities. The only exception is 'naive' induction, which will be the subject of our study in the next chapter, by virtue of its important role in mathematical conceptualization.

7.8 Summary

Information processing has the character of deduction in the interaction between the rheme and index positions, and the character of induction in the interaction between the index and legisign positions. See Fig. 7.14. Since an abduction of new qualia may demand a revision of the input analysis, abductive inference

---

[21]This view is supported by the logical expression of the index $(\neg A + \neg B, \neg A * \neg B)$ as a *sorting* representation of complementary input qualia $(\neg A, \neg B)$.

must have the character of both deduction and induction. As the processing schema has the character of abduction in the stages *predication*, *sorting* and *abstraction*, we may conclude that cognitive processing, and so 'naive' reasoning as a process, is basically abductive and, within that framework, deductive and inductive. Deduction and induction are coordinated by the index position, mediating premises in the rheme and legisign positions to a conclusion in the argument position.

Chapter 8

Mathematical signs

Besides logic, language and reasoning, mathematics is undoubtedly one of the most important domains of knowledge. According to experimental cognitive research, 'naive' mathematical or number concepts depend on our innate capacity to interpret stimuli as numbers.

A premise of this chapter is that 'naive' mathematical conceptualization can be modeled as a sign interpretation process, similar to conceptualization in other domains considered in this book. We will also suggest that 'naive' mathematical concepts mediate between 'naive' logic and natural language. The close relationship between 'naive' mathematics and sign processing opens the possibility for an interpretation of (naive) mathematics as a representation of observables, hence for the existence of a 'real' mathematical universe. (Wang, 1974) devotes an interesting section to natural numbers. In it Wang points to the subordinate relation in which cardinals stand to ordinals, ordinals being seemingly more basic. But he comes to the conclusion that the concept of more or equal is prior to both cardinals and ordinals. From there he follows the mathematical logical path in order to arrive at the recursive definition of natural numbers, made explicit by Peano's axioms (docens). We follow, so to speak, the same path in the other direction and try to find the phenomena (utens) of which the formalisations are developments. We think that origin can be found in the nature of information processes.

8.1 Introduction

The aim of this chapter is to show that the processing schema introduced earlier can be used to model mathematical conceptualization as well. As with our model of reasoning signs in Chapter 7, we restrict ourselves solely to the 'naive' or obvious meaning of number phenomena. As our focus is on a 'naive' mathematical interpretation, the prefix 'naive' can be omitted.

What makes the 'naive' mathematical domain especially important is that its concepts are involved in the more complex concepts of the math we learn at school. We will illustrate this relation with a 'naive' mathematical interpretation of infinity. In programming languages, infinite numbers are usually represented by means of some maximum value, e.g. 'max_int', which obviously cannot capture the full potential of infinite numbers. In this chapter we will foster the idea that infinity can be modeled by the use of a prototypical interpretation of memory signs.

Besides infinity, we will consider mathematical types (why are they necessary?), the relation of 'naive' mathematics with other domains such as 'naive' logic and natural language and, finally, mathematical induction. In particular, we will deal with the question of why this form of induction consists of three conceptually different stages.

8.2 Cardinality and numbers

In the model of 'naive' mathematical information processing we make use of evidence concerning the potential of the brain for an interpretation of multitudes as a cardinality.[1] To this end, the first part of this section is devoted to an overview of the neuro-physiological grounds for cardinality perception. In the second part, we will show how this ability of the brain can be used to model an interpretation of phenomena as numbers.

Recent neuro-physiological research by (Nieder, Freedman, & Miller, 2002) has experimentally shown the existence of number-encoding neurons in the brain. Such neurons fire maximally in response to a specific preferred number, correctly signifying a wide variety of displays in which the cues are not confounded. For instance, one such neuron might respond maximally to displays of four items, somewhat less to displays of three or five items, and not at all to displays of one or two items. It does not matter whether the displays are equalized according to perimeter, area, shape, linear arrangement, or density, such neurons attend only to number. The number-encoding neurons are able to recognize the number of similar items from 1 up to 5, but the representation of numbers gets increasingly fuzzy for larger and larger numbers. Many neurons fire selectively 120 ms after display onset, whatever the number on the screen, indicating that the neurons 'count' without enumeration (Dehaene, 2002).

The above experimental results suggest that a primary representation of the signals produced by the number-encoding neurons must be *iconic*. This is opposed to the mathematical interpretation of cardinality, which is *symbolic*. In this chapter we suggest that an intermediate *indexical* concept can be an ordering representation of cardinality. Thus we assume there are three principle levels of dealing with cardinality. Note that the lower levels are involved in the higher. The hidden agenda of this chapter is to show that in spite of their differences the three levels can be modeled in a uniform manner.

The signal of the number-encoding neurons is already vague for low numbers, contradicting the common experience that the brain is able to accurately stipulate cardinality (up to a limit) without symbolic counting. In this chapter

---

[1]See also (Dehaene, 1997), (Pica, Lemer, Izard, & Dehaene, 2004).

we suggest that the signal of number-encoding neurons could be processed by the brain analogously to the signal of color receptors.[2]

Below we introduce a model for cardinality processing as follows. In accordance with the findings of (Nieder et al., 2002) we suggest that objects that are perceived as similar are represented in the brain by cardinality qualia.[3] As these qualia arise in the brain, not in the senses, we assume that number perception comprises a higher level process. This means that we interpret cardinality as a *memory* sign.[4] In line with the results of the above neuro-physiological study, in our model we assume that the brain is able to sort input state (cardinality) qualia into three classes:

- no_num
  The input is interpreted as a single object. The number-encoding neurons are not active or their signal is not in focus.

- one_or_more
  The input is interpreted as a small collection of similar items. Some of the number-encoding neurons are active. Cardinality arises as a quale that can be recognized as a number.

- many
  The input is interpreted as an undefined but large numerosity of similar items. The number-encoding neurons are all active. Although cardinality does arise as a quale, its value is too vague to be recognized as a number.

The boundary between no_num and one_or_more is determined by the question of whether number plays a role or not.[5] If not, attention will go to the qualities of the phenomenon offering itself. If number plays a role and the size of the collection of similar input entities in principle allows the attribution of a definite number, the phenomenon belongs to the one_or_more category. The boundary between one_or_more and many is less sharp.[6] We assume that many begins just above numerosity two. In English, linguistic evidence for the above boundaries can be found in the distinction between singular, two, and plural. But they also show themselves through words like one, both, but all three, all four, and a trouser, a pair of trousers, but many trousers. If the signal of the counting neurons is vague,

---

[2]The attribution of a color is independent of the number of receptors simultaneously discharged.

[3]The important assumption is that cardinality appears as a quale.

[4]We use the term cardinality ambiguously. First, as a term for qualia arising for each similar input item (state), second, as a (cardinal) number representing a collection of qualia as a single object.

[5](Nieder, 2010, pers. comm.) suggests that "many of the numerosity selective neurons are not exclusively tuned to numerical information, but also to other stimuli dependent on which larger network they might be embedded in." His suggestion is backed up by the findings in (Tudusciuc & Nieder, 2007). These findings may indicate input ambiguity, comparable to the vase–face ambiguity in Fig. 3.7.

[6]A plausible explanation for the rapidly increasing vagueness as a consequence of a growing number of responding neurons in the case of an increased input numerosity is to be found in (Nieder et al., 2002).

the S_S may focus on (contiguous) input segments which are countable, process their number and estimate the number of the entire input by means of counting.

8.3 Finite numbers

From the assumption that cardinality as a memory sign is independent of the input effect, and the fact that cardinality is not our immediate interpretation of the input state, we conclude that cardinality must be furnished by complementary type memory signs (a'_c). If an immediate interpretation of input (cf. perceptual judgment) is found unsatisfactory, the brain may suggest another interpretation by an abductive process. Modeling issues of abduction have been discussed in the previous chapter.

Having said this, a model for number-interpretation is introduced below. We consider three levels of interpretation: iconic , indexical and symbolic, which correspond to three manners of how counting can be operational.

8.3.1 Iconic number signs

Mathematical information processing starts with an *iconic* interpretation of cardinality qualia. This can be illustrated with a numerical interpretation of a collection of cubic shapes.[7] Let us assume that the input state (**cube**) triggers a memory response in the sense of agreement (memory-sign-of-cube) and possibility (memory-sign-of-cardinality). And also assume that the appearing effect (**cubic-form, size**) generates a memory response in the sense of agreement (memory-sign-of-cubic-form) and in the sense of possibility (memory-sign-of-size). This completes a specification of the input for the process of perception. As usual, the final signs generated by this process are used as input qualia of a subsequent cognition process. Note that signs can be synonymously referred to by their Peircean sign aspects and their 'naive' logical expressions as in earlier chapters.

The input signs of the perception process:

$$
\begin{array}{lll}
a & = \textbf{cube} & \%\ a_f \\
a' & = \textsf{memory-sign-of-cube, memory-sign-of-cardinality} & \%\ a'_f,\ a'_c \\
b & = \textbf{cubic-form, size} & \%\ b_f,\ b_c \\
b' & = \textsf{memory-sign-of-cubic-form, memory-sign-of-size} & \%\ b'_f,\ b'_c
\end{array}
$$

The input signs of the cognition process:

$$
\begin{array}{lll}
A & = a{*}a' \quad = cube & \%\ \textbf{cube}{*}\textsf{memory-sign-of-cube} \\
\neg A & = a{+}a' \quad = cardinality & \%\ \textbf{cube}{+}\textsf{memory-sign-of-cardinality} \\
B & = b{*}b' \quad = form & \%\ \textbf{cubic form}{*}\textsf{memory-sign-of-cubic-form} \\
\neg B & = b{+}b' \quad = size & \%\ \textbf{size}{+}\textsf{memory-sign-of-size}
\end{array}
$$

---

[7]Through their shape bodies can be perceived as similar entities. See the distinction between sinsign (token) and legisign (type).

a)   b)   c)

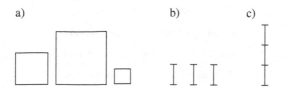

Figure 8.1: Sample cubic bodies (a), their representation as a collection of cardinality qualia (b), and stacked, as an iconic number (c)

If the final proposition, '*cube is form*' or, alternatively, 'some cubes are there' is rejected, the interpreting system (S_S) will, so we assume in this example, proceed with an abductive analysis of the input qualia.[8] Earlier we have shown (see Sect. 7.4.1) that abducted state qualia (*new-a*) always form a subset of the input state qualia (*a*). In other words, abductively generated new state qualia cannot contribute to a new interpretation of the input. This is opposed to the case that new effect qualia (*new-b*) are introduced via abduction. Those new qualia may enable novel conceptualizations, in this case, by the transformation of cubic entities (*a*) to their cardinalities (*a'*). The latter may trigger (new) memory response signs. In our presentation below, abductively introduced qualia are indicated by the subscript "*new*".

In our example (see Fig. 8.1) we restrict ourselves to the definition of abductively introduced new qualia as qualisigns of the process of perception. These are the new state, cube-cardinality$_{new}$ ($a'_f * a_f$) with its memory response sign, cube-cardinality-unit-value$_{new}$, and the new effect, cube-cardinality$_{new}$ ($a'_c \setminus a_f$) with its memory response sign, cube-cardinality-growth$_{new}$. Note that the sign cube-cardinality represents the input as a countable state and as such an effect, ambiguously. The corresponding memory response signs are labelled cube-cardinality-unit-value (e.g. 'one') and cube-cardinality-growth (e.g. 'incrementation' by one), respectively. The current status of information processing can be recapitulated as follows.

The input signs of the perception process:

a	$=$ **cube**, cube-cardinality$_{new}$	% $a'_f * a_f$
a'	$=$ memory-sign-of-cube, memory-sign-of-cardinality,	
	cube-cardinality-unit-value$_{new}$	
b	$=$ **cubic-form**, size, cube-cardinality$_{new}$	% $a'_c \setminus a_f$
b'	$=$ memory-sign-of-cubic-form, memory-sign-of-size,	
	cube-cardinality-growth$_{new}$	

The input signs of the cognition process:

A	$= a * a'$ $= cube$	% cube-cardinality$_{new}$ *memory-sign-of-cardinality
$\neg A$	$= a + a'$ $= unit\text{-}value$	% cube-cardinality$_{new}$ +cube-cardinality-unit-value$_{new}$

---

[8] In our example, the abductive process shifts attention from the appearance to the existence of the form. See the distinction between icon (quality of percept) and sinsign (existence of percept).

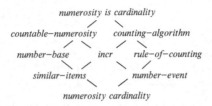

Figure 8.2: Conceptualization of iconic number-phenomena. In concrete cases of counting the demonstrative pronoun '*this*' ought to be added. For instance, *this-countable-numerosity, this-numerosity IS this-cardinality*

$$B = b*b' = cardinality \quad \% \textbf{ cubic form}*\text{cube-cardinality}_{new}$$
$$\neg B = b+b' = growth \quad \% \text{ cube-cardinality}_{new}+\text{cube-cardinality-growth}$$

Number interpretation may proceed as follows (see also Fig. 8.2). The icon $(A+B)$ and sinsign positions $(A*B)$ are an expression of the input qualia as a collection of simultaneously present similar objects (*similar-items*), and as an appearing cardinality property (*number-event*), respectively. As cardinality qualia may arise for any countable phenomenon, the sinsign represents the input as an appearing number, independently from the *sort* of similar objects observed.

The rheme position $(A*\neg B, \neg A*B)$ is an expression of the cubic bodies and cardinalities as countable abstract entities (*number-base*). The legisign position $(A*\neg B+\neg A*B)$ is an expression of a rule for counting cubic entities (*rule-of-counting*). An example is the accumulation of input cardinality qualia in a single value or measure, iconically representing the input collection as a 'number'. An essential parameter of the law-like rule involved in mathematical legisigns is a unit of counting, representing an increment (value) and an act of incrementation (property). For example, small cubes can be counted in steps of 1/10, if ten small cubes are equivalent to one large cube. A synonymous interpretation of such a value and property as a *type* (*incr*) is the contribution of the index position $(\neg A+\neg B, \neg A*\neg B)$, representing complementary information or the *context* of the input number-phenomenon.

The dicent position expresses the input as an actually existent numerosity $(A+\neg B)$ and a corresponding cardinality value $(\neg A+B)$, representing the view of the *subject* of the input number-phenomenon. The symbol position provides an analogous representation of a conventional (cardinality) property or, in other words, the *predicate* $(A*B+\neg A*\neg B)$ involved in the input phenomenon. It is *this* property that determines how the subject can be interpreted as a number. In a computational setting, the predicate sign of iconic number-phenomena can be called an algorithm for 'counting B-number of A-entities by means of accumulation'. The argument position, merging the mathematical dicent and symbol signs in a proposition represents the input as a measure of similar entities, which is iconic knowledge (*numerosity is cardinality*).

Evidence for counting by means of accumulation can be found in a recent experimental study by (Wittlinger, Wehner, & Wolf, 2006), showing that desert ants measure distances by means of some kind of step integrator or "step counter". In the reported experiment, the legs, and thereby the stride length, of freely walking ants were manipulated. Animals with elongated or shortened legs took larger or shorter strides, respectively. Travel distance is overestimated by ants walking on elongated legs, and underestimated by ants walking on shortened legs.

8.3.2 Inclusion ordering

A subsequent (second) level in mathematical conceptualization is an ordering interpretation of cardinality qualia. We assume that our potential for an *indexical* interpretation of number-phenomena enables us to order numerosities as more or less, without symbolic counting. This ability is shown to be present in children of age two (Bullock & Gelman, 1977).

The running example of this section consists of a pair of collections of cubes, on the left- and right-hand sides of a separating line. The task is to establish an order relation between the two collections. This can be solved by making use of an iconic interpretation of number-phenomena, as follows. Let us assume that the cardinality of the left-hand side collection is already available in a memory sign (n_l) and that, in the context of this value, we are concerned with a number interpretation of the collection of cubes on the right-hand side (n_r). An interpretation of this phenomenon as an order relation between two collections, which is indexical knowledge, may be explained as follows.

Let us assume that a number interpretation of the left-hand side collection (n_l) is degenerately represented by a complementary input quale as follows: $a_c := n_l$, $a'_c := n_l$. Note that a_c and a'_c refer to n_l as a cardinality, and a number, respectively. Such a twofold interpretation of n_l is possible, as cardinality arises in memory and, following our model of abductive inferencing (cf. Sect. 7.4.1), memory signs can be used to define new input qualia.[9] In addition let us assume that the subsequently generated number sign of the right-hand side collection (n_r) can be represented analogously, this time by a quale which is in focus: $a_f := n_r$; $a'_f := n_r$.

The above qualia can be interpreted as an order relation. By considering a' and a as previous and current percepts, respectively, new input qualia can be introduced through abduction. See also Fig. 8.3. Given that a relation in the sense of agreement ('*') is only possible between qualia that are in focus (a'_f, a_f), and that a relation in the sense of possibility ('+') may exist between all other combinations of focused and complementary qualia, such as a'_c and a_f, a'_f and a_c, and a'_c and a_c (cf. Sect. 7.4.1), we get:

$$
\begin{aligned}
\textit{new-a} \quad &:= \quad a' * a \\
&= \quad a'_f * a_f \\
&= \quad n_r
\end{aligned}
$$

---

[9]Note that n_l can be interpreted as *new-a* (a_c) and as a memory sign triggered by that sign (a'_c).

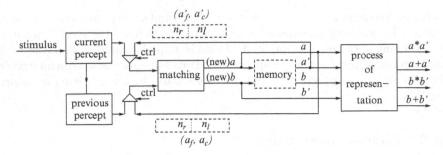

Figure 8.3: An ordering interpretation of number-phenomena. According to our assumption in Sect. 7.4: $a=(a_f,a_c)$, $a'=(a'_f,a'_c)$

$$
\begin{aligned}
\textit{new-b} \quad &:= \quad a'\backslash a \\
&= \quad a'_c\backslash a_f + a'_f\backslash a_c + a'_c\backslash a_c \\
&= \quad n_l\backslash n_r + n_r\backslash n_l
\end{aligned}
$$

In order to establish an order relation we need a substraction operation on collections of qualia. Subtraction of (iconic) numbers represented as sets can be implemented by means of a relative difference operation (\\). The result of this operation may not always be meaningful, however. For example, $n_r\backslash n_l$ can be interpreted as an order relation ('<'), only if $n_l<n_r$. Conforming to our model of perception, in Sect. 5.1, the relative difference operation between the previous and current input percepts can represent qualia that were not there (previous percept), but are there now (current percept). Similarly, $n_l\backslash n_r$ can be interpreted as an order relation ('>'), only if $n_l>n_r$. In other words, a relative difference operation on iconic numbers can be interpreted as an ordering if the value of the accumulated cardinality of the subtrahend is not less than that of the subtracter. If both ordering relations can be interpreted, then n_l and n_r must be equal ('=').

In sum, abductively generated new qualia may enable an interpretation of the input as an ordering-phenomenon, representing the observed phenomenon as an *inclusion relation* of the right-hand side collection (r), with respect to the collection on the left-hand side (l). In a propositional form: '$r\,\mathcal{R}\,l$' for $\mathcal{R}\in\{`<`,`=`,`>`\}$.

8.3.3 Symbolic number signs

A next (third) level in mathematical conceptualization consists of a symbolic interpretation of cardinality qualia. The importance of indexical number-signs resides in their potential to contribute to a conceptualization of symbolic numbers. This potential of ordering signs will be illustrated below with the rheme position (*number-base*) in a symbolic interpretation of cardinality.

Symbolic counting makes extensive use of primary symbolic numbers (cf. cardinal numbers), representing cardinalities that we are able to 'naturally' interpret as numbers. As the properties of symbolic counting are common knowledge, we restrict our focus to an analysis of the relation between symbolic and indexical interpretations of number-phenomena. To this end, let us re-visit our earlier example of cubic bodies and assume that the task is to rearrange the cubes on the left- and right-hand sides of the separating line such that eventually equally many cubes are left on both sides.

Children not in possession of the rules of symbolic counting tend to solve this problem by collecting all cubes on one side of the separating line. By moving cubes one by one, they 'iconically count' (cf. Sect. 8.3.1) their number on the two sides, in order to 'indexically' determine their equality (cf. Sect. 8.3.2). Those familiar with symbolic numbers may attain the same goal by symbolic calculation.

If the above task is supervised and an act of moving a cube is repeatedly followed by the articulation of the symbol "one", the move operation and a reference to a cube may become rule-like associated with the numeral "one". By applying the same operation to different numbers of cubes and to different objects as well, the prototypical meaning of "one", representing 'anything countable' (cf. *number-base*), may arise through abstraction. This way, eventually, a finite number of numerals can be learned. A prototypical interpretation of symbolic numbers, emerging from earlier observations of number-phenomena, can be modeled by means of average and domain formation. This can be illustrated with the interpretation of "one" as a value or state ('1') and also as an operation or effect ('incrementation by 1').

Large numerosities can be interpreted as a number, by focusing on contiguous segments of input qualia and interpreting the segments as nested number-phenomena. Large number-phenomena are more conveniently counted by making use of symbolic numbers, of course. As the rules of symbolic counting are basically syntactical, the definition of a model for symbolic number processing is omitted.

8.4   A 'real world' of mathematics

It is *only* possible to interpret naive mathematical signs as representations of 'real' world phenomena if the mathematical universe is 'real'. That mathematical world too must consist of phenomena that are interactions between states and effects. We content that the effects must be of a special kind because cardinality effects must have the potential to interact with *any* mathematical (number) state. This is a consequence of our earlier assumption that cardinality qualia may arise for any (countable) numerosity.

As we use existence with regard to phenomena that we call 'real', so we may use cardinality when we look at the world from the perspective of numerosity. As in the mathematical 'world' states are always related to cardinality effects, states can be interpreted from the perspective of number, in short, as 'state-number' or '*a*-number'. For instance, in our earlier example of cubic objects, each *cube* is marked by a cardinality quale. Those quale values can be generalized in the concept, 'cube-type-cardinality' or, simply, '*cube*-number', representing a unit value for counting cubic entities.

Number signs or, briefly, numbers can be degenerately represented by state type qualia in a subsequent interpretation process. Such qualia being *similar* to each other, hence countable, can be interpreted as a number. An example is the symbolic number-phenomenon: $sin^2(x)$.[10] The function, $sin(_)$, interpreted as an effect, is interacting with the parameter x, represented as a state. In addition, $sin(_)$ is functioning as a state, in the interaction with $\uparrow^2$ (second power), appearing as an effect.

This flexibility of representation is not typical for natural language, in which symbols representing a state or an effect cannot be used interchangeably. An example is the verb run, which syntactically is interpreted as an effect. An interpretation of this symbol as a state requires that the verbal relational properties of run are replaced by nominal relational ones. Mathematical signification is free from this rigidity of symbol use. The effect involved in $sin(_)$ is invariantly present in the expression $sin^2(x)$, as is witnessed by the potential of $sin(_)$ to map its parameter, x, which is a state, to its image, $sin(x)$, which too is a state, in the function application $\uparrow^2$. The rigidity of natural language symbols could be a consequence of their more specific objects; mathematical signs are more abstract.

As in the mathematical world objects (state) can interact with any cardinality (effect), mathematical symbol interactions are free from constraints. However, from the assumption that mathematical signs arise from 'real' world phenomena, possibly through a series of representation events, it follows that the mathematical 'universe' must be part of the 'real' world, in which interactions *are* subject to constraints, i.e., an object can interact with certain other objects, not with *any* object.

In order to avoid chaos in mathematical interpretation, phenomena need to be checked for correctness, for example, for a 'well-formedness' of the involved state and effect qualia, which may explain the necessity for the introduction of mathematical *types*. In the next section, we will advocate that 'naive' mathematical types may arise through refinement and generalization, from the indexical concept of 'increment' (*incr*).

8.4.1 'Naive' mathematical types

Establishing mathematical well-formedness of phenomena may require (complementary) type information about the input state and effect qualia. As, in our model, complementary information can be represented by the index position, this comes down to the requirement that an indexical interpretation of the input phenomenon must be possible. Through *complementation*, background information present in the context (index) can be used to generate a dicent and a symbol sign, furnishing them with information necessary for an interpretation

---

[10]The qualia involved in this phenomenon are: $sin(_)$, $\uparrow^2$, x, as well as their combinatory properties ($sin(_)$ is related to x, $\uparrow^2$ to $sin(_)$).

of the input qualia as a number (argument position). As complementary input qualia may inform, amongst others, about a relation between input and memory qualia in the sense of possibility ('+'), mathematical context signs may represent input phenomena in a general sense, that is, as *types*. More specifically, the context signs may express (i) that between input qualia a relation of type compatibility exists ($\neg A + \neg B$), and (ii) what the type is that results from the mathematical operation involved in their interaction ($\neg A * \neg B$). By making use of type information, mathematical processing can 'find out' (cf. type checking) whether the input phenomenon can be a meaningful combination of qualia or whether it arises through malfunctioning like in hallucinations.

In our view, context or index signs are the *key* to a 'naive' mathematical interpretation of phenomena. Just as in the mathematical 'universe' cardinality effects can be used as states, an interpretation of input phenomena as a number needs certain measures to be taken. In particular, since mathematical functions, interpreted as a state, preserve their potential to function as an effect, well-formedness of mathematical operations requires that the involved symbol interactions are correctly typed. Roughly, if the input can be interpreted as a mathematical type (index position), the observed number-phenomenon can be meaningful (argument position).

The basic type of cardinality, 'natural' numbers, arises through generalization from an obvious interpretation of mathematical index signs (*incr*), which is enumeration. By applying this type to the input interpreted as an abstract state (*number-base*) and effect (*rule-of-counting*), a representation of the observed phenomenon as a natural number can be obtained. For example, a 'naive' mathematical interpretation of a collection of cubes may arise by interpreting each cube as an abstract item ("one") and by accumulating their cardinality in a single value ("counting one by one"). Formal mathematical types such as natural ($\mathcal{N}$), rational ($\mathcal{Q}$), and real ($\mathcal{R}$) may arise from this 'naive' mathematical conception of number-phenomena, through an iconic, indexical and symbolic interpretation of '*incr*', as a constant, a quotient and a process, respectively. For instance, $\mathcal{N}$ can be interpreted as an abstraction of (natural) numbers, $\mathcal{Q}$ as that of an infinite sequence of natural numbers, and $\mathcal{R}$ as an abstraction of an infinite sequence of rationals.

8.5 Infinite numbers

How can we represent infinite numbers, what information and knowledge is involved? In this section we suggest the idea that the prototypical representation involved in memory signs provides an answer to this question.

Earlier (see Sect. 6.7.2) we introduced memory signs as prototypical representations of memory qualia responding to the input trigger. This conception of memory signs enables a twofold interpretation of the relation between input and memory. According to the first interpretation, $a * a'$ (A) is an expression of a as a value complemented by a', and $b * b'$ (B) an expression of b as a measure hence a value of b'. Both relations involve reference to individual qualia. Following the second interpretation, A stands for *all* qualia involved in the average value (a') triggered by the input a, and B for *all* qualia involved in the dense domain (b') triggered by the input b. According to this interpretation, both A and B involve reference to a collection of qualia as a whole (not to its individual elements). Below we suggest that this 'infinite' interpretation of memory signs represents a 'naive' concept of infinite numbers.

In line with the results of the neuro-physiological study in (Nieder et al., 2002), we assumed that the brain is able to distinguish number-phenomena into three classes: no_num, one_or_more, many. The last one, many, refers to numerosities that possess the quality of cardinality but miss the notion of increment (both as a value, and as a property). In our view, such number-phenomena could underly our 'naive' concept of infinity. Because, in interpretation of 'infinite', memory signs are assumed to refer to an entire collection (not to its elements), such signs do not possess the concept of an increment, hence are uncountable.

The above relation between a 'naive' mathematical interpretation of phenomena on the one hand and a twofold interpretation of the relation between input and memory signs on the other hand is supported by linguistic analogy. For instance, in the utterance, 'the police are going to lunch', the subject ('the police') can be interpreted as a whole, and as individual persons. The suggested link between a 'naive' interpretation of infinite numbers and a prototypical interpretation of memory signs such as nouns implies that in all memory signs infinity is involved as a possibility.

8.6 Naught

The condition for cardinality to appear as a quality is the existence of similar objects in the input. This implies that naught cannot be *perceived* as a cardinality, it is only through inferences that we arrive at the concept. This can be illustrated by an interpretation of qualia that belong to the category 'no_num', but that we nevertheless want to interpret according to their numerosity.[11] As those qualia do not allow their perception as a cardinality, but a number interpretation is anticipated, we may abductively infer that those qualia must have been there earlier, but disappeared. If those qualia refer to a countable state, their cardinality can be represented by naught or zero. In sum, zero can be defined as a hypothetical number sign, not having the quality of cardinality nor that of an increment (cf. *incr*).

8.7 The secondness of 'naive' mathematics

In human knowledge representation, 'naive' mathematics mediates between 'naive' logic and natural language. This may be explained as follows.

---

[11]For instance, qualia introduced through abduction.

From a categorical perspective, 'naive' logic, 'naive' mathematics and 'naive' or natural language exhibit the aspects of firstness, secondness, and thirdness, respectively. 'Naive' *logic* is concerned with the types of relations between dual qualia involved in phenomena. Such a relation exhibits the category of:

- 1stness, if it is a unary relation, such as an interpretation of a quale as a state or an effect (a, a', b, b');

- 2ndness, if it is a binary relation, such as an interpretation of a link between input and memory qualia $(A, \neg A, B, \neg B)$;

- 3rdness, if it is tertiary relation, such as an interpretation of a relation between input qualia $(A+B, A*B, \ldots, A \text{ is } B)$.

'Naive' *mathematics* is concerned with a number representation of logical relations involved in input phenomena. In addition, 'naive' mathematics introduces types for and shared by the incomparable (dual) qualia occurring in input phenomena. Those types are the foundation for the primary concept of natural language: the relational needs of symbols. It is important to remark that 'naive' mathematical types involve the notion of an increment. By means of this property we are able to derive an induced ordering of (consecutive) numbers and introduce a 'boundary' between collections of similar items separating those collections from each other. Note that a 'separation' is less meaningful than a classification which involves differentia. The introduction of boundaries is crucial for language processing, as information about potentially different objects can be necessary to determine the reference of a language sign, which, for example, occurs in syntactic modification phenomena.

Natural *language* 'lifts' the three types of logical relations mediated by 'naive' mathematics, to the concepts of a potentially existing or 'neutral' (n), a lexically defined possible or 'passive' (p), and an actual or 'active' relational need (a). These are the three types of combinatory properties of language symbols.

8.7.1 Levels of mathematical conceptualization

'Naive' mathematical concepts have other interesting properties that deserve our attention (see also Fig. 8.4). The first 'level' (*level-1*) in number interpretation, including the icon and sinsign positions, represents the input as a constituency and a simultaneity relation, respectively. These representations that arise through a sorting of the input qualia into two types express a logical relation. As the icon and sinsign positions are still too primordial to invoke any notion, including the notion of number, this level of interpretation can be called a *logical* level. In morpho-syntactic symbol processing, analogous icon and sinsign representations are a morphological root (that can be subject to affixation) and an affix (that requires a root), respectively.

The second 'level' (*level-2*) in number interpretation, introduces abstract concepts of number-phenomena. The rheme and legisign positions represent

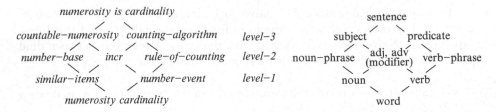

Figure 8.4: A comparison of 'naive' mathematical and language concepts

the input as a countable abstract entity or a '*number-base*' (it makes no difference whether houses or cats are counted), and a '*rule-of-counting*', respectively. The index position represents the concept of increment(ation), as a type. Through that type, the index enables an interpretation of '*number-base*' and '*rule-of-counting*', in context. As the 'naive' mathematical rheme, index and legisign positions represent a mathematical (term) structure involved in the input phenomenon, this level of interpretation can be called a *mathematical* level. Just as in language processing, the index position contains the adjective- and adverb-phrases, the rheme position the noun-phrases and the legisign position the verb-phrases.

The third 'level' in the interpretation of number-phenomena (*level-3*) defines the concepts of a countable numerosity (cf. subject) and a counting algorithm (cf. predicate). This level can be called a *language* level, by virtue of its potential to express the relation between the mathematical 'subject' and 'predicate', as a mathematical operation. Analogous concepts, in language processing, are the syntactic subject, the predicate, and the sentence.

Since a mathematical subject and predicate representation of the input only arises if an indexical representation exists (cf. context), phenomena that are not well-formed cannot be interpreted (their process does not exist). An example of an ill-formed number-phenomenon is '2/1.5' (assuming '/' stands for integer division). A semantical counterpart is the famous nonsensical sentence originated by Chomsky: 'colorless green ideas sleep furiously' (Chomsky, 1957).

8.8   Meta-mathematical signs

Mathematical induction is an instance of inductive inferencing. By showing that mathematical conceptualization involves mathematical induction, we open the way to merge 'naive' mathematics with inferencing in a single process. We will use the close relationship between the two domains, mathematics and reasoning, in order to reveal why mathematical induction consists of three conceptually different stages.

Our classification of logical inferences as symbol interactions is recapitulated in Fig. 8.5. As the qualisign, icon and sinsign positions play a less important role in 'naive' mathematical induction, abduction associated with *sorting* and *abstraction* is omitted in this diagram (cf. Sect. 7.2.1).

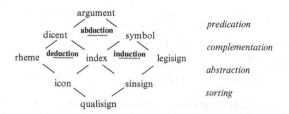

Figure 8.5: A classification of logical inferences (recap.)

8.8.1 Mathematical induction

According to the first principle of mathematical induction: If for a property P, $P(0)$ holds and, for $k>0$, from $P(k)$ it follows that $P(k+1)$ holds too, then P is true for all natural numbers. From this definition, the second principle of induction can be derived, which is more suitable for the purposes of this section:

> If for an arbitrary n,
>> from the statement that $P(k)$ holds for all $k<n$
>
> $P(n)$ follows,
>> then $P(n)$ is true for any n.

Formally: $\forall n \forall k.(k<n \rightarrow P(k)) \rightarrow P(n) \rightarrow \forall n.P(n)$, with $\forall k.(k<n \rightarrow P(k))$ as the induction hypothesis. The goal of this section is to show that the second principle of mathematical induction is involved in a 'naive' mathematical interpretation of phenomena.

The above definition of mathematical induction enables us to identify the stages of interpretation, as follows. Initially we know that $P(k)$ holds, for all $0 \leq k < n$. As our knowledge must arise from a 'naive' mathematical interpretation of n different phenomena, we may assume the existence of n states, satisfying the property P: $P(0), \ldots, P(n-1)$.[12] According to the above definition, in order to prove that $P(n)$ holds too, we have to consider the next state (next number) satisfying P. To this end we interpret the change which is brought about by the effect of incrementation (*succ*) affecting the state of the interpreting system (defined by $P(0), \ldots, P(n-1)$), in the context of P. Below we use the convention that braces and angle brackets stand for set and domain formation, respectively. We assume that P can be 'lifted' from elements to collections of elements. $P\{0, \ldots, k\}$ and $P\langle 0, \ldots, k \rangle$ are short for $\{P(0), \ldots, P(k)\}$ and $\langle P(0), \ldots, P(k) \rangle$, respectively. A specification of the signs generated by the perception process is omitted.

The input signs of the *cognition* process (an explanation is given below):

$$A = P\{0, \ldots, n-1\} \qquad \neg A = P$$
$$B = succ \qquad\qquad \neg B = P$$

---

[12] Here, n can be a constant or an arbitrary value. In the latter case, an interpretation of P itself involves induction as a nested phenomenon. Such a process is no different from the one described in this section and can be treated alike.

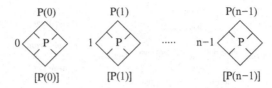

Figure 8.6: Earlier observations as deductive inferences. For i ($0{\leq}i{<}n$), [P(i)] is an expression of an uninterpreted input object involving the property P

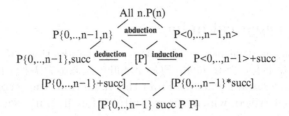

Figure 8.7: Logical relations involved in mathematical induction as a process (complementary qualia are omitted, except in the qualisign and index positions)

According to the initial condition set by induction, P must hold for all k ($0{\leq}k{<}n$). This implies the existence of n phenomena and corresponding deductive inferences, $P(0),\ldots,P(n-1)$, as shown in Fig. 8.6. The above definition of A is obtained by merging the proposition signs of those individual observations, $P(0),\ldots,P(n-1)$, into a single sign, through coordination, and by representing the resulting expression by a single state-type quale.[13]

In order to prove the inductive statement about P, we have to show that P holds for the next element satisfying P or the successor of $P(n-1)$. This can be established by applying the effect of incrementation (*succ*) to those known P-type objects as states. This may explain the above definition of B as well. The complementary signs, $\neg A$ and $\neg B$, defined by P, are interpreted as a state and an effect, respectively; they represent qualia involved in the context of the interaction between A and B.

In the interpretation of the above input qualia the first interesting moment is the rheme position. At this point the meaning of $P\{0,\ldots,n-1\}$ and *succ* is abstracted in the concept 'P-number' (*number-base*). The legisign position is an expression of a compatibility relation between $P\{0,\ldots,n-1\}$ and *succ*. It is by virtue of this rule-like relation that the collection of P-type input entities can be systematically extended by a subsequent next element. This interpretation of the legisign makes use of the representation of $P\{0,\ldots,n-1\}$ as a dense domain: $P\langle 0,\ldots,n-1\rangle$. The fact that this domain exists and can be extended by a next element proves the existence of a property shared by all elements in this domain.

Complementation of the rheme by the index may generate a representation of the input as a collection of P-type cardinalities. In context, *succ* can be

---

[13]The resulting quale represents all of $P,0,\ldots,n-1,P(0),\ldots,P(n-1)$.

interpreted as "+1", referring to such a P-type element and an incrementation event, ambiguously. Information deduced from the rheme and index can be used to generate the dicent sign that represents $P\{0,\ldots,n-1\}$ and $P\{n\}$ as existent entities, in short: $P\{0,\ldots,n-1,n\}$. The underlying symbol interaction, including an application of P to the next possible element, represented by "n", or, alternatively, an extension of the collection of $P\{0,\ldots,n-1\}$ by the next element, has the character of a deductive inference.

Complementation of the legisign amounts to a test of new elements in the extended domain for compatibility under P (the legisign is an expression of a rule-like compatibility of $P\langle0,\ldots,n-1\rangle$ and the incrementation operation *succ*). This requires the hypothesis that, in context, $P\langle0,\ldots,n-1\rangle$ can be inductively generalized for the next element of this domain. If testing is successful, it means that $P(0),\ldots,P(n-1)$ and $P(n)$ can be related to each other in the sense of agreement. This is expressed by $P\langle0,\ldots,n-1\rangle*P(n)$ or, briefly, $P\langle0,\ldots,n-1,n\rangle$, which represents a conventional property involved in the observed number-phenomenon (cf. symbol position).

In the final step, the interaction between the dicent and symbol signs is interpreted by a hypothetical proposition of an equivalent interpretation of the input as a collection of P-type entities (*state-view*) and a P-type operation (*event-view*). See also Fig. 8.8. A 'naive' mathematical interpretation of this relation can be expressed by the formula: ALL $n.P(n)$. Note that the involved quantification by 'ALL' is short for 'generalization on the basis of all objects we have knowledge of'. Those objects, their representation by a dense domain, and an interpretation of that domain as an infinite number are all involved in 'naive' mathematical induction phenomena.

The reader may have noticed the secondary role of P in the above process. What really matters in 'naive' mathematical induction is testing a next element in the domain of interest; the concept of infinity arises in this process as a tacit 'ingredient'. This enables us to draw the conclusion that infinity involved in 'naive' mathematical induction is a perspective that we had all the time. Hence it is only used, *not* generated during mathematical interpretation.

8.8.2 An example

Assume we want to prove that $P(n)=0+1+2+\ldots+n=(n^2+n)/2$ holds for all $n\geq0$. *Complementation* of the rheme by the index position obtains the expression: $(n^2+n)/2+(n+1)$; that of the legisign the expression: $((n+1)^2+(n+1))/2$ (calculations realized by nested processing are omitted). By postulating equality of these expressions, by *predication*, P is presented as an inductive property: ALL $n.P(n)$. Note that infinity involved in 'ALL' is a consequence of a continuous domain interpretation of $P\langle0,\ldots,n-1\rangle$ and $P\langle0,\ldots,n\rangle$.

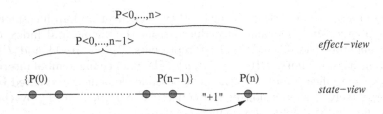

Figure 8.8: Sample mathematical induction. Initially we know $P(0)$, ..., $P(n-1)$. These elements can be deductively generalized in a collection by deriving the next P-type element (state-view), and inductively generalized in a dense domain by testing that element for the property P (effect-view). In the two generalizations, "+1" is used as a value and as a measure, respectively. The essence of 'naive' mathematical induction is a hypothesis that the results of deductive and inductive generalization are equivalent

8.9 Summary

As a consequence of an earlier assumption of this book, knowledge arises from the interpretation of interactions between dual qualia. This duality is captured by 'naive' logic, interpreting that property as a relation or fact. A generalization of qualia in types is a contribution of 'naive' mathematics. Language goes one step further, in the sense that it abstracts the mathematical concept of a type in the concept of a relational need. In other words, 'naive' logic, 'naive' mathematics, and natural language can be interpreted as increasingly more meaningful levels of human knowledge representation. An interesting 'feature' of mathematical information processing is that, to some extent, it contains the feats of all three levels: although mathematical interpretation is about mathematical signs, its interpretation moments show strong affinity with those involved in 'naive' logical and language processing.

Chapter 9

Text summarization

Redundancy is frequent in natural language. Words, phrases, clauses and even complete sentences can sometimes be removed without essentially changing the content of a text. Text summarization, a technique to generate concise summaries, capitalizes on this feature of language. Experience with traditional text summarization, using a statistical analysis of syntactic relations (Sparck Jones, 1993), (Endres-Niggemeyer, 1998), (Hovy, 2005), (Mani, 2001) shows its limitations. In our view, those limitations are related to the use of formal ontologies and the lack of a uniform method of knowledge representation. Formal ontologies do not respect the properties of cognitive activity and cannot support a meaningful summarization of concepts. As traditional knowledge representation can be complex[1] and text summarization may require an analysis of the input from different perspectives, the use of uniform representation, enabling a combination of knowledge from different domains in a single representation, by means of structural coordination, can be beneficial for reasons of efficiency.

The premise of this chapter is that the theory introduced earlier in this book enables an alternative for text summarization that may not suffer from the above limitations. Because of the immense complexity of meaningful text summarization, in this chapter we restrict ourselves to an illustration of the theoretical possibilities of our approach. Let us emphasize that 'meaningfulness' associated with our model of interpretation, is qualitatively less than meaningfulness involved in authentic (triadic) interpretation.

9.1 Introduction

The idea underlying the text summarization technique suggested in this chapter is straightforward. We assume that a pair of subsequent sentences, a previous and a current sentence, can be interpreted as a state-transition, which transforms the state involved in the previous sentence to the (next) state represented

---

[1] Formalisms using unification can lead to exponential complexity (Dwork, Kanellakis, & Mitchell, 1984).

by the current sentence. Following this line of thinking, text summarization can be defined as a process that combines state-transitions, induced by consecutive sentences into a single transition induced by the entire text. By removing symbols not contributing to that state-transition, a summary of the text can be generated.[2] Symbols can be superfluous for various reasons. For instance, a syntactic modification can be unimportant if there is no reference to the modifier elsewhere in the text; a verb-phrase can be redundant if it is an expression of a semantically 'neutral' effect. As summarization must depend on the perspective taken, the process of text summarization will, in general, have different results.

The idea behind sentences interpreted as transitions can be illustrated with our earlier metaphor of apparent motion perception. In this phenomenon, a series of steady pictures is displayed, that arouses in us a sense of motion. Although the pictures can be meaningful in themselves, we are capable of interpreting them from the perspective of their contribution to the input series. In this chapter we suggest that a summarized meaning of a text may arise in an analogous way. The individual pictures can be associated with a clause or a sentence representing a single state-transition; motion perception with an interpretation of the entire text as a *summarizing* transition. Motion perception and text summarization can be different, however. Motion perception requires, amongst others, that subsequently displayed pictures do not differ from each other too much, that the speed of presentation is correctly adjusted, etc.[3] This is opposed to text summarization, in which subsequent sentences may refer to semantically distant phenomena. That nevertheless we may be able to combine their series in a summarizing single sentence, proves our potential to mentally 'bridge' the gap between information elements conveyed by the individual sentences of a text.

In our summarization algorithm we capitalize on an interpretation of the input from different perspectives. Roughly, a text can be summarized in a single sign (potentially paraphrased by a sentence), if it can be summarized in some domain(s). Summarization may introduce new symbols (cf. summaries), enabling further summarization in a recursive fashion. In conformity with the experimental evidence, found in (Hagoort et al., 2004), for (quasi-)simultaneous information processing by the brain in different domains, we assume that parsing and summarization can be elaborated in a (quasi-)simultaneous fashion as well. Important elements of the approach introduced in this chapter are a uniform representation of knowledge, a systematic (categorical) framework for ontological specification and a process model of interpretation.

It is possible to compare our approach with playing a game of sudoku, with only a few exceptions. As with sudoku the goal is to establish a consistent interpretation. In contradistinction with sudoku however, summarization has to deal with more complex rules and more indeterminacy. Even up to the point that the value to insert in a cell may depend on another sudoku game.

---

[2]The focus of this chapter is on texts describing a single phenomenon.

[3]For the complex spatial and temporal conditions that have to be satisfied, see (Wandell, 1995), for example.

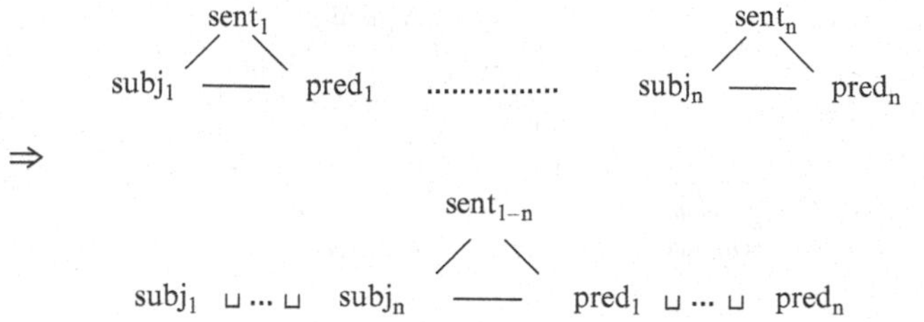

$$\begin{array}{ccc}
\text{sent}_1 & & \text{sent}_n \\
\diagup \diagdown & & \diagup \diagdown \\
\text{subj}_1 \text{------} \text{pred}_1 & \dots\dots\dots & \text{subj}_n \text{------} \text{pred}_n
\end{array}$$

$$\Rightarrow$$

$$\begin{array}{c}
\text{sent}_{1-n} \\
\diagup \diagdown \\
\text{subj}_1 \sqcup \dots \sqcup \text{subj}_n \text{------} \text{pred}_1 \sqcup \dots \sqcup \text{pred}_n
\end{array}$$

Figure 9.1: Summarization of a text consisting of n sentences ($\text{sent}_1, \dots, \text{sent}_n$), in a single sentence (sent_{1-n}). 'Subj', 'pred', 'sent' are short for subject, predicate and sentence, respectively. Unification is represented by the infix operator '$\sqcup$'

The running example of this chapter is the fairy tale "Snow White" (Grimm & Grimm, 1988). Our goal is to develop a concise summary. In the process of achieving this goal, we show the potential of our language model (cf. Chapter 6) for an analysis of complex utterances characterizing actual language use.

9.2 Sentences as state transitions

The input for summarization consists of sentences and clauses, commonly referred to as *sentences*.[4] In this chapter, sentences are interpreted as a result of a change or 'modulation' of a state (cf. subject) by an effect (cf. predicate). A modulated state will be called the *current state*, an act of 'modulation' a *state-transition*. The analogy with our process model of cognitive activity (Sect. 4.3) must be clear. The state, preceding a state-transition corresponds to the observer's state (q_1) or the *previous state*, the effect to the input stimulus (q_2).

We define a summarization as a cumulative effect of state-transitions induced by individual sentences of a text. Summarization is a process to achieve this goal. In the simplest case this comes down to covering the transformations occurring from the initial state, involved in the first sentence, up until the final state represented by the last one. See also Fig. 9.1. In this chapter we assume that it is always possible to (re)present a summarization in a single sentence. A pair of subsequent sentence signs, previous and current sentence, can be summarized in a single sign, if a state-transition from the previous sentence to the current sentence can be defined.

Text summarization can be simplified by requiring that, in a state-transition, the states (cf. subjects) and effects (cf. predicates), defined by the previous and current sentence, can be pairwise unified and that the two unifications share a common context. In this chapter, *unification* is used as a polymorphic operation, that establishes a connection between its arguments. If those arguments refer to

---

[4]Following Sect. 4.3 the input for information processing is defined by a collection of qualia. In natural language, such collections correspond to a contiguous segment or a series of symbols defined by clauses, sentences, and certain phrases.

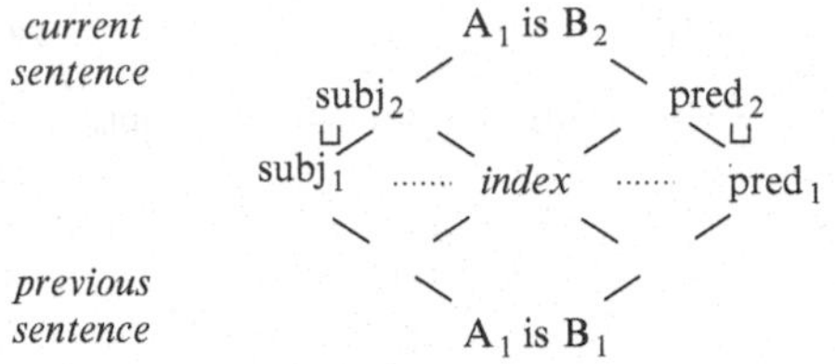

$$
\begin{array}{ccc}
& A_1 \text{ is } B_2 & \\
current & \nearrow \qquad \searrow & \\
sentence & \text{subj}_2 \qquad\qquad \text{pred}_2 & \\
& \sqcup\nearrow \qquad \searrow \qquad \nearrow \qquad \searrow\sqcup & \\
& \text{subj}_1 \cdots\cdots index \cdots\cdots \text{pred}_1 & \\
& \searrow \qquad \nearrow \qquad \searrow \qquad \nearrow & \\
previous & \searrow \qquad \nearrow & \\
sentence & A_1 \text{ is } B_1 &
\end{array}
$$

Figure 9.2: Sample coordinated unification. A pair of subsequent sentences are represented as interpretation moments of a hypothetical phenomenon. The previous sentence is represented in the qualisign ('A_1 is B_1'), rheme (subj_1) and legisign positions (pred_1), the current sentence in the dicent (subj_2), symbol (pred_2) and argument positions ('A_2 is B_2'). Pairwise unification ('$\sqcup$') of the subjects and the predicates is coordinated by the *index*. Dotted lines stand for induced sign interactions

a single position of the processing schema, unification can be realized by means of an accumulation operation (see Sect. 6.1.1). Otherwise, we assume that unification requires the introduction of a context, that enables the realization of a connection between the arguments through binding.[5] As the arguments of a unification operation may arise through interpretive processes in different domains, the potential of our theory to uniformly represent comes in handy.

If a state-transition is possible, the previous and current sentences can be merged in a summarizing single sentence or a *summary*. Otherwise, the current sentence can be interpreted as a nested phenomenon or an 'episode', later intertwining with the nesting phenomenon marked by the previous sentence.[6]

The suggested interpretation of sentences as state-transitions is supported by our language model (see Chapter 6). As the subject and predicate symbols of a sentence arise from the rheme and legisign positions, respectively, through complementation by the index, the rheme can be interpreted as a candidate for the subject and the legisign as a rule-like property constituting the predicate. The index, providing a shared context, coordinates the complementation of the signs in the rheme and legisign positions. Having said this, an algorithm for text summarization can be defined as follows.

First, the input sentences are analyzed syntactically, as well as in the knowledge domains pertinent to the actual summarization process. Second, the text is split into overlapping pairs of subsequent sentences and the sentences are pairwise re-analysed. So, in a summarization event, the first or previous and the second or current sentence of a pair are represented in the qualisign and argument sign positions, respectively. See Fig. 9.2. Next the syntactic rheme, index, and legisign representations of the previous sentence are re-generated, 'bottom-up', and those of the dicent, index, and symbol sign representations of the current sentence are re-generated, 'top-down'. In this preparatory phase the

---

[5] Accumulation and binding are used in a broader sense, as types of sign interaction.

[6] This is a consequence of our assumption that the input text is referring to a single phenomenon that can be represented by a single sign.

representations generated may not define a consistent collection of interpretation moments of an instance of the processing schema. In fact, the generation of such a consistent collection of representations *is* the goal set for text summarization as a process.[7] A unification of signs in the rheme and dicent positions on the one hand, and in the legisign and symbol sign positions on the other hand, can be used to generate the subject and predicate symbols of a summarizing single sentence. This process generates representations that can be used for the definition of qualia of an underlying (summarizing) phenomenon. The summarization of the following pair of sentences may serve as an example.

> John left the house.
> The door closed.

The domains pertinent to the summarization we present below are the domains of 'naive' syntactic, semantic-syntactic and reasoning signs (cf. Sect. 7.7). In the first, syllogistic analysis, comments are added, clarifying the intended meaning of a premise. In the subsequent semantic analysis we show how semantic information processing can be combined with the syllogistic analysis. Unification is designated by a '⊔' symbol. In the syllogistic analysis quantifiers are omitted.

In the sample text above, the syntactic subjects are John and the door (in short door), the predicates are left the house (in short left)[8] and closed. See Fig. 9.3. A unification of John and door is possible (John⊔door), for instance, if we have semantic-syntactic information about the agent's (John) ability to open something and the patient's (door) potential to undergo such an event.

> open *IS* door % the door is open
> John *IS* open % John opened something
> ⇒ John *IS* door % it is John who opened the door

Similarly, a unification of left and closed is possible (left⊔closed), if we have semantic information that left and closed can affect door as a state.

> door *IS* closed % the door is closed
> door *IS* left % somebody left (the house) through that door
> ⇒ left *IS* closed % (the door through which somebody) left (the house)
> % (is the door that somebody) closed

The two unification operations above reveal the existence of a common property (open), possessed by the subjects (cf. deduction), as well as the existence of a common state (door), compatible with the rule-like meaning of the predicates (cf. induction). Summarization is possible if *this* property and state can be interpreted as dual representations of a common context (open/door). If this condition holds, a summarizing single sentence can be generated. In the context specified by the sentence, 'John who opened the door, left the house and the door closed', this facilitates the summary: 'John left (the house)'. Note that in our analysis above we focussed on the agent (John).

---

[7]Interpretation conceived as a 'game' has been illustrated in Sect. 7.6.

[8]The complement of 'left', 'the house', can be represented by a sign in the index position.

```
              /      \
          door  ——  closed          scheme-1        scheme-3
        /  \      /  \ 3
   John ——  open/door  —— left          X  B            C  B
   1    \      /  \      /               A  X            C  X
          \  /      \  /                 A  B            X  B
              \      /
```

Figure 9.3: Sample summarization (left) and a definition of the syllogistic inference schemes used (right). See also Fig. 7.13. Accumulation is designated by a '/' symbol

The above syllogistic analysis can be justified by making use of additional semantic information about the major and minor terms of the premises. A semantic analysis of our text may reveal that John and door can be unified by John, as John can be the agent and door the patient of an open event and that, from a semantic point of view, patient(1)<agent(3) (a trichotomic specification of thematic roles is given later in this chapter). In sum, John (unifier) can be interpreted as 'John who opened the door'. Similarly, semantic information can be used to show that left and closed can be unified by left, representing the property 'left behind a closing door'. Unification is possible, as (door) closing can be interpreted as a measure in the domain of 'leave' effects. By virtue of its indexical content, e.g. the involved direction, left(2) can be more meaningful than closed(1). By revealing that open and door can be interpreted as converse representations of a single phenomenon (see Sect. 6.7.5), we can show that John and door can be unified ('door' can be interpreted as the patient of an 'open' event). Put differently, if we observe an open event, then there can be the occurrence of a door, which is affected by that event.

This closes our analysis of a unification of subjects and predicates. The above results enable the pair of input sentences to be replaced by their summary, 'John left (the house)'. Summarization may proceed however if the sample text is part of a larger discourse.

A potential benefit of an intertwined 'naive' syntactic, semantic-syntactic, and reasoning analysis is the introduction of related signs, enabling further summarization repeatedly. This aspect however is not illustrated by the above example. Note that text summarization may put a great burden on the lexical specification of symbols. An analysis of this aspect of summarization falls outside the focus of our book.

9.3   An extended example

We illustrate our approach with a summarization of the fairy tale "Snow White". See Fig. 9.4. Dialogs occurring in the text, which do not contribute to the generated summary, are removed. Sentences are marked by a letter 's', followed by a hexadecimal number.

SNOW WHITE

(s_0) In a far off land, there lived a very beautiful Queen who had a stepdaughter called Snow White. (s_1) The wicked Queen ordered a servant to take Snow White to the forest and put her to death, but the poor man had not the heart to do it, and told her to hide in the forest. (s_2) Snow White ran into the thickest part of the forest and walked for many long days, until she came upon a tiny little house. (s_3) The Princess thought that in such a lovely place as that, there must live kind people who would give her shelter. (s_4) The house, which at that moment was empty, was in a state of complete disorder. (s_5) The furniture and everything inside was small. (s_6) Snow White cleaned and tidied the little house until it shone. (s_7) Then she lay down exhausted on one of the little beds and fell asleep. (s_8) When she woke up, she found herself surrounded by seven little dwarfs who, on hearing what had happened to her, promised to protect her from her stepmother. (s_9) They were all very happy and contented. (s_A) One day, the Queen, who had heard that Snow White was still alive, disguised herself as an old woman and invited her to try an apple which she had poisoned. (s_B) The Princess was tempted by the lovely apple the old woman was offering her. (s_C) The old woman insisted, assuring her that she had nothing to fear, until at last, she accepted. (s_D) But ... when she bit into the apple, Snow White fell senseless on the ground, and how those dwarfs cried and cried. (s_E) A Prince who was passing by saw the beauty of Snow White and kissed her on the forehead, whereupon she wakened from that bad dream and the dwarfs were happy again. (s_F) Snow White and the Prince married and were happy ever after. (Grimm & Grimm, 1988)

Figure 9.4: Sample text for summarization

Important parameters of summary generation are, amongst others, the perspective taken and the degree of conciseness required. In this section we assume that the focus is on the main character, Snow White, and that the goal of summarization is the derivation of a single catchy sentence, for instance, for a program guide. The price for pushing summarization this far is that other important aspects such as the narrative structure of the text will not be respected by the summary.

In the analysis below, individual summarization steps can be simplified by omitting less meaningful signs in favor of more meaningful ones.[9] As signs in the index position may interact with signs in the rheme and the legisign positions, our representation can be simplified by indicating the reference of an index sign. An arrow pointing to the left ('←') and right ('→') is used to indicate the reference of an index sign to the rheme and the legisign position, respectively. By virtue of their different referential content, index signs can be accumulated typewise.[10] A temporal analysis of the input, e.g. verb-phrases, is left out of consideration. We assume that the order of appearance of the input

---

[9]More meaningful, according to a trichtomic ordering of signs in some knowledge domain.

[10]In Sect. 6.1.1 we used this potential of index signs for a uniform representation of syntactic modification and complementation phenomena.

nouns:
    possible existence < actual reference < conventional function
actual reference:
    general < indefinite < definite
adjectives:
    intersective < subsective compatible < subsective incompatible
verbs:
    existence < modification < transformation
transformation:
    neutral < modulation < change

nouns:
    patient < instrument < agent
nouns:
    unnamed < episodic < title

Figure 9.5: Semantic trichotomies used in the example. The classification of lexical categories is given in an ordering. For instance, general<indefinite<definite represents a classification of referential symbols: general(1), indefinite(2), definite(3). In each trichotomy, the perspective of comparison taken is assumed, but not explicitly mentioned. For instance, in 'adjectives', the perspective used is complexity in nomen–adjective combinations (see Sect. 6.7.6)

sentences and the temporal order associated with their effects are isomorphic. This enables us to summarize subsequent sentences in any order (note that summarized sentences can be replaced by their summary).

In a semantic analysis of verb–complement relations we make use of thematic relations (Fillmore, 1968), (van Valin, 1993). We assume that semantic-syntactic information used in this chapter is lexically defined in trichotomies. Trichotomies used in the example are recapitulated in Fig. 9.5. Stages of summarization are indicated by the label "Step", followed by an integer. Stages used in the example are recapitulated in Fig. 9.13.

A (morpho-)syntactic analysis of the first two sentences of our text, s_0 and s_1, can be found in Appendix E. Interpretation moments of s_0 that play a role in the summarization process described in this section are depicted in Fig. 9.6, those of the first clause of s_1 in Fig. 9.7. Since in that clause the predicate complement itself is realized by a syntactic clause, a summarization of the predicate complement can be postponed.[11] For the time being we assume the verb ordered to function as the predicate of the sentence (this view is also supported by the lexical definition of this symbol as an intransitive verb).[12]

Is a state-transition possible from s_0 to s_1? What can be the summary of this transition? In order to answer these questions we have to analyse the relation between the rheme, index, and legisign positions of s_0 on the one hand, and the dicent, index, and symbol sign positions of s_1 on the other (through their common reference (Queen), the symbols wicked, very beautiful and who had... can be merged into a single sign in the index position). See also the diagram in Fig. 9.8 on the left-hand side.

---

[11] In our model, clauses and sentences are treated in a uniform fashion.
[12] Note the tacit use of the syntactic trichotomy: intransitive<transitive<ditransitive.

Figure 9.6: Signs of s_0 (previous sentence) for summarization with s_1 (current sentence). Who had... is short for who had a stepdaughter called Snow White

Figure 9.7: Signs of the first clause of s_1 (current sentence), preceding their summarization with s_0 (previous sentence)

Step 1

A unification of the subjects may proceed as follows. A Queen (rheme) and the wicked Queen (dicent) can be unified by the Queen as, following an ordering of nouns as actual reference signs, in Fig. 9.5, a(2)<the(3), implying that the indefinite reference of the article symbol can be removed. According to a trichotomic characterization of adjectives as intersective, subsective compatible, and subsective incompatible (cf. Sect. 6.7.6), the index expressions, wicked(1) and very beautiful(1), are less meaningful than who had a stepdaughter called Snow White(2) (in short who had...), enabling those meaningful adjectives to be ignored.

A unification of the predicates obtains the sign ordered, as, according to a trichotomy of verbs, in Fig. 9.5, lived(1) can be classified as an act of existence and ordered(2) as a modification of a state[13] (in both events, Queen's thematic function is actor). Summarization is possible, by virtue of the index expression, who had..., coordinating the above unifications of the subjects and predicates.[14] This is depicted by the right-hand side diagram in Fig. 9.8. In the index position the sign, in a far off land, can be removed, as it does not change the interpretation of lived as an existence(1) event.

Step 2

The complement of ordered contains embedded clauses, enabling further summarization.[15] To this end we make use of a classification of verbs as transformation(3) events: neutral<modulation<change, representing a neutral (e.g. told

---

[13]In the current analysis, ordered is considered to be an intransitive verb. This is opposed to its interpretation as a transitive verb, in Table E.7 (which may explain the representation of ordered in the legisign (ord), not the symbol sign position).

[14]who had... can be interpreted as an appearing property (effect) as well as the actor (state) of an event.

[15]In this part of the analysis, ordered is interpreted as a transitive verb.

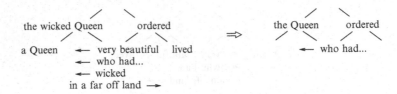

Figure 9.8: Signs of s_0 and s_1 (left) and their summarization (right)

Figure 9.9: Combined coordination and summarization. The complement of ordered, which is a servant to take Snow White to the forest and put her to death, is coordinated (but) with the clause the poor man had not the heart to do it, and told her to hide in the forest

her), a reversible (e.g. take her to the forest), and an irreversible transformation (e.g. put her to death). See also Fig. 9.5. In the analysis below we tacitly assume the existence of a trichotomy of preposition–complement signs (cf. Sect. 6.4), which can be specified analogously to the above classification of verbs as 'transformation' acts.

Step 3

A summarization of the complement of ordered, which is the coordination structure to take Snow White to the forest and put her to death, may proceed as follows (see also Fig. 9.9). Coordination and summarization can be elaborated simultaneously. As to take(2) and to put(2) are both reversible transformation events, but their modifications by to the forest and to death are semantically different (to the forest(2)<to death(3)), the first conjunct, to take Snow White to the forest, can be removed. The resulting expression, (to) put her to death, can be summarized with the second conjunct of but. This requires a unification of the subjects (servant and the man) and the predicates (to put her to death and had not the heart...). The unification of the subjects obtains the sign the servant, because the coordination (but) does not affect the interpretation of the subjects. The index sign, poor, which does not refer to a lexically defined semantic relation of the servant, can be removed.

A unification of the predicates may proceed as follows. Since told her...(1) is a neutral transformation event, it can be removed. Coordination of the predicates obtains: to put her to death, but had not the heart to do it. By making use of the trichotomy of verbs as transformation events, this enables the introduction of the order relation: had not the heart to do it(2)<put to death(3). Indeed, the first conjunct can be interpreted as an intention of a certain reversible change

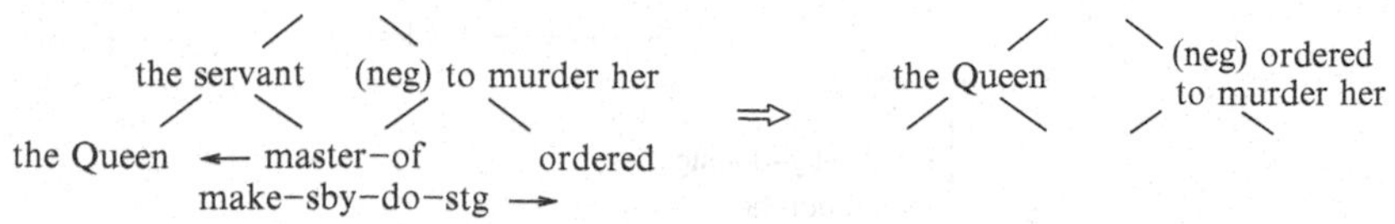

Figure 9.10: Summarization of s_0 and s_1 (cont.)

or 'modulation' of a state (for example, the emotional status of an actor), as opposed to the second conjunct, which can be associated with the effect of an irreversible change. Since the negative content of 'but' can be treated as syntactic complementation by negation ('neg'), and, because put to death can be paraphrased as murder (her is a reference to Snow White) and it is anaphorically linked with the first conjunct, summarization of the predicates eventually obtains: '(neg) to murder her'.

Step 4

The resulting expression of the complement of ordered, which is a non-finite syntactic clause with an explicit subject, can be interpreted as a proposition (argument position). A summarization of this clause and the result of the earlier summarization of s_0 and s_1 (see Fig. 9.8) is depicted in Fig. 9.10 (the sign who had..., which does not refer to a lexically defined relation of the Queen, is omitted in the index position). Summarization is possible if the subjects (the Queen and the servant) and the predicates (ordered and murder her) can be pairwise unified and a common context coordinating the two unification operations exists. The Queen and the servant can be unified (the Queen⊔the servant) as the Queen can be the master of the servant (we assume master of to be a lexically defined semantic relation of Queen). As a result, master of can be introduced as a new sign in the index position. See Fig. 9.10.

At this point, summarization can make use of a trichotomic classification of thematic roles: patient(1), instrument(2), agent(3). Because the Queen is the agent and the servant the patient of ordered and this verb links its agent (the Queen) with its theme ((neg)to murder her) through its patient (servant), we may draw the conclusion that the mediating sign (servant), that could be introduced in the index position, can be omitted. Put differently, by using ordered's potential to 'make somebody do something' (in short, make-sby-do-stg), the Queen can be exposed as the 'master mind' or the real actor behind the murder event. As a result of summarization, the above potential of order for mediation can be represented by a complementary sign in the index position (make-sby-do-stg).

A summary can be generated if the context used in the unification of the subjects is compatible with the context used in the unification of the predicates. That this condition can be satisfied too, is explained below.

In the unification of the predicates we may capitalize on the 'naive' induction involved in *complementation* (cf. Sect. 7.2.1). The representation of ordered in the legisign position is based on an interpretation of this verb as a measure in the domain of 'ordering'-effects. That measure, indicated by make-sby-do-stg (index

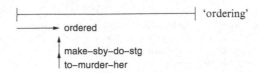

Figure 9.11: The verb 'ordered' interpreted as a measure in the domain of 'ordering' effects. The continuity that constitutes the domain is realized by a dense domain represented by a set of stored values. In this example, the actual measure is associated with the symbols 'make-sby-do-stg' and 'to-murder-her'

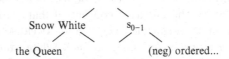

Figure 9.12: Final summarization step

position), can be represented by the event, ordered to murder her (see Fig. 9.11). From here on, summarization of the predicates, ordered and (neg)to murder her, follows trivially. The index expressions used in the unification operations above are compatible with each other, because master-of and to-make-sby-do-stg can be interpreted as synonymous signs which are semantic counterparts (cf. converse sign in Sect. 6.7.5). In the end, the summarization process may generate the subject and the predicate of a summary: the Queen and (neg) ordered to murder her, respectively. As ordered can be interpreted as a transformation(3) event and neg as a reference to the denial of an event, the predicate can be expressed by means of the converse expression of failure: failed. Finally, the above interpretation of neg can be merged with ordered, by means of syntactic coordination: (s_{0-1}) The Queen ordered to murder her, but it failed (note the use of it as a reference to murder).

Further summarization is possible by interpreting the title of the text as an incomplete clause, the predicate of which is defined by the tale itself: s_{0-1} (see Fig. 9.12). A unification of the Queen and Snow White needs a trichotomy of roles realized by personages of a story, for instance: unnamed(1), episodic(2), title(3). Since the predicate of s_{0-1} can be interpreted as a measure of an 'ordering'-effect ((to) murder her), and to murder (event) can be represented by its counterpart sign, the noun murder, the final summary can be expressed by the sentence:

Snow White: A murder failed

An overview of the summarization process is given in Fig. 9.13. Interestingly, the above sentence may function as the summary of the entire text as well. An analysis of the rest of the tale shows that the remaining sentences do not affect the above summary (assuming the focus of summarization is invariantly on Snow White). Indeed, when the Queen discovers that the servant was disloyal to her, she begins her 'apple project', that eventually fails as well.

A summarization of the remaining sentences may proceed as follows. Below we restrict our presentation to an overview of the summarization steps. A

9.3 An extended example

Step 1

A very beautiful Queen lived who had ... ⊔ The wicked Queen ordered

⇒ {wicked(1), very beautiful(1) < who had ...(2); lived(1)<ordered(2)}

The Queen ordered

Step 2

a servant to take Snow White to the forest and put her to death,
but the poor man had not the heart to do it, and told her to hide in the forest.

⇒ {take(2)=put(2), to the forest(2)<to death(3); put to death=murder;
but='neg'; told(1)<had not the heart(2)<put her to death(3)}

a servant (neg) to murder her

Step 3

The Queen ordered ⊔ a servant (neg) to murder her

⇒ {servant(1)<Queen(3); ordered(1)<ordered to murder her(2); 'neg'=but it failed}

The Queen ordered to murder her, but it failed.

Step 4

The Queen ordered to murder her, but it failed ⊔ Snow White: <entire text>

⇒ {Queen(2)<Snow White(3); to murder her=a murder}

Snow White: A murder failed

Figure 9.13: An overview of the stages of summarization. Conditions used in a summarization step are given in curly brackets. Unification is designated by an infix '⊔' symbol

state-transition is designated by a '⇒' symbol. Expressions generated by the summarization are labeled by the sentences involved. For example, the summary of s_2 and s_3 is labeled by s_{2-3}.

s_2: Snow white ran into the forest denotes the beginning of a new episode. This sentence can be summarized with s_3, assuming that Snow White and the Princess can be interpreted as identical persons. $s_2 \Rightarrow s_3$: (s_{2-3}) Snow White ran into the forest and thought.... The sentence s_4 also marks the beginning of a new episode. Since, in the summarization of s_2, house (index position) can be removed, the entire sentence s_4 can be ignored. Because the possibility to summarize s_5 depends on s_4, that sentence can be removed as well.

$s_{2-3} \Rightarrow s_6$: (s_{2-6}) Snow White ran into the forest and cleaned and tidied (some) house. s_7: She lay down and fell asleep. $s_{2-6} \Rightarrow s_7$: (s_{2-7}) Snow White ran...and lay down and fell asleep. s_8: She found herself.... $s_{2-7} \Rightarrow s_8$: (s_{2-8}) Snow White ran...and lay down...and fell asleep and found herself.... s_9: They were.... As the dwarfs (referred to by they) have been removed in s_8, the entire sentence of s_9 can be ignored.

s_A: The Queen disguised herself and invited her to try an apple. $s_{0-1} \Rightarrow s_A$: ($s_{0-1,A}$) The Queen ordered...but it failed, and disguised herself.... Assuming that her refers

163

to Snow White, the stories of the Queen and Snow White can be merged by means of the element of linking involved in the event, 'invited'. As a result, all events that only refer to one of the personages, such as ran and found herself, can be removed. $s_{0-1,A} \Rightarrow s_{2-8}$: ($s_{0-A}$) The Queen invited Snow White to try an apple (here also we tacitly assume that her is referring to Snow White).

s_B: The Princess was tempted.... This sentence can be summarized with s_{0-A}, but it will not have an effect on the summary so far. s_C: The woman insisted. This sentence too can be merged with s_{0-A} and, again, there will be no change in the summary. s_D: Snow White bit...and fell. As the dwarfs have been ignored in s_8, they can be omitted in this sentence too. $s_{0-A} \Rightarrow s_D$: (s_{0-D}) The Queen invited Snow White to try an apple and Snow White bit into the apple and fell.

s_E: A Prince saw Snow White and she wakened from (a) dream. This sentence marks the beginning of a new episode. s_F: Snow White and Prince married. $s_E \Rightarrow s_F$: (s_{E-F}) A Prince saw Snow White and they married.

Finally we have two sentences: s_{0-D} and s_{E-F}, which can be combined into a single sentence through reasoning. By taking the first part of s_{0-D} (Snow White bit into the apple and fell) as the first or major premise, and using information about the apple (which she (Queen) had poisoned) as the second or minor premise, we can deduce that Snow White could have been poisoned. As a poisoned person (who fell) must be dead, we can infer that Snow White must be dead as well. However, according to s_{E-F}, which occurs later than s_{0-D}, Snow White gets married. From this we may infer that Snow White must be alive. Assuming poisoning is a lexically defined counterpart of murder, we get again: (s_{0-F}) a murder failed.

9.4   Conclusion

This chapter introduces a blueprint for a systematic approach to text summarization. The proposed technique makes beneficial use of the potential of the process model to uniformly represent knowledge in different domains as well as to trichotomously specify signs.

The sample text, "Snow White", is commonly known and almost everybody is able to recapitulate its meaning in a few sentences. The summary generated in this chapter may be different from that, by virtue of the specific goal set for summarization, which is the generation of a single catchy sentence. Nevertheless the results illustrate the theoretical potential of our approach, which was our major goal. A practical realization of the proposed method requires the development of suitable lexicons, consisting of a trichotomic specification of signs in the domains of interest.

Chapter 10

Reflexive analysis

Our assumption that knowledge arises from observations of phenomena enables us to summarize our book in a unique way. Since knowledge representation itself can be perceived as an appearing problem or phenomenon, the theory of this book can be applied to itself, reflexively. Accordingly, the goal of this final chapter is to suggest that the chapters of this book can be interpreted as events in a process that aims at conceptualization of knowledge representation as a phenomenon.

10.1 A meta-theory of knowledge representation

As part of the reflexive analysis we re-visit the chapters of our book in the order of presentation, and characterize their contribution from the perspective of the book as a whole. The resulting classification is depicted in Fig. 10.1. We associate characteristic concepts with the different sign aspects. For instance, the concept 'relation' with the legisign position. Besides that we provide imputed concepts in bold-face. For example, the concept imputed by 'relation' is 'logic'.

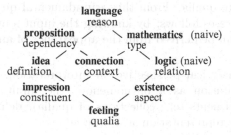

Figure 10.1: A meta-level analysis of knowledge representation as a process

Ch. 1–3: Signs and interpretative processes

Because interpretation is intimately tied up with signs, if we are interested in the properties of signification, we best approach it by studying sign processes. According to Peirce, a sign stands for something other than itself. That which the sign stands for, Peirce calls the sign's object. Since phenomena are inter-actions, and interactions involve duality, it follows that phenomena interpreted as signs must involve duality as well. The duality involved in signs and the teleological nature of interpretation (i.e., the compelling need for completeness) are the grounds for our model of interpretive processes.

In perception phenomena appear as qualia. Sign processing takes qualia as potential signs (representamina) in order to interpret their impact. For our attempt to apply the processing model to the phenomenon of knowledge representation this means that uninterpreted knowledge elements (cf. feeling or information) appear as qualia. In the first stage the qualia are to be sorted into more meaningful units (icon, terms) and their existence (sinsign) in the domain to be covered is to be admitted. Since, however, a real process of interpretation always initiates on a sheet in its actual modality (S_S^A), the potentially relevant signs must be present in the primordial soup on which the book runs its interpretation process. To ensure that the primordial soup is relevant for the goal set, is the task of the introductory chapters.

Qualisign = qualia, **feeling**

Ch. 4: A world of signs

Phenomena can be interpreted from different perspectives. As interpretation is always related to some relevant aspect(s) of a phenomenon, not to all aspects, representations are always approximations of the full meaning of phenomena.

By looking at input phenomena (which are interactions, hence a duality) from the viewpoint of knowledge representation, we may conclude that the co-occurrence of two types of input qualia, state and effect, conveys information about a change (impression). This change enables us to interpret effect qualia with respect to state qualia. From this a fundamental question for the study of information processes follows: by knowing the input state (which is a sign), what information can be derived from the appearance of an input effect (which is another sign)?

Following an analytical perspective on interpretation, we can say that in knowledge representation as a phenomenon, the input stands for the co-occurrence of constituents (cf. collections of qualia), defining the immediate object of knowledge representation as a process.

Icon = constituent, **impression**

Ch. 5: Perception and cognition

According to our theory, information processing can be subdivided into two processes, perception and cognition. These processes can be modeled by isomorphic instances of the processing schema. The goal of perception is an analysis of input qualia in themselves; the goal of cognition is to establish a relation between those perceived qualia.

We raised the hypothesis that the processing schema can be uniformly applied to the modeling of information processing in different knowledge domains. What distinguishes those domains is the perspective from which we look (aspect). Phenomena, for instance, can be interpreted from a logical, a (morpho-)syntactic, and a semantic-syntactic perspective. In this sense, what is deemed existent in a domain depends on the perspective taken.

In knowledge representation as a process, the actual perspective taken can be interpreted as an appearing property (cf. actual event).

> Sinsign   =   aspect, **existence**

Whatever the perspective from which we represent, a relation between sign and object is always involved. This relational aspect of knowledge representation is generalized in the habitual production of relations. This is what we called 'naive' logic. By offering a logical analysis of the processing schema, we revealed 'naive' logic as a process or a 'term procedure' (cf. term algebra) that generates Boolean logical expressions on two variables.

> Legisign   =   relation, 'naive' **logic**
> Index   =   Boolean logic, process

By capturing an abstract relation between qualia (idea), 'naive' logic represents knowledge as a combinatory property or a relational potential of the involved phenomena. This is akin to a lexical definition of symbols. From the point of view of knowledge representation as a process, the combinatory potential of input qualia (which are signs) is abstracted in the concept of (immediate) interpretant or rheme.

> Rheme   =   definition, **idea**

Ch. 6: Language signs

Natural language is one of the few knowledge domains in which a lexical specification of combinatory properties can be available. In order to model language processing, we introduced a sequential version of the processing schema. We applied the revised model to morpho-syntactic and syntactic symbols. By offering an analysis of semantic symbol processing we revealed the need for a dual representation of memory qualia, as an average value (state) and a measure of a dense domain (effect).

By making use of Peirce's categorical schema, we introduced a trichotomic specification of combinatory properties in different domains. For the existence of semantic trichotomies in human language processing, we found experimental evidence in psycholinguistic research of nomen-adjective combinations.

In knowledge representation as a process, relations involved in signs are abstracted in combinatory needs (that define the relational possibilities for connections between signs) and in rules (that express the conditions for the constituents of sign-sign relations).

Legisign = 'naive' language, **combinatory rules**
Rheme   = relational need, **lexical definition**
Index   = average, domain, trichotomy

Ch. 7: Reasoning signs

Following a 'naive' logical interpretation of our model, we offered an analysis of the processing schema from the perspective of 'naive' reasoning. The results reinforced our conjecture that higher level information processing as well can be modeled by means of our theory.

From the stance of knowledge representation as a process, the introduction of a model of 'naive' reasoning revealed the potential of signs to function as a premise in deductive, inductive, and abductive 'naive' logical inferencing.

Legisign = 'naive' reasoning, **inference rules**
Index   = deduction, induction, abduction

Ch. 8: Mathematical signs

Besides natural language and 'naive' logic, another important knowledge domain is 'naive' mathematics or the domain of number symbols. Justified by experimental evidence that cardinality originates in qualia, we introduced a model for 'naive' mathematical information processing. As cardinality arises in the brain, not in the senses, we suggested that 'naive' mathematical processing is based on abductive reasoning.

An analysis of mathematical concepts, such as infinite and naught, revealed the potential of memory signs to represent types (cf. prototypes). From the perspective of knowledge representation as a process, types delineate conventional properties involved in phenomena. The close relationship between 'naive' reasoning and mathematics is illustrated with an account of mathematical induction as an instance of 'naive' reasoning.

Symbol = 'naive' mathematics, **type**

Ch. 9: Text summarization

Uniform knowledge representation can be beneficial for text summarization, by virtue of its potential to merge knowledge in different domains in a single representation, by means of structural coordination. An important element of our approach to text summarization is an interpretation of sentences as state-transitions. State-transitions induced by a series of sentences can be summarized in a single transition, transforming the initial state involved in the first sentence into the final state represented by the last one. The proposed summarization algorithm makes extensive use of trichotomic specifications of signs, in which the trichotomies are used as order relations.

We capitalize on an interpretation of sentences (argument position) as subject–predicate relations (dicent and symbol position). From the point of view of knowledge representation, as a process, the dicent position is an expression of a proposition about a structural relation or (f)actual dependency between (input) qualia. This is opposed to the argument position, which is an expression of a proposition or premise in a process of communication. Communication is related to reason. As, basically, all signs are symbolical hence involve consensus, sign interpretation and so knowledge representation is inherently related to the languages native to any sense, including the inner sense which is the seat of natural language.

> Dicent   =   dependency, **proposition**
> Argument   =   reason, **language**

Ch. 10: Reflexive analysis

In the current, final chapter, we offer an analysis of our theory itself. In order to simplify the presentation of results (see also Fig. 10.2), we introduce labels for classes of concepts associated with positions of the processing schema. For instance, concepts introduced in the index position, such as 'Boolean logic', 'process', 'memory model', etc., referring to background knowledge, are represented by the term 'context'. In conformity with the potential of the above notions to signify a link between input and memory information, the imputed meaningful concept at the index position is called **connection**.

The classification depicted in Fig. 10.2 can be interpreted as a sign interpretation process, as follows. The input for knowledge representation as a process is an interaction between an interpreting system occurring in some state, and a stimulus. The interaction appears as a feeling.

Sorting transforms the input feeling to a constituency relation involved in the input (impression), and also to a simultaneity relation involved in the co-existence of the input qualia. This latter relation offers an interpretation of the input from a certain perspective (aspect).

Abstraction has two interpretations, which can be explained by means of relative difference operations. The first, '*constituent\aspect =definition*' represents the constituents of interpretation, irrespective of the actual perspective

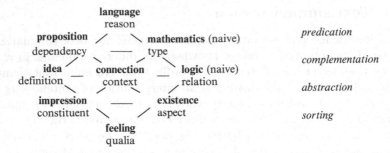

Figure 10.2: A meta-level analysis of knowledge representation as an interpretation process (cf. Fig. 10.1). A horizontal line denotes a sign interaction, a diagonal one a representation relation. Operations associated with involved sign interactions are indicated on the right-hand side of the diagram

of interpretation taken, as pure combinatory needs; this is akin to a lexical definition of a term capturing its meaning as just an idea. The second, '*aspect/constituent=relation*' represents the input interaction as a logical dependency or rule, irrespective of the nature of the actual constituents of the interaction.

Complementation has two instances as well. The first is an expression of the constituent input signs as actually existent entities in context. To this end, the knowledge representation process takes the abstract (lexical) *definition* of the input signs and puts them in the current context. The duality involved in signs is represented as a *dependency* relation or structure. The second instance of complementation represents the rule-like compatibility *relation* between the input signs in a context, thereby generalizing the involved interpretation aspect in the concept of *type*.

Predication represents knowledge as a proposition of a *dependency* relation, by means of the involved conventional property or *type*. The existence of such a *sentence* is an expression of completeness (from a certain point of view) of knowledge representation as a process. Other examples of completeness are syntactic wellformedness (in natural language processing), and the successive generation of all Boolean expressions on two variables (in a 'naive' logical interpretation). From the perspective of knowledge representation as a process, the final proposition is an expression of a *reason* for the interpretation of the input (potential sign) as a (meaningful) sign.

The concepts displayed in Fig. 10.1 can be arranged in trichotomies, in two different ways (the induced order relations are denoted by a '<' symbol).

I. As 'phenomenological dependencies' (how signs can appear):[1]

   (1)   feeling < impression < idea
   (2)   existence < connection < proposition
   (3)   logic < mathematics < language

---

[1] The ordering, logic<mathematics<language, refers to a relation between a 'naive' interpretation of these domains. According to Peirce, (full) mathematics precedes (full) logic.

II. as 'ontological dependencies' (how signs can mediate):

  (1)   qualia < aspect < relation
  (2)   constituent < context < type
  (3)   definition < dependency < reason.

The above 'phenomenological' and 'ontological' trichotomies of sign aspects correspond to the two 'dimensions' Peirce used to characterize his nine sign aspects. Briefly, the phenomenological type of a sign can be firstness, secondness or thirdness, depending on the category exhibited by the sign. The ontological type of a sign can be a first, a second, or a third, depending on the category associated with the mediation (event) realized by the sign (Liszka, 1996).

An indispensable element of knowledge representation is the underlying paradigmatic view of knowledge. According to the view suggested in this book, knowledge arises from interactions that reveal themselves as events in our experience of change. In Peircean terms, signs (interaction) mediate their objects (change) to their interpretants (event). This 'triangular' relation of sign, object and interpretant characterizes the entire process of interpretation as well as its individual events. As for the entire process, interpretation generates a reaction (interpretant) from the feeling appearing as a 'primordial soup' (sign). As for the individual events of this process, the interaction of a pair of proto-signs (cf. sign aspects), functioning as sign and object, is interpreted by a more developed proto-sign. In a degenerate representation of such an event, a proto-sign, functioning as ground, is analyzed in a sign and an object, which are involved. A 'triangular' picture of the processing schema is depicted in Fig. 10.3, on the left-hand side. A pair of degenerate and genuine representations can be combined in a quadrangle, generating an interpretant from a proto-sign (ground), through the mediation of the interaction of an involved sign and object pair. The processing schema as a collection of quadrangles is given in Fig. 10.3, on the right-hand side.

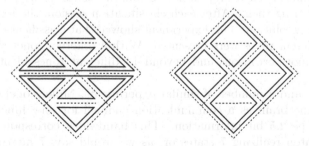

Figure 10.3: The processing schema as a structure of triangles (left) and quadrangles (right). A triangle represents the constituents of a genuine sign interpretation (see e.g. the positions rheme, index, dicent), or those of a degenerate sign interaction (see e.g. the positions qualisign, sinsign, icon). A quadrangle is defined by a pair of triangles connected by a mediating sign interaction

10.2 Potential cognitive relevance

In the previous pages we incidentally referred to evidence found in cognitive research. Although we cannot prove that our theory provides a naturalistic account of how we, humans, process information, it is tempting to explore the question. The remark that has to be made beforehand is that drawing a full analogy between human cognitive processes and our model is feasible only if we include the human capacity to learn something new, while the computational approach advocated thus far only covers habitual or 'already learned' cognitive behavior.

The tasks differ as building a concept car from scratch[2] differs from assembling a car on a production line. In the latter case all the parts are known. They are known in themselves, but foremost with respect to their place in the assembly process and in the final product. On top of that, if incidentally a part proves to be missing, an embedded-process is initiated in order to obtain it. In case of regular production lines this subprocess has the same general characteristics as the embedding process. Presently we stick to assembly-like or habitual information processing. Note that we assume that in habitual interpretation a fit of the combinatory needs at all positions is sufficient for an acceptance of the result of the process.

Since the point of departure for our model is not brain tissue but our mind at the moment some qualia are knocking at its door, a natural point of departure for our short detour is our working memory.

Channel Capacity of working memory

In an early paper, Miller reported experiments that measured the capacity of the immediate memory (Miller, 1956), nowadays known as 'working memory'. In this article, Miller considered the brain as a communication channel: he examined the effect of input growth on the reliability of the output. In one of the experiments, listeners were asked to identify tones between 100 Hz and 8 kHz by numbering them. After each classification session, the test person was told the correct solution. This experiment showed that classification was precise when 2-3 different tones were presented. With 4 different tones the result was increasingly more erroneous and beyond 14 different tones identification was very bad.

From this and a number of similar experiments, Miller concluded that the capacity of the brain as a communication channel for one dimensional judgments could be 2.5 bit information. This bandwidth corresponds to a finite state automaton realizing 7 states or, as we would say, 7 interpretation moments approximately. This capacity is invariant, whether the entities are simple (e.g. simple words) or complex (e.g. large numbers). Broadbent, who repeated Miller's experiment fifteen years later, writes (Broadbent, 1975):

---

[2]Note that making a concept car nowadays is far less demanding with respect to learning, than doing the same at a time preceding the invention of the steam engine or, for that matter, the discovery of the principle of the wheel.

> Human processing is limited to handle a fixed number, say 7, inde-
> pendent units at one time. Each unit could nevertheless be divided
> into sub-units so that facts and actions of enormous complexity could
> be handled by calling up a fresh ensemble of sub-units at each stage
> when it became necessary.

The hypothesis about the size of the working memory can be interpreted in the context of the theory of this book as follows. According to our model, sign interpretation consists of nine types of interpretation moments. The first or qualisign position represents the input as a collection of qualia. In human cognition, however, such qualia, which are only a potential for interpretation by the mind, are stored outside the working memory. The last interpretation moment, the argument position, represents the output of the process. If the output generates signals for motor control, such signs fall outside the recognition process and can be stored in brain areas dedicated to motor control. If used in a subsequent or future process, the output enters a subsequent process by triggering a change in the qualisign position.

In sum, the proposed model has seven interpretation moments that have to be 'remembered' during input processing. This number fits nicely with the Miller–Broadbent conjecture about the span of the working memory.

It should be mentioned that, according to their conjecture, the working memory may simultaneously contain seven independent, one-dimensional infor-mation units. As, in our model, all interpretation moments are representations of a single input, they are not independent. This is not the case in text summa-rization, for instance, in which expressions, representing different perspectives of a hypothetical phenomenon, have to be combined in a single interpretation process.

Chunking

According to Miller, there are several ways to overcome the limit of seven units or 2.5 bit information for unidimensional, absolute judgments, set by the channel capacity of the working memory:

(1) to use relative instead of absolute judgments

(2) to use multi-dimensional instead of uni-dimensional judgment

(3) to arrange a task in such a way that several judgments are put in a row, increasing the information of the judgments along the way.

Miller adds a comment to possibility (3) when he states that it turns memory into a handmaiden of the working memory and that there are many ways to recode input in such a way that the manifold is brought to a manageable unity. For our present purpose the third suggestion is of particular interest because our process model provides a procedure for the formation of a judgment; in that sense we specified the model for chunking procedures.

Miller and Broadband concentrated on capacity measurements and looked at the working memory as an information channel, but more recent work on the working memory goes into more detail by asking what other processes are running on it. Some suggestions of processes performed in working memory are:

(1) active maintenance of ordered information for short periods of time

(2) context relevant updating of information

(3) rapid biasing (control) of task-relevant cognitions and behaviors in the service of active goals (Hassina, Bargh, Engell, & McCulloch, 2009).

Interestingly enough, the research on working memory provides a means to investigate the question whether indeed the model we propose for interpretation processes provides a naturalistic account of what we do. Below we sketch the direction of what ought to be done to settle the question.

Possible measurement of the model

Since the number of states of our model and the number of states necessary for the realization of the working memory as an automaton are equal, it must be possible to match the positions (interpretation moments) of our model to brain tissue in the basal ganglia.[3] Since it is possible to measure activation of brain tissue during information processing by making use of suitable experimental procedures,[4] a difference between matching and analysis mode operation can be established.[5] In matching mode operation, we expect less activation in tissue corresponding to functions typical for the 'icon', 'sinsign', 'dicent' and 'symbol sign' positions in our model. By making use of characteristic properties associated with positions in the processing schema, predictions can be derived from our model and experimentally tested. One of the predictions is this. In analysis mode operation, we should observe more intensive data transfer between 'rheme' tissue and cortex (this as a consequence of the need to select a fitting element) than between 'legisign' tissue and cortex. This prediction is a consequence of the difference in properties of the rheme and legisign positions: the rheme is an expression of a 'range of possibilities', while the legisign is an expression of 'habitual' interpretation.[6]

What makes measurement of our theory important is the answer it provides to the conjecture that the processing schema captures the events of cognitive activity, thus can be interpreted as the 'program' of information processing.

---

[3]The basal ganglia (striatum, globus pallidus, subthalamic nucleus, substantia nigra) is interconnected with the sensory systems and the neocortex. Specifically, the anterior portion of the frontal lobes projects to the head of the caudate nucleus (amygdala) whereas the more posterior putamen receives converging and overlapping input from the primary and secondary motor and somesthetic cortices. See also (Joseph, 2000).

[4]See (Melrose, Poulin, & Stern, 2007).

[5](Shen, Lin, & de Wilde, 2008) experimentally showed the existence of the Hebb's cycle (reverberating circuits), thereby giving evidence for two possible modes of information processing by the brain: 'meaningful', and 'automatic' (in our proposal we make a link between these modes and the two operation modes of our process model: 'analysis' and 'matching').

[6]Recent research presented in (Cohen, Elger, & Weber, 2008) reveals the existence of the above two modes of information processing by the brain, by showing an analogous difference in information flow between the amygdala and the orbitofrontal cortex, and between the amygdala and the hippocampus.

10.3 Conclusions

This chapter illustrates that the theory introduced in this book can be applied to itself reflexively. Our analysis reveals that the order of presentation of the various topics is not arbitrary, but dictated by the dependencies between them, as events in an interpretation process.

Properties of the model

The possibility to reflexively apply our theory reinforces the conjecture that the proposed model of knowledge representation could indeed be generic. The uniform representation enables knowledge in different domains to be merged in a single representation by means of structural coordination.

The representation is robust. Adjustments demanded by the need to cope with new phenomena in a domain can be reduced to adjustments of the lexicon; the processing algorithm can be used invariantly.

The close relationship between Peirce's sign aspects and his categorical scheme enables the definition of lexical entries in a systematic fashion, by a trichotomic specification of combinatory properties.

Conjectures

Paradigmatic differences between our theory and traditional approaches of knowledge representation make a full comparision difficult. In our view the proposed model will reveal its usefulness in dealing with complex tasks that require a simultaneous interpretation of knowledge pertaining to different domains. By virtue of the need to make translations between different representations, such a task can be computationally too complex for traditional modeling.

Following the theory that human information processing must be characterized as a process, we conjecture that, if the computational process respects the properties of cognitive activity, information generated by the computer can be more easily processed by humans. Preliminary evidence is provided by a few experiments (Couwenberg, 2007), (Draskovic et al., 2010), (Klomp, 2008).

An important aspect of knowledge representation, learning, is not in the focus of this book. In our view information processing and learning can be considered to be independent, enabling our theory to be combined with any algorithm for learning (Bishop, 2006).

Present and future research

In our current research the focus is on the development of a procedure that tests the possible neuro-physiological reality of our model. We are also interested in a computational implementation of our knowledge representation. An application of our knowledge representation in problem specification and for modeling information processing in organizations is on our agenda as well (van Breemen, 2010).

Up until now our approach provides insight into the potential contribution of the sign to its interpretation as meaningful (cf. the ten classes of signs). Future refinements are possible by analyzing and modeling the actual and the habitual contributions. For the sake of completeness we end with the remark that already in the writings of Peirce corresponding attempts are made resulting in the conclusion that there must be 28 and 66 sign classes, respectively. We believe that the 'Knowledge in Formation' model derived in the Introduction (see below) is sufficiently rich to enable the completion of this plan.

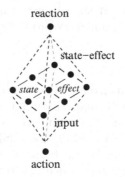

Appendix A

The Peircean categorical schema

Since Aristotle wrote his Categories, philosophers have been searching for the most general categories in which all that is, can be caught. Merriam-Webster defines category in its first meaning as: "any of several fundamental and distinct classes to which entities or concepts belong." Since the categories have to be fundamental and distinct, it will be clear that only those classes that can not be reduced to other classes are candidate for inclusion in the list of most fundamental categories.

The history of thought about categories is a complex one. So every summary is bound to distort. That being said, in general one could say there is a tendency that can be nicely illustrated with three philosophers: Aristotle (384–322 BC), Immanuel Kant (1724–1804) and Ch. S. Peirce (1839–1914). Aristotle was the least critical of the three about the distinction between the object on the one hand and our knowledge of objects on the other. So, he tended to look at the task as a matter of finding out the most general concepts needed to class the entities. He drew up a list of ten categories by means of which all that possibly exists can be sorted out. The categories are: Substance, Quantity, Quality, Relation, Place, Date, Posture, State, Action, and Passion.

With Kant critical philosophy came into full swing; objects in themselves (Ding an sich) were regarded as unknowable. As a consequence he concentrated on the concepts by which we know objects as they appear to us. His table of categories is based on a sorting out of all the kinds of judgments (posed propositions). According to him it can be asked of every judgment what its Quality, its Quantity, its Relation and its Modality is. Each of these main categories is sub-divided threefold:

Quantity:	universal, particular, singular
Quality:	affirmative, negative, infinite
Relation:	categorical, hypothetical, disjunctive
Modality:	problematic, assertoric, apodictic

So, all judgments can be classified by giving a score on the sub-division for each of the main categorical distinctions.

C.S. Peirce started his quest for the most fundamental categories as an attempt to simplify the list Kant provided, however without having to conclude that objects in themselves remain out of the reach of our knowledge. For in the end that comes down to the statement that there is a reality that, in principle, is unknowable. He did acknowledge that we will always have to work with what we know, however false that may be, but, so he assumed, reality will keep forcing itself upon us and in the end, provided we stick to the scientific method, our errors will be corrected. This take on the problem opens up new possibilities with regard to our conception of objects.

For most of us the concept of object is associated with things of which we gain knowledge through our senses, that is through perception. But how to look at consistency, the idea of justice or the mathematical straight line? Do they not count as objects because in the end we do not perceive them through our senses? Some have drawn that conclusion, but not Peirce; he drew a radically different one. Being an object to him is being resistant to what we individually think. The element of resistance here is more important than the idea of materiality and sense perception. This does not mean that he discarded perception –it is an element even in abstract thought– but it does entail that for Peirce experience must complement perception in order to gain knowledge. The following passage provides a nice example.

> A whistling locomotive passes at high speed close beside me. As it passes the note of the whistle is suddenly lowered from a well-understood cause. I perceive the whistle, if you will. I have, at any rate, a sensation of it. But I cannot be said to have a sensation of the change of note. I have a sensation of the lower note. But the cognition of the change is of a more intellectual kind. That I experience rather than perceive. It is [the] special field of experience to acquaint us with events, with changes of perception. Now that which particularly characterizes sudden changes of perception is a shock. A shock is a volitional phenomenon. The long whistle of the approaching locomotive, however disagreeable it may be, has set up in me a certain inertia, so that the sudden lowering of the note meets with a certain resistance. That must be the fact; because if there were no such resistance there could be no shock when the change of note occurs. Now this shock is quite unmistakable. It is more particularly to changes and contrasts of perception that we apply the word 'experience'. We experience vicissitudes, especially. We cannot experience the vicissitude without experiencing the perception which undergoes the change; but the concept of *experience* is broader than that of *perception*, and includes much that is not, strictly speaking, an object of perception. It is the compulsion, the absolute constraint upon us to think otherwise than we have been thinking that constitutes experience. Now constraint and compul-

sion cannot exist without resistance, and resistance is effort opposing change. Therefore there must be an element of effort in experience; and it is this which gives it its peculiar character. (CP 1.336)

It becomes clear that Peirce looked closely at the role of perception and experience in interpretive processes, which is the domain of a branch of philosophy called Phenomenology. This had consequences for his treatment of the categories.

Phenomenology is "the Doctrine of Categories", whose business it is to unravel the tangled skein [of] all that in any sense appears and wind it into distinct forms; or in other words, to make the ultimate analysis of all experiences the first task to which philosophy has to apply itself. (CP 1.280)

So, one must study what appears (to the mind) if one wants to make a list of categories. Peirce, like Kant, noticed that in fact there are two lists: one generally applicable and one for particular cases. Let's first look at Kant's list from this perspective. Every judgment has a quality, a quantity, a relation and a modality. But the quantitative, qualitative, etc. value is in particular cases not so generally applicable. It is either affirmative, negative or indefinite, etc.

For Peirce there are three basic categories to which he gave content in lots of different areas. In experience they are:

1. The monad (unity), like the sensation of a note of the whistle.

2. The dyad, the event of the change in perception from the higher into the lower note (but only as an event, not as a cognized happening).

3. The triad, or the mediative thought, that resolves the shock in the understanding by taking a whistle that is passing by as the reason.

Other ways of stating things are easy to find in (Peirce, C.S, 1931-58). On the most general level they are: Firstness, Secondness and Thirdness. In the domain of metaphysics they are: possibility, existence and law (or habit or rules to which appearances cohere). In semiotics a sign can be looked at as a possible, then we look at the sign in itself. A sign can also be looked at as an existent, then we look at the relation of the sign with its object. And it can be looked at as a habit, then we look how the sign affects the interpreter. These are the general categories.

If we go into more particular detail when studying signs, we always make a choice out of threes: icon, index and symbol, for example. An icon is something in itself, it is a monad just offering the possibility to be used as a sign by means of similarities. An index has a dyadic character, its function is to connect 'what is said' with 'of what' something is said, but only as a blind connection. A triadic symbol glues things together in habits of interpretation. We may err, but brute intrusions leading to new experiences, as well as unwanted consequences following from erroneous conclusions, may exert a corrective influence.

This all too sketchy introduction to Peirce's work on categories, may be unsatisfactory. Its main purpose here however, is to show an ingenuous trait. For it is the *repeated* application of the categorical distinctions, with which he tries to develop the long list of categories in semiotics.

Appendix B

The ten classes of signs according to Peirce

Peirce defines a sign as a First (1, representamen) related to a Second (2, object) and addressing a Third (3, interpretant) in such a way that it brings the Third into the same (or a more developed) relation to its object as it stands itself. From this it follows that in a Third, a Second and a First are involved ('<'), but not the other way around. Just so, in a Second a First is involved, but not the other way around (1<2<3 but not 3<2<1).

Signs can be sub-divided into classes. To that end, first the categories are applied to themselves. This results in three trichotomies:

1.1 Qualisign	1.2 Sinsign	1.3 Legisign
2.1 Icon	2.2 Index	2.3 Symbol
3.1 Rheme	3.2 Dicent	3.3 Argument

By taking a value from each of the trichotomies, we specify a class of signs, e.g. [1.1,2.1,3.1]. As a consequence of the asymmetrical involvement relation not all combinations yield a class; out of the 27 possible classes of signs, 10 are really possible. The rule applicable here is that a categorical aspect belonging to a trichotomy of a higher category can combine with an equal or a higher categorical aspect of a lower category, but not with a lower categorical aspect of a lower category.

Note by the way that this does not preclude lower valued sign aspects of lower categories from being involved in a sign class characterized by higher categorical aspects. Just as the definition of a sign class does not preclude that a lower valued sign class is involved in a higher sign class. Or, cast in a metaphor: If we regard interpretational processes as described by our model as educational careers, each year grade is a sign type, the sign aspects are the intermediate grades that you earn throughout the year. Without the latter you can not earn a year grade, but if you leave the system the year grade has a formal status, while the intermediate grades lose their value.[1]

Below we provide Peirce's description of the 10 general classes of signs.[2] Higher numbered categories involve the lower, but not the other way around. A categorical aspect (2nd) of a higher category (3) may involve a higher (3rd) or a like valued (2nd) categorical aspect of a lower category (2) but never a lower valued aspect of a lower category (2.2nd<3.2nd and 2.3rd<3.1st are possible, 2.2nd<3.3rd and 1.1st<3.2nd are not possible combinations of categorical aspects). The ten sign classes the system yields are:

i) A **Rhematic** [3.1] **Iconic** [2.1] **Qualisign** [1.1] (e.g., a feeling of "red") is any quality in so far as it is a sign. Since a quality is whatever it is positively in itself, a quality can only denote an object by virtue of some common ingredient or similarity; so that a Qualisign is necessarily an Icon. Further, since a quality is a mere logical possibility, it can only be interpreted as a sign of essence, that is, as a Rheme.

ii) A **Rhematic** [3.1] **Iconic** [2.1] **Sinsign** [1.2] (e.g., an individual diagram) is any object of experience in so far as some quality of it makes it determine the idea of an object. Being an Icon, and thus a sign by likeness purely of whatever it may be like, it can only be interpreted as a sign of essence, or Rheme. It will embody a Qualisign.

iii) A **Rhematic** [3.1] **Indexical** [2.2] **Sinsign** [1.2] (e.g., a spontaneous cry) is any object of direct experience so far as it directs attention to an Object by which its presence is caused. It necessarily involves an Iconic Sinsign of a peculiar kind, yet is quite different since it brings the attention of the interpreter to the very Object denoted.

iv) A **Dicent** [3.2] **Indexical** [2.2] **Sinsign** [1.2] (e.g., a weathercock) is any object of direct experience, in so far as it is a sign, and, as such, affords information concerning its Object. This it can only do by being really affected by its Object; so that it is necessarily an Index. The only information it can afford is of actual fact. Such a Sign must involve an Iconic Sinsign to embody the information and a Rhematic Indexical Sinsign to indicate the Object to which the information refers. But the mode of combination, or Syntax, of these two must also be significant.

v) A **Rhematic** [3.1] **Iconic** [2.1] **Legisign** [1.3] (e.g., a diagram, apart from its factual individuality) is any general law or type, in so far as it requires each instance of it to embody a definite quality which renders it fit to call up in the mind the idea of a like object. Being an Icon, it must be a Rheme. Being a Legisign, its mode of being is that of governing single Replicas,[3] each of which

---

[1]The simile can be pushed even further: all lower sign types are involved in higher, as all lower year grades are involved in the higher year grades.

[2]Quotes are taken from (CP 2.254–2.263). We changed the lay out, completed the sign type labels where they were incomplete, added categorical values, but left the descriptions as they are provided.

[3]A replica is an instance of a form, or to put it in semiotical terms a sinsign that is governed

will be an Iconic Sinsign of a peculiar kind.

vi) A **Rhematic** [3.1] **Indexical** [2.2] **Legisign** [1.3] (e.g., a demonstrative pronoun) is any general type or law, however established, which requires each instance of it to be really affected by its Object in such a manner as merely to draw attention to that Object. Each Replica of it will be a Rhematic Indexical Sinsign of a peculiar kind. The Interpretant of a Rhematic Indexical Legisign represents it as an Iconic Legisign; and so it is, in a measure – but in a very small measure.

vii) A **Dicent** [3.2] **Indexical** [2.2] **Legisign** [1.3] (e.g., a street cry) is any general type or law, however established, which requires each instance of it to be really affected by its Object in such a manner as to furnish definite information concerning that Object. It must involve an Iconic Legisign to signify the information and a Rhematic Indexical Legisign to denote the subject of that information. Each Replica of it will be a Dicent Sinsign of a peculiar kind.

viii) A **Rhematic** [3.1] **Symbolic** [2.3] **Legisign** [1.3] (e.g., a common noun) is a sign connected with its Object by an association of general ideas in such a way that its Replica calls up an image in the mind which image, owing to certain habits or dispositions of that mind, tends to produce a general concept, and the Replica is interpreted as a Sign of an Object that is an instance of that concept. Thus, the Rhematic Symbol either is, or is very like, what the logicians call a General Term. The Rhematic Symbol, like any Symbol, is necessarily itself of the nature of a general type, and is thus a Legisign. Its Replica, however, is a Rhematic Indexical Sinsign of a peculiar kind, in that the image it suggests to the mind acts upon a Symbol already in that mind to give rise to a General Concept. In this it differs from other Rhematic Indexical Sinsigns, including those which are Replicas of Rhematic Indexical Legisigns. Thus, the demonstrative pronoun "that" is a Legisign, being a general type; but it is not a Symbol, since it does not signify a general concept. Its Replica draws attention to a single Object, and is a Rhematic Indexical Sinsign.
A Replica of the word "camel" is likewise a Rhematic Indexical Sinsign, being really affected, through the knowledge of camels common to the speaker and auditor, by the real camel it denotes, even if this one is not individually known to the auditor; and it is through such real connection that the word "camel" calls up the idea of a camel. The same thing is true of the word "phoenix." For although no phoenix really exists, real descriptions of the phoenix are well known to the speaker and his auditor; and thus the word is really affected by the Object denoted. But not only are the Replicas of Rhematic Symbols very different from ordinary Rhematic Indexical Sinsigns, but so likewise are Replicas of Rhematic Indexical Legisigns. For the thing denoted by "that" has not affected the replica of the word in any such direct and simple manner as that in which, for example, the ring of a telephone-bell is affected by the person at the other end who wants to make a communication. The Interpretant of the

---

by a legisign and has the function to convey that legisign is a replica sinsign; otherwise it functions as a sinsign.

Rhematic Symbol often represents it as a Rhematic Indexical Legisign; at other times as an Iconic Legisign; and it does in a small measure partake of the nature of both.

ix) A **Dicent** [3.2] **Symbolic** [2.3] **Legisign** [1.3], or ordinary Proposition, is a sign connected with its object by an association of general ideas, and acting like a Rhematic Symbol, except that its intended interpretant represents the Dicent Symbol as being, in respect to what it signifies, really affected by its Object, so that the existence or law which it calls to mind must be actually connected with the indicated Object. Thus, the intended Interpretant looks upon the Dicent Symbol as a Dicent Indexical Legisign; and if it be true, it does partake of this nature, although this does not represent its whole nature. Like the Rhematic Symbol, it is necessarily a Legisign. Like the Dicent Sinsign it is composite inasmuch as it necessarily involves a Rhematic Symbol (and thus is for its Interpretant an Iconic Legisign) to express its information and a Rhematic Indexical Legisign to indicate the subject of that information. But its Syntax of these is significant. The Replica of the Dicent Symbol is a Dicent Sinsign of a peculiar kind. This is easily seen to be true when the information the Dicent Symbol conveys is of actual fact. When that information is of a real law, it is not true in the same fullness. For a Dicent Sinsign cannot convey information of law. It is, therefore, true of the Replica of such a Dicent Symbol only in so far as the law has its being in instances.

x) An **Argumentative** [3.3] **Symbolic** [2.3] **Legisign** [1.3] (e.g., a syllogism) is a sign whose interpretant represents its object as being an ulterior sign through a law, namely, the law that the passage from all such premisses to such conclusions tends to the truth. Manifestly, then, its object must be general; that is, the Argument must be a Symbol. As a Symbol it must, further, be a Legisign. Its Replica is a Dicent Sinsign.

Please note that it is on this sign class level of analysis that, besides the type–instance relation, the matter of compositionality is addressed through the notion of sign classes being involved in other sign classes. As, for instance, when it is stated that terms make up a proposition or that an argument is made up of propositions. Also notice (see Appendix A) that mediated through the sign class level, the lower valued aspects of lower categories are involved in sign classes originating from a composition of sign aspects of higher categorical value. Sign class **vi** involves **ii** and **iii**; **iii** involves **ii** and **ii** involves **i**.

Appendix C

Towards a computational implementation

In our model of cognitive processing we assumed that the input qualia arise from a pair of percepts through a comparison operation. Qualia occurring in the current percept are defined by the input trigger, those in the previous percept must come from memory. In this appendix we combine the above approach to input generation with the memory representation suggested in Sect. 6.7.2 and introduce a revised version of our process model (S_S) that better suits a computational interpretation. Below we start with a renewed definition of the input for information processing. This is followed by a model of the S_S as a graph interpretation system.

C.1 Input signs revisited

Input stimuli that trigger memory generate a response. Responding neurons can be ordered according to their activation intensity, which is proportional to the degree of match.[1] Neurons showing high activation intensity can be used as a representation of a current percept; those responding with less intensity as representations of previous percepts. A positive difference between a pair of interconnected matching neurons (consisting of a larger and a smaller collection of qualia) can be interpreted as an effect. Through this effect the larger collection (cf. current percept), interpreted as a current state, can be said to arise from the smaller collection (cf. previous percept) interpreted as a previous state.

The above interpretation of states and effects conforms with their earlier definition in Sect. 4.3. Neurons involved in the computation of a difference through comparison are triggered by the input stimulus, hence contain qualia that were there and remained there (cf. state); the difference between their contents represents qualia, which, though they were not there, are there now (cf.

---

[1] We assume that a single neuron has the potential to represent a collection of qualia.

Figure C.1: A sample S_S^A. Dashed lines represent the stimulus, solid lines a connection between neurons. Black bullets stand for an active neuron, white bullets for a passive one

effect). In our model, a positive difference between qualia collections is always associated with the neuron (or previous state) containing the smaller collection, i.e., the collection which is affected by the effect. A chain of differences is interpreted as a measure; a collection of related measures is regarded as a domain of effects (b'). An average value of qualia stored in neurons included in a chain is interpreted as the average value associated with those neurons as a state (a'). See also Sect. 6.7.2.

Responding neurons represent active states. Neurons that do not respond to the input stimulus may become active by virtue of their connection to an active state. Such neurons, which are available for inspection by the active state, represent passive states. A large (small) difference between a pair of collections of qualia stands for an active (passive) effect. Neurons that fall outside the collection of active and passive states represent neutral states. The network of active and passive neurons, which is a graph, defines the S_S^A. A sample S_S^A is illustrated in Fig. C.1.

By linking input and memory response qualia with each other, the signs a, a', b, b', introduced in Sect. 5.2 arise again. Note that a is given, b, a' and b' are hypothetical and arise through a process of interpretation generating increasingly better approximations to their value. This implies that the processes of perception and cognition must be quasi-simultaneous. Having said this, the input of information processing is defined as follows.

The relation between the stimulus (a) and its memory response (a') referring to a large (small) intensity of activation can be used for the definition of A ($\neg A$); the relation between a large (small) difference (b) with the qualia collection associated with the previous state (b') affected by the difference, can be used for the definition of B ($\neg B$).

Information processing concerns the responding active neurons and the connected passive ones. Connections between neurons represent a potential for information flow between them. Initially, all connections are assumed to be unevaluated (cf. neutral effect). During information processing the status of a connection may change from neutral to a passive ($\neg B$) or an active effect (B). Information flow involved in active and passive effects is modeled by means of qualia assignments (cf. relational needs, in Sect. 6.3.1). For instance, for a pair of connected neurons containing the qualia 'color' and 'black', information flow from black to color is represented by the quale assignment: 'color⟵ black'.

In the diagrams below, the three types of a state (neuron) are depicted

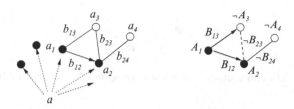

Figure C.2: Sample representations generated by the processes of perception (left) and cognition (right). For $1 \leq j \leq 4$, a'_i is the collection of qualia stored by a_i; a is the input stimulus, $b = b_{12} = a'_2 \setminus a'_1$. $A_1 = a*a'_1$, $A_2 = a*a'_2$, $\neg A_3 = a + a'_3$, $\neg A_4 = a + a'_4$. An average value (a') and a domain (b') representation of the input a and b is defined by the expressions ('avg' stands for some averaging function): $a'_f = \mathrm{avg}(a'_1, a'_2)$, $a'_c = \mathrm{avg}(a'_1, a'_2, a'_3, a'_4)$, $b'_f = a'_1 \setminus a'_3 + a'_3 \setminus a'_2$, $b'_c = a'_4 \setminus a'_2$ (we assume that b'_f is a best approximation of b, according to some measure)

by a circle: active ($\bullet$), passive ($\bigcirc$), neutral ($\because$); those of an effect (difference) by an edge: active ($\rightarrow$), passive ($\cdots$), neutral ($-$). The three types of state and effect are related to each other by a relation of involvement ('$<$'): neutral$<$passive$<$active. For example, a subset of qualia of an active neuron or state (A) can be interpreted as a passive state ($\neg A$) which is involved. In conformity with the proposed interpretation of the difference between qualia collections, active effects are represented by a directed edge, pointing from the more active to the less active neuron or state. Passive effects are bi-directional; in the diagrams their direction can be omitted. Instances of the different types of states and effects are indicated by integer subscripts. Sample representations generated by the interpretation process are displayed in Fig. C.2.

C.2 The S_S as a graph system

The graph defined by the active and passive neurons (states) and their connections (effects), is written in the S_S. We assume that interpretation by the S_S can be characterized by means of operations on graphs consisting of a pair of active states, a single passive state, and any number or neutral states.

If the active states in the graph of the S_S are directly connected, then the S_S is in *matching* mode (which is also the default mode of operation by the S_S). Note that the connection must stand for an active effect (B), otherwise the two states would be similar hence there would be no change and no input interaction. Information flow between the active states corresponds to habitual interpretation; see Fig. C.3. An illustration of this mode of operation is the following. If we have a high intensity response on our visual perception of 'Mary with a hat' (A_1) and a lower intensity response on 'Mary without a hat' (A_2), then the connection between the active states, A_1 and A_2, is an expression of the propositional sign: 'Mary is wearing a hat' (as usual).

If the active states are *not* connected, the S_S is in search of a passive state ($\neg A$), transitively connecting A_1 with A_2. This is when the S_S is in *analysis*

Figure C.3: Matching mode operation corresponding to habitual interpretation

Figure C.4: A sample graph (left) and its interpretation as a triad (right) in analysis mode operation

mode. For instance, if our focus is on 'Mary' (A_1), but the qualia of hat are not part of the input,[2] then by using complementary information about wearable 'hat's ($\neg A$), we may be able to derive how our current percept (A_1) arose from a previous percept (A_2). Our propositional sign can be: 'Mary must be wearing a hat'.

In matching mode operation, initially, the passive state ($\neg A$) is connected to the active states by neutral effects. Analysis will be successful if those neutral connections can be interpreted as active effects. We call such a relation between A_1, $\neg A$ and A_2, a *triad* relation. See Fig. C.4. In order to establish a triad relation, the S_S analysis the information flow enabled by the active (B) and passive ($\neg B$) effects between the states of the S_S^A. This can be illustrated as follows.

Assume that A_1 (Mary) and A_2 (Mary without a hat) are not connected, but, through a pair of neutral effects they are both connected to some passive state, $\neg A$ (hat), as shown in Fig. C.4. The difference between A_1 and $\neg A$ must be large (B), as the qualia occurring in the current observation of 'Mary' must be very different from the qualia defining 'hat'.[3] This difference can be made small if, through qualia assignment, $\neg A$ can be shown to be Mary's hat. This can be achieved in two ways: via $A_1 \leftarrow \neg A$, by showing that Mary's potential for 'wearing headgear' can be satisfied by hat, and, via $\neg A \leftarrow A_1$, by showing that the potential of hat 'to be worn by somebody' can be satisfied by Mary. As a result, the relation between A_1 and $\neg A$ can be shown to be bi-directional. The relation between A_2 and $\neg A$ can be evaluated analogously.[4]

If a triad relation cannot be established, the S_S may abductively extend its focus, by considering neutral states connected to the passive state. If this search

---

[2]E.g. because we do not look at or cannot see Mary's hat. We assume that Mary (A_1) contains qualia signifying the possibility of wearing headgear, however.

[3]But see *The man who mistook his wife for a hat* (Sacks, 1985).

[4]Note the symmetrical character of the assumed representation. If, in another observation, we perceive hat, then we may derive Mary ($\neg A$) as a person wearing this or a similar hat. This potential of the graph system for a dual interpretation of the difference between a pair of qualia collections underlies our concept of a relation of 'conversion' as well (cf. Sect. 6.7.5).

Qualisign $(A, B, \neg A, \neg B)$

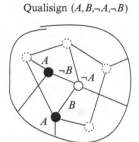

Figure C.5: The graph associated with the qualisign position. A, B, $\neg A$, $\neg B$ are monadic s/e-relations

is successful, the triad relation found can be represented by a single passive state, degenerately. An analysis of this mode of operation (cf. abductive reasoning) is beyond our current goals, however. Through qualia assignment the graph in the S_S may change. If, through analysis, a triad relation can be established, the S_S introduces a temporary connection between the active states (cf. 'A *is* B'). Temporary connections may become more steady as a result of learning.

In the next section we show that the generation of triad relations requires a (graph) realization of the types of interpretation moments defined by the processing schema.

C.3   Interpretation moments

On the basis of state–effect relations (in short s/e-relations) in the S_S^A (the actual state of the S_S), the graph can be used to simulate the different stages of information processing. Following our model, a state s is in relation to an effect e if and only if s is affected by e; otherwise they are independent. This is represented by the expression $s*e$. Independent s/e-relations involved in the S_S^A can be combined in a single expression by means of '+' symbols. An s/e-relation is called neutral, passive or active, if it satisfies a neutral, passive or an active relational need, respectively.

In our model we acknowledge monadic and dyadic s/e-relations. Monadic s/e-relations are designated by the expressions: A, B, $\neg A$, $\neg B$; dyadic ones are pictorially represented by their graphs (a bullet stands for a state, an edge for an effect): ●—▸, ○—▸, ●-▸, ○-▸. Monadic s/e-relations involved in dyadic ones can be omitted in relational representations of the S_S^A. States (nodes) and effects (edges) defining a graph are called *elements* of the graph.

The pair of active states of the S_S^A are defined by the input stimulus, the mediating passive state is defined by the S_S itself. The different stages of interpretation are characterized by their different perspectives. In the qualisign position the perspective is the collection of monadic relations. These are potentials for developing into dyadic relations. A sample graph and its relational interpretation associated with the qualisign position is depicted in Fig. C.5.

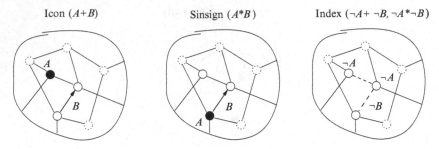

Figure C.6: S/e-relations of active elements with each other (left, middle) and those of passive elements with each other (right)

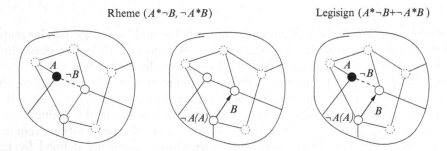

Figure C.7: S/e-relations between active and passive elements (note that the S_S^A corresponding to the rheme position enables two interpretations)

This graph will be used for an illustration of all more developed stages of the S_S^A as well.

Sorting

The graphs of the icon and sinsign positions, in Fig. C.6, are an expression of possible s/e-relations between active elements in the S_S^A, as a co-existence (icon) and a co-occurrence (sinsign). The graph of the index position in Fig. C.6 represents identical relations this time between the (potential) passive elements of the S_S^A.[5]

Abstraction

In this stage the S_S analysis the possible s/e-relations of active elements with passive ones. See Fig. C.7. There may be different potential passive states (and neurons) as possibilities. Note the correspondence between an interpretation of active and passive states as current and previous percepts on the one hand, and an interpretation of those states from an agent and a patient perspective on the other. In the graph corresponding to the legisign position the relations

---

[5]A subset of qualia of an active neuron can be interpreted as a passive state which is involved.

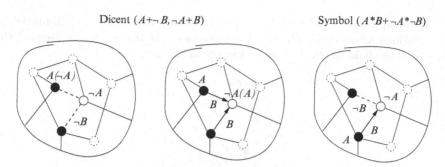

Figure C.8: *S/e*-relations of active elements following qualia assignment (note that the S_S^A corresponding to the dicent position enables two interpretations)

associated with the rheme position are merged. The condition for merging is the existence of a shared passive state ($\neg A$), enabling a common interpretation of the two relations of the rheme (cf. compatibility). The collection of such common values or possibilities cannot be empty. If it were empty, then a legisign would not arise and sign interpretation as a process would not occur. An example for such an input is the sentence 'the house flew out through the window': A_1:=the house, A_2:=window, $\neg A$:=flying through. By imposing contradictory conditions on $\neg A$, a common interpretation of the passive state cannot be defined.[6]

Complementation

By making use of qualia included in $\neg A$ (cf. context information), the S_S selects an element from the range of possibilities offered by the rheme position which can satisfy the relation associated with the legisign position as well. In the graphs corresponding to the dicent and symbol positions, the S_S establishes a relation between the active states through the mediation of the shared passive state. This is achieved by means of qualia assignments, via $A \dashrightarrow \neg A$ and $\neg A \dashrightarrow A$, actualizing relations involved in the graphs of the rheme and legisign positions.

In this stage the focus of the S_S is on *s/e*-relations between active and passive elements, *after* qualia assignment. See Fig. C.8. In the left-hand side diagram of the dicent position $\neg A$ is connected to A through a passive effect. As in this interpretation of the S_S^A the difference between A and $\neg A$ is small, the used qualia assignment does not change the active status of A, but it may turn the status of $\neg A$ into an active state. In the diagram, following qualia assignment, the active state is labelled $A(\neg A)$; the arising relation is represented by the expression $A+\neg B$. The right-hand side diagram of the dicent position (in Fig. C.8) illustrates the interpretation of the S_S^A in which A is connected to $\neg A$ through an active effect (B). As now the difference is large, the qualia assignment does not change the passive status of $\neg A$ (cf. the state with the label $\neg A(A)$ and the expression $\neg A+B$).

---

[6]We disregard the possibility that the sample sentence is referring to a cartoon.

The graph associated with the symbol position represents a combination of the relations associated with the dicent position. At this stage the focus of the S_S is on the chain of effects connecting the active states.

Argument (*A is B*)

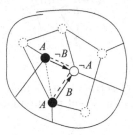

Figure C.9: An induced s/e-relation between the active states of the S_S (see the dotted bi-directional edge)

Predication

By combining the interpretations associated with the dicent and symbol positions, a realization of a triad relation comes in sight. The relation between A and $\neg A$, defined by the graph of the dicent position, can be realized by the effect defined by the graph of the symbol position. The arising relation between the active states is of a hypothetical nature, however. This is illustrated in Fig. C.9 by using a dotted bi-directional edge. The induced effect can be assigned to a direction if the S_S^A prefers an agent- or a patient-perspective or suggests a certain causal interpretation of the relation between the active states of the S_S^A.

Appendix D

A derivation of 'naive' logic

Earlier we defined 'naive' logic as a procedure that generates relations on collections of qualia (see Sect. 5.3). In this section we suggest that the hierarchy of logical expressions, recapitulated in Fig. D.1, can be interpreted as a 'term-procedure' (cf. term-algebra). In this chapter we use '+' and '∗' as commutative binary operators. A, B are initial terms; X, Y are variables. The empty term is designated by a '$\emptyset$' symbol. The monadic operator '$\neg$' is defined on terms: $\neg(X)=\neg X$, $\neg(\neg X)=X$; and on operators: $\neg('\ast')= '+'$, $\neg('+') ='\ast'$. Expressions treated as synonymous from some perspective are separated by a ',' symbol. Terms generated by 'naive' logic are linked with the graph interpretation introduced in Appendix C.

Sorting

The expressions $[q_1]=A+B$, $[q_2]=A\ast B$, $[C]=\neg A+\neg B, \neg A\ast\neg B$ are trivially generated from the initial terms and their negated forms: A, B, $\neg A$, $\neg B$.

Abstraction

The expressions of q_1 and q_2 are generated from the expressions of $[q_1]$ and $[q_2]$ by means of a relative difference operation. The differences between $[q_1]$ and $[q_2]$ ask for two versions of a relative difference operation, that we represent by the symbols '\' and '/'. Below we assume that $X\backslash Y=X/Y=\emptyset$ for $X=Y$, and $X\ast\neg Y$ for $X\neq Y$. A derivation of q_1 and q_2, including a definition of the two kinds of relative difference operations, is given as follows. We begin with q_1.

In the derivation of q_1, simultaneity involved in $[q_2]$ is 'removed' from the constituency involved in $[q_1]$. That this operation is feasible is witnessed by the interpretations of $A+B$ as constituent: A, B, $A\cdot B$.[1] Each one of these terms is an expression of a possible co-existence of A and B. For instance, A is an expression of a possible co-occurrence of the input state (A) with a suppressed input effect (B). Alternatively, A can be designated by A_B. From

---

[1] $A\cdot B$ is short for 'A and B' as a possible co-existence.

193

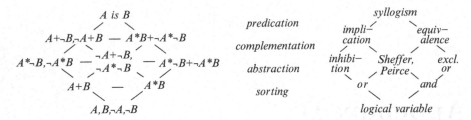

Figure D.1: Logical expressions (left) and their mundane terms (right)

the perspective of constituency, $A \cdot B$ can be interpreted as A or B, $A*B$ as A and B. By 'removing' simultaneity involved in $[q_1]$ (cf. $A \cdot B$), $A+B$ 'falls apart' into a pair of terms: A, B.

$$
\begin{aligned}
q_1 &= [q_1]\backslash[q_2] \\
&= (A+B)\backslash(A*B) \\
&= A\backslash(A*B), \ B\backslash(A*B) \\
&= A\backslash A, \ A\backslash B, \ B\backslash A, \ B\backslash B \\
&= A\backslash B, \ B\backslash A \\
&= A*\neg B, \ \neg A*B
\end{aligned}
$$

This closes the derivation of q_1. Let us proceed with the derivation of q_2. By 'removing' constituency from the simultaneity involved in $[q_2]$ we obtain a relation which is less intense than simultaneity but more tight than constituency. The resulting relation is represented below by the expression $A*\neg B+B*\neg A$ (cf. 'exclusive-or').

$$
\begin{aligned}
q_2 &= [q_2]/[q_1] \\
&= (A*B)/(A+B) \\
&= (A*B)/A+(A*B)/B \\
&= A/A+A/B+B/A+B/B \\
&= A*\neg B+B*\neg A
\end{aligned}
$$

From the 'graph' perspective of Appendix C, the relative difference operation involved in *abstraction* enables an interpretation of existing neutral s/e-relations as passive ones (the terms, $A\backslash A$ and $B\backslash B$, that provide no new information are removed). See Fig. C.7. In $[q_1]$ these neutral relations are represented by the sub-graph associated with A and B, and in $[q_2]$ by the undetermined hence neutral relation between A and B.

Complementation

The expressions associated with (q_1,C) and (q_2,C) are generated from the expressions associated with q_1 and q_2, by means of complementation. Indexicality (involved in $[C]$) is represented by the negation operation '$\neg$'. In the definition of (q_1,C) below, the operand of '$\neg$' is interpreted as a *collection* of constituents ('state' view). For instance, the constituents of $A*\neg B$ are: 'A', '$*$', '$\neg B$'.

$(q_1, C) = \neg q_1$
$$= \neg(A*\neg B), \neg(\neg A*B)$$
$$= (\neg A)(\neg *)(\neg\neg B), (\neg\neg A)(\neg *)(\neg B)$$
$$= \neg A + B, A + \neg B$$

From the 'graph' perspective (cf. Fig. C.8), the first term, $A + \neg B$, arises through qualia assignment, from $\neg A$ to A. As a result, the involved s/e-relation is resolved ('$\neg *$'), the relation not involved is incorporated ($\neg B$). As the latter does not affect A and so does not affect $\neg A(A)$ either, the relation between A and $\neg B$ must be a relation of a possible co-existence (cf. '$+$').

The second term above, $\neg A + B$, arises through qualia assignment from A to $\neg A$. By virtue of the large difference between the states involved, this operation does not change the passive status of $\neg A$. As a result of qualia assignment the involved active effect is resolved, the effect not involved is incorporated. As the latter effect does not affect $\neg A$, the relation between $\neg A$ and $\neg B$ must be a relation of a possible co-existence ('$+$').

In the definition of (q_2, C) below, the operand of complementation is interpreted as a *single* object ('effect' view). As the existence of an effect always implies the existence of a state, complementation must interpret its operand both as a state and an effect. These possibilities are indicated by making use of square brackets and boldface symbols. In the first term of (i), '$\neg$' is applied to terms representing a state ($\mathbf{A}$, $\neg\mathbf{A}$), in the second term to those representing an effect ($\neg\mathbf{B}$, $\mathbf{B}$).

$(q_2, C) = \neg q_2$
$$= \neg(A*\neg B + \neg A*B))$$
$$= [\neg(\mathbf{A}*\neg B) + \neg(\neg\mathbf{A}*B)] + [\neg(A*\neg\mathbf{B}) + \neg(\neg A*\mathbf{B})] \qquad (i)$$
$$= [(\neg\mathbf{A}*\neg B) + (\neg\neg\mathbf{A}*B)] + [(A*\neg\neg\mathbf{B}) + (\neg A*\neg\mathbf{B})]$$
$$= A*B + \neg A*\neg B$$

Predication

For the sake of completeness we mention that (q_1, C)–(q_2, C) can be interpreted as a syllogistic conclusion, defined by the expressions (q_1, C) and (q_2, C) as premises. Below we make use of Łukasiewicz's interpretation (Dumitriu, 1977), according to which premises can be represented by an implication. From the major premise $A*B + \neg A*\neg B = A + B \rightarrow A*B$, and the minor premise, $A \rightarrow B = A \rightarrow A + B$, the conclusion '$A$ *is* B' syllogistically follows (by taking $A + \neg B$ or $A \leftarrow B$ as the minor premise, 'B *is* A' can be obtained; the two propositions represent the input in an 'active' and 'passive' sense). In the derivation below quantifiers are omitted.

$$
\begin{array}{lll}
& A+B & IS \ A*B \\
& A & IS \ A+B \\
\Rightarrow & A & IS \ A*B \quad \% \ A \rightarrow A*B = \neg A + A*B = \neg A + B = A \rightarrow B \\
= & A & IS \ B
\end{array}
$$

Appendix E

Sample language parsing

The potential of our model for parsing complex linguistic phenomena is illustrated in this section with a number of examples. This includes an analysis of some of the sentences used for text summarization, in Chapter 9.

Besides the usual graphical illustration, presentation of an analysis is simplified by introducing a tabular form, in which a row corresponds to an evaluation moment (cf. Sect. 6.2), a column to a position of the processing schema.[1]

The following abbreviations are used: input(i), accumulation(a), coercion(c), binding(b). Degenerate representation is indicated by the subscript 'd'. Signs which are accumulated are separated by a '/'. Input symbols are given in boldface. Positions of the processing schema are referred to by their sign aspect label. These are abbreviated to four letters, e.g. 'qual' is short for 'qualisign'. The parsing of space and dot symbols is omitted, as well as the signs generated by *predication*.

A lexical definition of input symbols used in Sects. E.1–E.3 can be found in Appendix F.

E.1 PP-attachment

Our first example is the utterance 'Mary eats pizza with a fork'. A 'naive' morpho-syntactic analysis is depicted in Fig. E.1 and Table E.1. In step 9 (cf. Table E.1), the article symbol a (index) binds with fork (rheme), complementing it with the referential property 'non-definite'; a fork is represented degenerately, in the index position. This sign is used as the context in the sign interaction with the preposition with (legisign). Their binding is represented by the prep-complement symbol with a fork, having adjective- or adverb-like potential syntactic properties. The final representation obtained by the morpho-syntactic analysis elaborated in this section: *(Mary)(eats)(pizza)(with a fork)*. In this and later examples, items

---

[1]The first column in row i ($i>0$) contains the current input symbol, subsequent columns represent signs introduced in row $i-1$, the last column contains a list of symbol interactions associated with the current evaluation moment.

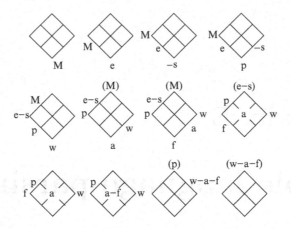

Figure E.1: A morpho-syntactic analysis of Mary eat -s pizza with a fork yielding *(Mary)(eats)(pizza)(with a fork)*. Items in parentheses represent morpho-syntactically finished symbol

enclosed in parentheses stand for morpho-syntactically finished symbols. Syntactic relational needs of morpho-syntactically finished symbols are defined by a perception process (cf. lexical analysis). In the current analysis this obtains:

$$
\begin{aligned}
\text{eats} &= \{legi, symb\} \\
\text{with a fork} &= \{indx\}
\end{aligned}
$$

The input is syntactically ambiguous. One of the possible analyses is depicted in Fig. E.2 (and Table E.2), another in Fig. E.3 (and Table E.3). In the second analysis, only symbol interactions differing from the first analysis are illustrated.

A combined syntactic *and* 'naive' logical interpretation of the input reveals that Mary (A) can be interpreted as a possible for the subject (rheme; $A*\neg B$), and eats (B) as a rule-like effect involved in the predicate (legisign; $A*\neg B+\neg A*B$). See Fig. E.2. The two expressions are interrelated through the complementary state, pizza ($\neg A$), and, in a *later* interpretation moment, via the complementary effect, with-a-fork ($\neg B$). These complementary signs, which are independent, together represent the context of the sentence (index; $\neg A+\neg B$).

This is opposed to the second analysis, depicted in Fig. E.3. In this analysis, first, pizza (A) is assumed to be a possible (cf. rheme) for the subject. The appearance of with-a-fork (B) asks this assumption to be reconsidered. As a result, pizza (rheme) *binds* with with-a-fork (index). The interpreting sign, pizza-with-a-fork, is degenerately represented as the context of the sentence (index; $\neg A*\neg B$).

nr.	qual	icon	sins	rhme	indx	legi	dcnt	symb	rule
0	Mary(M)								i
1	eat(e)	M							i, c
2	-s	e		M					i, c, c
3	pizza(p)	e	-s	M					i, c
4	with(w)	p		e-s			M		i, c, b, c
5	a(a)		w	p			e-s		i, c, c, c
6	fork(f)		a	p		w	e-s		i, c, c
7		f			a	w	p		c, c, c, c
8				f	a	w	p		b_d
9					a-f	w	p		b, c
10								w-a-f	c

Table E.1: A tabular representation of the analysis displayed in Fig. E.1

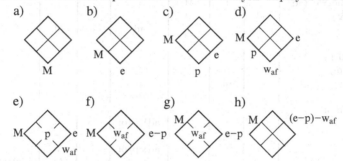

Figure E.2: A syntactic analysis of Mary eats pizza with a fork (alternative #1) yielding *Mary eats-pizza with-a-fork* (w_{af} is short for *with-a-fork*)

nr.	qual	icon	sins	rhme	indx	legi	dcnt	symb	rule
0	Mary(M)								i
1	eats(e)	M							i, c
2	pizza(p)		e	M					i, c, c
3	with a fork(w_{af})		p	M		e			i, c, c
4				w_{af}	M	p	e		c, b_d
5					M	w_{af}	e-p		c
6						w_{af}	e-p	M	b
7							M	M	e-p-w_{af}	b

Table E.2: A tabular representation of the analysis displayed in Fig. E.2

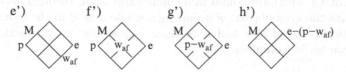

Figure E.3: A syntactic analysis of Mary eats pizza with a fork (alternative #2) yielding *Mary eats pizza-with-a-fork*

nr.	qual	icon	sins	rhme	indx	legi	dcnt	symb	*rule*
3'	with a fork(w_{af})	p		M		e			i, c, c
4'			w_{af}	p		e	M		c
5'				p	w_{af}	e	M		b_d
6'					p-w_{af}	e	M		b
7'							M	e-p-w_{af}	b

Table E.3: A tabular representation of the analysis displayed in Fig. E.3

nr.	qual	icon	sins	rhme	indx	legi	dcnt	symb	*rule*
0	Mary(M)								i
1	is(i)	M							i,c
2	a democrat (ad)		i	M					i,c,c
3	and(&)	ad		M			i		i,c,c
4					ad	i	M		c,c
	save								
5	proud(p)								i
6	of it(oi)		p						i,c
7			oi		p				c,c
8					p/oi				c,a
	coordination								
9					ad&p/oi				
	restore								
10					ad&p/oi	i	M		
11							M	i-ad&p/oi	b

Table E.4: A syntactic analysis of Mary is a democrat and proud of it

E.2 Coordination

We consider the sample coordination structure 'Mary is a democrat and proud of it', morpho-syntactically analyzed: *(Mary)(is)(a democrat)(and)(proud)(of it)*. The syntactic relational needs of the symbols used are defined as follows:

$$
\begin{aligned}
\text{is} &= \{legi, symb\} \\
\text{proud} &= \{indx\} \\
\text{of it} &= \{indx\}
\end{aligned}
$$

A syntactic analysis of the input sentence is depicted in Table E.4. In step 8, proud and of it (index) are bound in a single expression, through accumulation. This obtains the symbol proud of it, having a single *a*-need in the index position. Coordination of proud of it and a democrat is possible, as, syntactically, both symbols can be 'is'-complements.

nr.	qual	icon	sins	rhme	indx	legi	dcnt	symb	*rule*
0	a man (a_m)								i
1	entered(e)	a_m							i,c
2	who(w_h)		e	a_m					i,c,c
recursion									
3	was covered (w_{cd})	w_h							i,c
4	with mud (w_m)		w_{cd}	w_h					i,c,c
5			w_m	w_h		w_{cd}			c,c
6				w_h	w_m	w_{cd}			c
7					w_m	w_{cd}	w_h		c
8							w_h	w_{cd}-w_m	b
return									
9	who-...-mud(w_{cm})		e	a_m					i
10			w_{cm}	a_m		e			c,c
11				a_m	w_{cm}	e			c
12						e	a_m-w_{cm}		b
13						e	a_m-w_{cm}	e	c

Table E.5: A syntactic analysis of A man entered who was covered with mud

E.3 Discontinuous modification

We analyse the sentence 'A man entered who was covered with mud', morpho-syntactically parsed as: *(A man)(entered)(who)(was covered)(with mud)*. In the syntactic parsing, displayed in Table E.5, the series of symbols beginning with who and closed by the sentence ending dot is analyzed recursively. A specification of the syntactic relational needs is the following:

entered	=	*{legi, symb}*
was covered	=	*{legi, symb}*
with mud	=	*{indx}*

In the recursively analyzed segment, 'who' is interpreted as the syntactic subject. The propositional (sentence) sign of the nested series is degenerately represented by a single quale (w_{cm}). In conformity with the referential properties involved in the symbol who, w_{cm} is defined as a syntactic quale having adjective-like properties.

E.4 Parsing complex sentences

This section contains a (morpho-)syntactic analysis of the sentences s_0 and s_1, which were used for text summarization in Chapter 9. Below, symbols generated by *sorting* (icon and sinsign positions) and *predication* (argument position) are omitted. Coordination is designated by a generic '&' symbol, subscripted by the actual coordinator, for example, '$\&_{but}$'. Symbol interactions are indicated by a '-' symbol. Coinciding semantic and syntactic signs are merged in a single representation. In a syntactic analysis, signs used for text summarization are given in bold face.

The nesting structure of s_0 and s_1 is illustrated by Fig. E.4. A syntactic analysis of s_0 may be found in Table E.6. A syntactic analysis of the first clause of s_1 is displayed in Table E.7, that of the second clause in table E.8.

input	rhme	indx	legi	dcnt	symb	action
in						
far off(foff)			in			c
a land(alnd)		foff	in			c
	alnd	foff	in			c,b
		foff-alnd	in			b
there(t)		inffl→				d
lived(lvd)	t	inffl→				c
very beautiful(vb)		inffl→	lvd	t		c,c
a Queen(aQ)		←vb,inffl→	lvd	t		c,a
	aQ	←vb,inffl→	lvd	t		c
recursion(1)						
who(wh)						
had	wh					c
	wh		had			c
recursion(2)						
a stepdaughter(st)						
called(ca)	st					c
Snow White(SW)	st		ca			c
	st	SW	ca			c
	st	ca-SW				b
				st-ca-SW		
return(2)						
	wh	stcsw	had			d,c
		stcsw	had	wh		b
				wh	had-stcsw	b
return(1)						
	aQ	**←vb/hadst, inffl→**	**lvd**	**t**		**d,b**
. . .						
				t/aQ-hadst...	lvd-inffl	b

Table E.6: A syntactic analysis of s_0. Recursive parsing is indicated by the labels *recursion* and *return*, and by the recursion depth, given by an integer in parentheses. The abbreviations used are: in a far off land (inffl), a stepdaughter called Snow White (stcsw), who had a stepdaughter called Snow White (hadst)

s_0:   (In)(far off)(a land)
      (there)(lived)(very beautiful)(a Queen)
        [(who)(had)
           [(a stepdaughter)(called)(Snow White)]]

s_1:   (Wicked)(the Queen)(ordered)
        [(a servant)(to take)(Snow White)(to the forest)
          $\&_{and}$ (put)(her)(to death)]
      $\&_{but}$ (poor)(the man)
         (had not)(the heart)[(to do)(it)]
          $\&_{and}$ (told)(her)
            [(to hide)(in the forest)]

Figure E.4: Nesting structure of s_0 and s_1. Morpho-syntactically finished symbols are given in parentheses. Coordination is denoted by a generic '&' symbol, subscripted by the coordinator. Layout is used for an expression of nesting (nested segments are encapsulated by a pair of square brackets)

input	rhme	indx	legi	dcnt	symb	action
wicked(wk)						
the Queen(tQ)		wk				c
ordered(ord)	tQ	wk				c,b
			ord	**wk-tQ**		
recursion						
a servant(se)						
to take(ta)	se					c
Snow White(SW)	se		ta			c
to the forest(tf)		SW	ta	se		c,c
		tf	ta-SW	se		b
				se	ta-SW-tf	b
coordination						
put(pu)						
her(he)			pu			c
to death(td)		he	pu			c,b
		td	pu-he			b
					pu-he-td	
restore						
				se	**take&put**	
return						
	se-take&put		ord	wk-tQ		d,b
				wk-tQ	ord-se-take&put	b

Table E.7: A syntactic analysis of the first clause of s_1

input	rhme	indx	legi	dcnt	symb	action
coordination						
poor(po)						
the man(tm)		po				c
	tm	po				c
				po-tm		b
recursion(1)						
had not(hn)						
the heart(th)			hn			c
		th	hn			c
			hn-th			b
recursion(2)						
to do(td)						
it			td			c
		it	td			c
		td-it				b,d
return(2)						
		td-it	hn-th			
					hn-th-td-it	b
return(1)						
				po-tm	**hn-th-td-it**	
coordination(2)						
told(td)						
her(hr)			td			c
		hr	td			c
			td-hr			b,d
recursion						
to hide(hi)						
in the forest(tf)		tf	hi			c
					hi-tf	bd
return						
		hi-tf	td-hr			b
					td-hr-hi-tf	
restore(2)						
				po-tm	hd...&td...	
restore(1)						

Table E.8: A syntactic analysis of the second clause of s_1

Appendix F

Towards a syntactic lexicon

This section contains the blueprint for a lexicon of syntactic symbols, but the proposed lexical structure can be used for a specification of morpho-syntactic symbols as well. As opposed to Sect. 6.3.1, in which we defined a lexical entry by a set of relational needs, in this section we capitalize on the isomorphism between the types of relational needs and the levels of interpretation; in the lexical entries we refer to the corresponding sign interactions. Roughly, *abstraction, complementation*, and *predication* can be associated with a realization of a neutral, passive, and active relational potential, respectively.[1] Lexical specification is simplified by making use of two features of our language model (cf. Fig. 6.8): (1) that only signs in the icon and sinsign positions may undergo a *coercion* (cf. sect. 6.1.1) and (2) that passive relational needs can be optional, except in the dicent position (cf. syntactic subject). The latter conforms with the SV(O) rule, in English. As a result, a syntactic specification can be given in a 'natural' way, similarly to grammar (Aarts & Aarts, 1982), (Quirk et al., 1985). Lexical definitions presented in this section are restricted to symbols used in the examples in Chapter 6.

A syntactic lexicon is defined by a set. A lexical entry consists of two parts: a symbolic name (a string), and a trichotomic specification of relational properties (in tuples), defining neutral, passive, and active relational needs of a symbol, in different sign interactions. A tuple is divided into three parts, containing information: (1) about relational properties of the symbol in itself, (2) about relational needs which can affect the symbol, and (3) about relations the symbol itself can establish.

An example is the verb 'likes': (1) it cannot be neutral ($n()$); (2) it can be subject to coercion due to the neutral need of another sign[2], or can be subject to accumulation or binding due to the passive relational need of a syntactic modifier or a verb-complement ($p(verb,n/p,acc/bind)$); finally (3) it can actively trigger accumulation with another verb, syntactic complementation of another symbol

---

[1]From a syntactic perspective, the sign interactions *sorting* and *abstraction* are neutral.

[2]In the example of this section, the optional *p*-need of likes, which is not realized by a coercion operation, is represented by an *n*-need, ambiguously.

(the syntactic complement of likes), or predication of the subject of the sentence (a(trans,compl/subj,acc/bind)). In sum:

likes[n(); p(verb,n/p,acc/bind); a(trans,compl/subj,acc/bind)].

Following the theory of this book, we will assume that a syntactic lexical definition of a symbol can be generated (at least partly), from the morpho-syntactic constituents of that symbol. For instance, a lexical definition of likes can be defined on the basis of syntactic properties associated with like and -s, as well as those associated with a morpho-syntactic binding of these symbols.

F.1 A formal definition

A formal definition of a syntactic lexicon as a context-free grammar extended by regular expressions is given below. In order to keep the size of the grammar small, nonterminals representing identical concepts are unified in a single sign (clearly this may increase the size of the language generated by the grammar). For example, the three nonterminal symbols occurring in the definition of 'rel_needs' below, specifying neutral, passive, and active relational needs in tuples are generalized in the nonterminal symbol 'rel_tuple'.

The formal definition below capitalizes on grammatical concepts, but makes no reference to modeling of specific notions, such as interpretation moments and Peircean sign aspects (except the categorically inspired three types of relational needs), implying that a definition of a syntactic lexicon can be given in a 'natural' way. Information about the underlying language model is made available to the parser through a classification of syntactic symbols, depicted in Fig. 6.8.[3]

lexicon= {lex_entry}*
lex_entry= string, "[", rel_needs, "]".
rel_needs= n-needs, ";", p-needs, ";", a-needs.
n-needs= "n", "(", rel_tuple, ")".
p-needs= "p", "(", rel_tuple, ")".
a-needs= "a", "(", rel_tuple, ")".
rel_tuple= element_type, ",", implied_rels, ",", imputed_rels.
element_type= neutral_type; passive_type; active_type.
neutral_type= conjunction.
passive_type= {nominal_type; verbal_type; mod_type}$^+$.
nominal_type= common-noun; proper-noun; pronoun.
verbal_type= copula; intransitive; transitive.
mod_type= adjective; adverb; preposition-compl.
active_type= {complement; subject}$^+$.
implied_rels= {n; p; a}$^+$.
imputed_rels= {coercion; accumulation; binding}$^+$.

---

[3]In fact, this classification can be used as a skeleton for the parser.

Sample lexical specifications

We introduce a lexical specification for symbols used in the examples of Chapter 6. Below we use the convention that terminal symbols derived from a regular expression are separated by a '/' symbol. For example, 'p/a' stands for two values, 'p' and 'a', generated from 'implied_rels'. The following abbreviations are used: accumulation(acc), binding (bind), complement (compl), verbal (verb), transitive (trans), intransitive (intrans), subject (subj), conjunction (conj), adverb (adv), adjective (adj), preposition-compl (prep).

1. John likes Mary and Mary, John likes.

    John[n();p(proper-noun,n/p/a,acc); a()]
    likes[n(); p(verb,n/p/,acc/bind); a(trans,compl/subj,acc/bind)]
    Mary[n();p(proper-noun,n/p/a,acc); a()]

2. John likes Mary and Kim.

    John[n(); p(proper-noun,n/p/a,acc); a()]
    likes[n(); p(verb,n/p/,acc/bind); a(trans,comp/subj,acc/bind)]
    Mary[n();p(proper-noun,n/p/a,acc); a()]
    and[n(conj,(),()); p(); a()]
    Kim[n();p(proper-noun,n/p/a,acc); a()]

3. Mary eats pizza with a fork.

    Mary[n();p(proper-noun,n/p/a,acc); a()]
    eats[n(); p(verb,n/p,acc/bind); a(trans,compl/subj,acc/bind)]
    pizza[n();p(common-noun,n/p/a,acc); a()]
    with_a_fork[n(); p(); a(prep;p/a;acc/bind)]

4. Mary is a democrat and proud of it.

    Mary[n();p(proper-noun,n/p/a,acc); a()]
    is[n(); p(); a(copula,bind,compl/sub)]
    a_democrat[n();p(proper-noun,n/p/a,acc); a()]
    and[n(conj,(),()); p(); a()]
    proud[n(); p(adj,n/p,acc); a(adj,p/a,acc/bind)]
    of_it[n(); p(prep,n/p/0,()); a(adj,p/a,bind)]

5. A man entered who was covered with mud.

    a_man[n();p(proper-noun,n/p/a,acc,); a()]
    entered[n(); p(verb,n/p,acc/bind); a(trans,comp/subj,acc/bind)]
    was_covered[n();p(verb,p/a,acc,bind); a(trans,compl/subj,acc/bind)]
    with_mud[n(); p(); a(prep,p/a;acc/bind)]
    who[n(); p(pronoun,n/p/a,bind); a()]

References

Aarts, F., & Aarts, J. (1982). *English syntactic structures.* Oxford: Pergamon.

Aho, A., & Ullman, J. (1972). *The theory of parsing, translation and compiling, Vol. 1: Parsing.* Englewood Cliffs: Prentice Hall.

AITopics (2009). Representation. *In:* aaai.org/AITopics/pmwiki/pmwiki.php/AITopics/Representation.

Birkhoff, G., & Bartee, T. (1970). *Modern applied algebra.* New York: McGraw-Hill.

Bishop, C. (2006). *Pattern recognition and machine learning.* New York: Springer.

Bochenski, I. (1961). *A history of formal logic.* Notre Dame: University of Notre Dame Press.

Broadbent, D. (1975). The magic number seven after fifteen years. In A. Kennedy & A. Wilkes (Eds.), *Studies in long term memory* (pp. 1–18). London: Wiley.

Bullock, M., & Gelman, R. (1977). Numerical reasoning in young children: The ordering principle. *Child Development, 48*(2), 427–434.

Chomsky, N. (1957). *Syntactic structures.* The Hague: Mouton.

Chomsky, N. (1975). *The logical structure of linguistic theory.* New York: Plenum.

Churchland, P. (1997). Knowing qualia: A reply to Jackson. In N. Block, O. Flanagan, & G. Guzeldere (Eds.), *The nature of consciousness: Philosophical debates.* Cambridge: MIT.

Cohen, M., Elger, C., & Weber, B. (2008). Amygdala tractography predicts functional connectivity and learning during feedback-guided decision-making. *NeuroImage, 39,* 1396–1407.

Colgin, L., Denninger, T., Fyhn, M., Hafting, T., Bonnevie, T., Jensen, O., et al. (2009). Frequency of gamma oscillations routes flow of information in the hippocampus. *Nature, 462*(7271), 353–357.

Couwenberg, M. (2007). *Analyse van ontwikkeling van kenniselementen* (Master's thesis). Nijmegen: Radboud Universiteit.

Cowper, E. (1992). *A concise introduction to syntactic theory: The government-binding approach.* Chicago: The University of Chicago Press.

Davis, R., Shrobe, H., & Szolovits, P. (2009). What is a knowledge representation? *AI Magazine, 14*(1), 17–33.

Debrock, G., Farkas, J., & Sarbo, J. (1999). Syntax from a Peircean perspective. In P. Sandrini (Ed.), *Proc. 5th Int'l Congress on Terminology and Knowledge Engineering* (pp. 180–189). Innsbruck: TermNet.

Dehaene, S. (1997). *The Number Sense.* Oxford: Oxford University Press.

Dehaene, S. (2002). Single–neuron arithmetic. *Science, 297,* 1652–1653.

Dennett, D. (1991). *Consciousness explained.* London: Penguin.

Draskovic, I., Couwenberg, M., & Sarbo, J. (2010). New Concept Development Model: Explorative study of its usability in intelligence augmentation. In *Proc. 2nd Int'l Conf. on Computer Supported Education (CSEDU 2010)* (pp. 288–292).

Draskovic, I., Pustejovsky, J., & Schreuder, R. (2001). Adjective–noun composition and the generative lexicon. In P. Bouillon & K. Kanzaki (Eds.), *Proc. of the First Int'l Workshop on Generative Approaches to the Lexicon.* Université de Genève.

Dumitriu, A. (1977). *History of logic* (Vols. 1–4). Tunbridge Wells: Abacus.

Dwork, C., Kanellakis, P., & Mitchell, J. (1984). On the sequential nature of unification. *Journal of Logic Programming, 1*, 35–50.

Endres-Niggemeyer, B. (1998). *Summarizing information.* Berlin: Springer.

Engelbart, D. (1962). *Augmenting human intellect: A conceptual framework* (Summary Report No. AFOSR-3233). Menlo Park: Stanford Research Institute.

Fann, K. (1970). *Peirce's theory of abduction.* The Hague: Martinus Nijhoff.

Farkas, J. (2008). *A Semiotically oriented cognitive model of knowledge representation.* PhD thesis, Radboud University, Nijmegen.

Farkas, J., & Sarbo, J. (2000). A Logical Ontology. In G. Stumme (Ed.), *Working with conceptual structures: Contributions to ICCS'2000* (pp. 138–151). Aachen: Shaker Verlag.

Fillmore, C. (1968). The case for case. In E. Bach & R. Harms (Eds.), *Universals in linguistic theory* (pp. 1–90). New York: Holt, Rinehart and Winston.

Fisch, M. (Ed.). (1982). *Writings of C.S. Peirce: A Chronological Edition, 6 volumes.* Bloomington: Indiana University Press.

Fodor, J. (1998). *Concepts: Where cognitive science went wrong.* Oxford: Oxford University Press.

Gärdenfors, P. (2004). How to make the semantic web more semantic. In A. Varzi & L. Vieu (Eds.), *Proc. Third Int'l Conf. on Formal Ontology in Information Systems (FOIS'04)* (pp. 17–36). IOS Press.

Gibson, J. (1997). *The ecological approach to visual perception.* Boston: Houghton Mifflin.

Goldstone, R., & Barsalou, L. (1998). Reuniting perception and conception. *Cognition, 65*, 231–262.

Grimm, J., & Grimm, W. (1988). *Festival fairy tales.* Bridlington: Peter Haddock.

Guerri, C. (2000). Gebaute Zeichen: Die Semiotic der Architektur. In U. Wirth (Ed.), *Die Welt als Zeichen und Hypothese. Perspectiven des semiotischen Pragmatismus von Charles S. Peirce* (pp. 375–389). Frankfurt: Suhrkamp.

Hagoort, P., Hald, L., Bastiaansen, M., & Petersson, K.-M. (2004). Integration of word meaning and world knowledge in language comprehension. *Science, 304*, 438–441.

Halpin, T. (1998/2006). Object-role modeling (ORM/NIAM). In P. Bernus, K. Mertins, G. Schmidt, & J. Günter (Eds.), *Handbook on architectures of information systems.* Berlin: Springer.

Hardwick, C. (1978). *Semiotics and Significs: Correspondence between Charles S. Peirce and Lady Victoria Welby.* Indiana University Press.

Harnad, S. (1987). *Categorical Perception: The groundwork of cognition.* Cambridge: Cambridge University Press.

References

Harnad, S. (1990). The symbol grounding problem. *Physica D*, *42*, 335–346.

Hassina, R., Bargh, J., Engell, A., & McCulloch, K. (2009). Implicit working memory. *Consciousness and Cognition*, *18*, 665–678.

Hovy, E. (2005). Automated text summarization. In R. Mitkov (Ed.), *The Oxford handbook of computational linguistics* (pp. 583–598). Oxford: Oxford University Press.

Hudson, R. (1984). *Word grammar*. Cambridge: Basil Blackwell.

Jakobson, R. (1980). *The framework of language*. Ann Arbor: Michigan Studies in the Humanities.

James, W. (1890/1983). *Principles of psychology*. Harvard: Harvard University Press.

Joseph, R. (2000). *The head of the caudate nucleus*. New York: Academic Press.

Klomp, E. (2008). *Conceptualisatie in een requirements development proces* (Master's thesis). Nijmegen: Radboud Universiteit.

Korcsmáros, P. (1985). *Mesélő ceruza*. Budapest: Táltos Kiadásszerv.

Liszka, J. (1996). *A general introduction to the semeiotic of Charles Sanders Peirce*. Bloomington: Indiana University Press.

Mackay, D. (1987). *The organization of perception and action. A theory for language and other cognitive skills*. New York: Springer.

Mani, I. (2001). *Automatic summarization*. Amsterdam: John Benjamins.

McCloud, S. (1994). *Understanding comics: The invisible art*. New York: Harper Collins.

Melrose, R., Poulin, R., & Stern, C. (2007). An fMRI investigation of the role of the basal ganglia in reasoning. *Brain Research*(1142), 146–158.

Miller, G. (1956). The magical number seven, plus or minus two. *The Psychological Review*, *63*(2), 81–97.

Newton, I. (1959/1671). *The correspondence of Isaac Newton* (Vol. I; H. Turnbull, Ed.). Cambridge: Cambridge University Press.

Newton, I. (1999/1687). *The Principia*. Berkeley: University of California Press.

Nieder, A., Freedman, D., & Miller, E. (2002). Representation of the quantity of visual items in the primate prefrontal cortex. *Science*, *297*, 1708–1711.

Peirce, C.S. (1931-58). *Collected papers of Charles Sanders Peirce*. Cambridge: Harvard University Press.

Pica, P., Lemer, C., Izard, V., & Dehaene, S. (2004). Exact and approximate arithmetic in an Amazonian indigene group. *Science*, *306*, 499–503.

Pollard, C., & Sag, I. (1994). *Head-driven phrase structure grammar*. Chicago: The University of Chicago Press.

Popper, K. (1959). *The logic of scientific discovery*. New York: Basic Books.

Pribram, K. (1971). *Languages of the brain, experimental paradoxes and principles in neuropsychology*. New York: Wadsworth.

Prueitt, P. (1995). A theory of process compartments in biological and ecological systems. In J. Albus (Ed.), *Proc. of ISIC Workshop on Architectures for Semiotic Modeling and Situation Analysis of Large Complex Systems*. Monterey.

Pylyshyn, Z. (Ed.). (1987). *The robot's dilemma: the frame problem in artificial intelligence.* Norwood: Ablex.

Quirk, R., Greenbaum, S., Leech, G., & Svartvik, J. (1985). *A Comprehensive Grammar of the English Language.* London: Longman.

Ramachandran, V., & Hirstein, W. (1997). Three Laws of Qualia. *Journal of Consciousness Studies, 4*(5-6), 429–458.

Sabra, A. (1981). *Theories of Light: From Descartes to Newton.* Cambridge: Cambridge University Press.

Sacks, O. (1985). *The man who mistook his wife for a hat, and other clinical tales.* New York: Summit Books.

Sarbo, J. (2006). Peircean Proto-Signs. In D. M. Dubois (Ed.), *Computing Anticipator Systems, Proc. of the Third Int'l Conf. (CASYS'06), Vol. 839* (pp. 474–479). Liege, Belgium.

Sarbo, J. (2009). On Well-formedness in Requirement Elicitation Processes. In X. Feng, K. Liu, & G. Jiang (Eds.), *Proc. of the 11th Int'l Conf. on Informatics and Semiotics in Organisations (ICISO 2009)* (pp. 18–25). Beijing, China.

Sarbo, J., & Farkas, J. (2002). A linearly complex model for knowledge representation. In U. Priss, D. Corbett, & G. Angelova (Eds.), *Conceptual structures: Integration and interfaces (ICCS'2002), Proc. of the 10th Int'l Conf., Lecture Notes in Artificial Intelligence, Vol. 2193* (pp. 20–33). Berlin: Springer.

Sarbo, J., & Farkas, J. (2004). Towards a theory of meaning extraction. In H. D. Pfeiffer, H. Delugach, & K. E. Wolff (Eds.), *Conceptual structures at work, Proc. of the 12th Int'l Conf. (ICCS'04)* (pp. 55–68). Aachen: Shaker Verlag.

Schurger, A., Pereira, F., Treisman, A., & Cohen, J. (2010). Reproducibility distinguishes conscious from nonconscious neural representations. *Science, 327*, 97–99.

Shen, X., Lin, X., & de Wilde, P. (2008). Oscillations and spiking pairs: Behaviour of a neural model with STDP learning. *Neural Computation, 20*, 2037–2069.

Sippu, S., & Soisalon-Soininen, E. (1988). *Parsing theory, Vol. 1.* Berlin: Springer.

Solso, R. (1988). *Cognitive psychology.* New York: Harcourt Brace Jovanovich.

Sparck Jones, K. (1993). What might be in a summary? In G. Knorz, J. Krause, & C. Womser-Hacker (Eds.), *Information Retrieval '93: von der Modellierung zur Anwendung* (pp. 9–26). Konstanz: Universitätsverlag Konstanz.

Squire, L., Zola-Morgan, S., Cave, C., Haist, F., Musen, G., & Suzuki, W. (1993). Memory organisation of brain systems and cognition. In D. Meyer & S. Kornblum (Eds.), *Attention and performance xiv: Synergies in experimental psychology, artificial intelligence, and cognitive neuroscience* (pp. 393–424). Cambridge: The MIT Press.

Stamper, R. (2009). *Analysis of perception and meaning for information systems engineering.* Unpublished manuscript.

References

Tudusciuc, O., & Nieder, A. (2007). Neural population coding of continuous and discrete quantity in the primate posterior parietal cortex. *PNAS*, *104*(36), 14513–14518.

van Breemen, A. (2010). The semiotic framework: Peirce and Stamper. In R. Jorna, K. Liu, G. Jiang, K. Nakata, & L. Sun (Eds.), *Proc. of the 12th Int'l Conf. on Informatics and Semiotics in Organisations (ICISO 2010)* (pp. 87–95). Reading, UK: SciTePress.

van Breemen, A., & Sarbo, J. (2009). The machine in the ghost: The syntax of mind. *Signs – International Journal of Semiotics*, *3*, 135-184.

van Breemen, A., Sarbo, J., & van der Weide, T. (2007). Towards a theory of natural conceptualization. In K. Liu, J. Connolly, & S. O'Neill (Eds.), *Proc. 10th Int'l Conf. on Organisational Semiotics (ICOS'07)* (pp. 24–32). Sheffield, UK.

van Driel, H. (1993). *De Semiotiek van C.S. Peirce in verband gebracht met het verschijnsel 'film'*. PhD thesis, Landegem, Nevelland.

van Valin, R. (1993). A synopsis of role and reference grammar. In R. van Valin (Ed.), *Advances in role and reference grammar* (pp. 1–164). Amsterdam: John Benjamins.

Wandell, B. (1995). *Foundations of vision*. Sunderland: Sinauer.

Wang, H. (1974). *From mathematics to philosophy*. London: Routledge and Kegan Paul.

Wittlinger, M., Wehner, R., & Wolf, H. (2006). The ant odometer: Stepping on stilts and stumps. *Science*, *312*, 1965–1967.

Index